D1031969

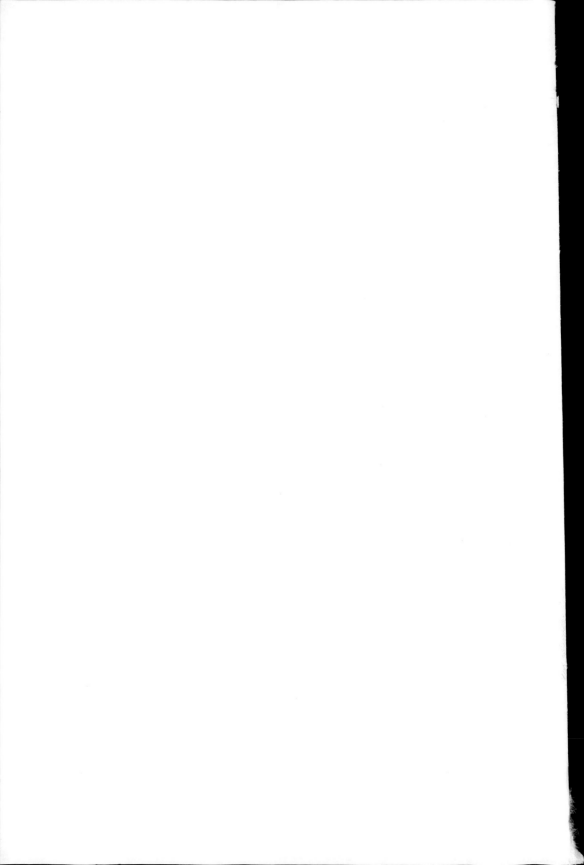

Psychological Agency

Theory, Practice, and Culture

edited by Roger Frie

A Bradford Book
The MIT Press
Cambridge, Massachusetts
London, England

MIT Press books may be purchased at special quantity discounts for business or sales promotional use. For information, please e-mail special_sales@mitpress.mit.edu or write to Special Sales Department, The MIT Press, 55 Hayward Street, Cambridge, MA 02142.

This book was set in Stone Sans and Stone Serif by SPi Publisher Services, Puducherry, India and was printed and bound in the United States of America.

Library of Congress Cataloging-in-Publication Data

Psychological agency : theory, practice, and culture / [edited by] Roger Frie.
p. cm.
Includes bibliographical references and index.
ISBN 978-0-262-06267-1 (hardcover : alk. paper)—ISBN 978-0-262-56231-7 (pbk. : alk. paper)
1. Self. 2. Agent (Philosophy) I. Frie, Roger, 1965–
BF697.P755 2008
155.2—dc22

2008017556

10 9 8 7 6 5 4 3 2 1

Contents

Preface

This book is premised on the belief that agency is a central psychological phenomenon that must be accounted for in any explanatory framework of human action. Broadly speaking, psychological agency refers to the human capacity for reflective action, and is based on the potential to imagine and create new ways of being and acting in the world. This generative potential is only possible within the collective meanings and social and material relations that shape our lives.

It is essential, in my view, that agency be seen as a *situated* psychological phenomenon. Psychological agency is not a fixed entity that conforms to traditional definitions of free will. It is an active process of meaning construction that is dependent on the self-interpretation of individuals and is grounded in biology, society, and culture. As such, agency can never be divorced from the contexts in which it exists, yet neither can it be wholly reduced to these contexts. Agency is based on the embodied, affective potential for reflective understanding and, as such, is central to the process of psychotherapy and psychological change and development.

Agency is a lived phenomenon that is evidenced in everyday experience and in those therapy clients who seek help for problems in living. The question of agency also relates to how we choose to live our lives and the responsibility we have for the decisions we make. As such, agency is both a psychological concept with direct clinical implications and a central philosophical issue pertaining to the ethics of choice. Because it is such a multidimensional concept, I believe that agency can only truly be appreciated and understood from a multidisciplinary perspective. In developing this book, I therefore invited a diverse group of scholars, researchers, and clinicians to provide discussions of agency that expand our appreciation of the complexity of the agential process. The contributors are all trained in either psychology or psychiatry, and many have academic philosophical backgrounds that they bring to bear in their explication of agency.

I have divided the book into three separate sections: theoretical contexts, clinical and developmental contexts, and social and cultural contexts. Each chapter, to a greater or lesser extent, touches on all three of these areas. I also asked contributors, where ever possible, to combine theoretical discussion with clinical case illustrations. Taken together, the chapters demonstrate that agency cannot be fully appreciated from any single disciplinary outlook, but, especially when considering its clinical implications, must be considered from multiple perspectives. As a group, the contributors approach and define agency as a central topic in clinical and theoretical psychology, yet their discussions also draw on the fields of philosophy and neuroscience and to a lesser extent, on sociology and anthropology. An underlying theme throughout the book is the utility of a contemporary psychodynamic perspective for understanding the affective dynamics at work in the emergence, development, and experience of agency.

This book developed over a number of years and with the help, both direct and indirect, of many people. I would like to thank first and foremost my students and clients. It is through the process of mutual reflection on the nature of psychological agency, whether in a pedagogical or clinical setting, that I have learned to appreciate both its importance and its complexity. Working in the Department of Psychiatry at Columbia University and the Department of Psychology at Long Island University, as well as at various doctoral and postdoctoral institutes, has enabled me to understand and appreciate the interconnections between theory, practice, and research, and to draw on each of these in formulating my approach to agency. In addition, my earlier academic training in continental philosophy in Cambridge and Berlin has been enormously helpful to my elaboration of agency as a "metatheoretical" subject. The majority of my published work to date has been geared towards developing the interconnections between the disciplines of psychology, philosophy, and psychoanalysis. I continue to believe strongly that clinical training in the mental health professions can benefit from the study and recognition of the philosophy of human development and experience. Unfortunately, pervasive disciplinary boundaries, reinforced by economic and social forces, often present challenges for substantive cross-disciplinary exchange. I hope that this book can help to foster such dialogue.

I wish to express my gratitude to Tom Stone, Senior Editor at The MIT Press, for taking on and supporting this project and to Sandra Minkkinen for her advice through the editing stage. I also owe thanks to the contributors to this book for their shared enthusiasm and belief in the value of the study of psychological agency. My work on agency has benefited greatly from discussions with many friends and colleagues over the past several years; I wish to acknowledge in particular John Fiscalini, Elliot Jurist, Jack Martin, Donna Orange, and Jeff Sugarman. However, I am without doubt most indebted to my family for their support: to Emily for her enthusiasm and boundless energy, and to Elena and Andreas for their wonderfully imaginative and endlessly creative acts of agency. It is to them that I dedicate this book.

Introduction: The Situated Nature of Psychological Agency

Roger Frie

The current fascination with the biophysical and sociocultural origins of human action has lent new importance to the question of agency. The capacity to be an agent, to act purposefully and reflectively, depends on the biological, social, and cultural contexts that inform and shape who we are. But agency is more than a mere effect of these contexts. Psychological agency also involves the capacity for imagining and creating potentially new and different ways of being and acting and, as such, cannot be explained purely in terms of its biological, social, or cultural determinants. The purpose of this introductory chapter is to develop a theory of situated agency that locates the origin of human action neither solely in the individual nor in the biophysical and sociocultural contexts. Rather, the potential for psychological agency and the creation of meaning is seen to exist within a web of intersecting biophysical, social, and cultural determinants in an ongoing generative and developmental process.

This edited collection is motivated by the belief that the question of agency, though often perplexing, is nevertheless central to psychological inquiry and practice. The contributors argue that the language of psychological agency and personal meaning must be maintained in any explanatory framework of human behavior. The version of agency this book seeks to promote is not based on rational self-mastery or cognitive certitude, but on the affective, embodied, and relational processing of human experience. While many social-scientific approaches face the challenge of accounting for the lived experience of agency, traditional definitions of agency in terms of free will and autonomy fail to account for the very contexts that make action possible to begin with. Without a satisfactory concept of agency, it becomes increasingly difficult to explain either the nature of psychological change or the role of the person in the shaping and reshaping of her world.

As a group, the contributors argue that a philosophically coherent and clinically consistent theory of agency must account for the complex intertwining of personal history, affectivity, embodiment, social and cultural context, and reflective capability. Drawing on the fields of psychology, philosophy, neuroscience, and psychoanalysis, they present agency as a central feature of the relational, embodied person, embedded within dynamically evolving social and interactive circumstances. Thus, this book maps out a space for agency and self-experience that transcends the distinction between modernist certainty and postmodernist fragmentation. The contributors maintain that agency is not reducible to biophysical properties, or to depersonalized social and cultural forces. And in the wake of widely held conceptions that equate agency with Western and gender-biased notions of individuality and autonomy, they argue that agency is not an isolated act of detached self-reflection and choice. The objective, rather, is to reconfigure agency as an emergent and developmental process that is fundamentally intersubjective and contextualized.

In framing the discussion and debate over agency, it is important to note that current psychological research and practice do not conceptualize agency with any consistency. Academic psychology and postmodernism offer accounts of human behavior that reduce agency to its biophysical and sociocultural origins respectively.[1] Professional psychology, on the other hand, assumes a robust and overly simplistic form of agency, according to which psychological change is dependent on rational self-knowledge and choice. Many forms of psychoanalysis, meanwhile, treat agency with considerable skepticism, if not complete disregard.

I begin by assessing four major critiques that support the need for a theory of situated agency: the function of naturalism in psychology; the postmodern critique; the growth of professionalism in clinical practice; and the skeptical tradition in psychoanalysis. In responding to each critique, I formulate an interdisciplinary conceptual approach through which to analyze the intersubjective, affective, and embodied dimensions of agency. I argue that traditional views of agency as disengaged, autonomous, and wholly rational are incomplete and that contemporary psychological inquiry and practice require a theory of situated agency. Such a theory is valuable because it can account for the biologically and socioculturally embedded nature of experience and for the personal construction of psychological meaning within these contexts. The introduction concludes with an overview of the individual chapters.

The Challenge of Naturalism

Advances in neuroscience and biology have created significant opportunities for understanding the nature of human life. Not surprisingly, psychologists increasingly look for neurological and biophysical explanations to answer questions about human behavior. They argue that psychological phenomena can be accounted for by "more basic" neurological and biophysical events. This approach is part of the wider naturalistic project in psychology, which views human activity in terms of physical causes and laws and increasingly affects psychological inquiry and practice, as illustrated in the rapid growth of evidence-based treatments. It is important to consider, therefore, to what extent a naturalistic framework can account for the situated nature of psychological phenomena in general, and agency in particular.

The naturalistic project is consistent with the broad mechanistic perspectives underlying the reigning conceptual paradigms of North American psychology over the past century. During the first half of the century, psychology was dominated by behaviorism, relying on a naturalistic view of human action. Behaviorism was initiated by the work of John B. Watson, who rejected introspective methods and sought to restrict psychology to experimental methods, thus introducing the "science of behavior." By midcentury, research psychology was chiefly identified with the radical behaviorism of B. F. Skinner. More recently, cognitive psychology has sought to explain human behavior in terms of its causal antecedents, focusing on the architecture of the mind, its organizational principles, and its computational rules. The contemporary focus on biology similarly offers explanations of human behavior in terms of physiological mechanisms.

The application of the methods and values of the natural sciences to human behavior has garnered valuable knowledge. But it means that contemporary research psychology deals with individual components, such as cerebral responses, neural structures, and other physiological mechanisms, not with the phenomenology of lived experience. The difficulty is that when the understanding of individual components is equated with a system as complex as human behavior, we inevitably end up with reductionism.

The appeal of reductionist thinking lies in its ability to offer clear and concise explanations for problems that might otherwise defy explanation. But psychological phenomena are not easily explainable as objects whose functioning can be formulated in causal explanations. Once psychological phenomena are reduced to their component status, they are essentially removed from the wider social and cultural contexts in which human action take shapes. As a result, the language we use to describe and explain human agency is curiously absent. In a critique of naturalism, Charles Taylor (1989, 58) argues that

> what we need to *explain* is people living their lives; the terms in which they cannot avoid living them cannot be removed from the explanandum, unless we can propose other terms in which they could live them more clairvoyantly. We cannot just leap outside of these terms altogether, on the grounds that their logic doesn't fit some

> model of "science" and that we know a priori that human beings must be explicable in this "science." This begs the question. How can we ever know that humans can be explained by any scientific theory until we actually explain how they live their lives in its terms?

Clearly, as Taylor suggests, the experience and language of agency—interpretation, reflection, understanding, affectivity, meaning, choice, and responsibility—contrast sharply with the predominant tendency of the discourse of science.

The potential disavowal of agency has its beginnings in psychology's embrace of the experimental method. In 1879, with the establishment of a scientific laboratory devoted to psychological experimentation at the University of Leipzig, Wilhelm Wundt made it possible to explore and understand the psyche on a mostly inductive, mechanistic basis. This new experimental psychology permitted the researcher to bracket out any subjective interference, and achieve an understanding of the psyche that was thought to be truly objective. What followed was a tendency to treat the psyche as an aseptic object, whose functioning could be formulated in causal, mechanistic laws.

The new experimental approach was not without its critics. Wilhelm Dilthey proposed that psychologists use their everyday experience as a basis for interpreting psychological meaning. Dilthey argued that psychological phenomena not only require interpretation, but are also constituted by human interpretive practices, thus giving rise to the field of hermeneutics—essentially the study of interpretation. Dilthey (1977) developed a "descriptive and analytic psychology" that began with the examination of the totality of life experience: the lived reality that precedes distinctions between mind and body and self and world. He argued that it is only against this ever-present, mostly unarticulated, background of their experience that humans are able to perceive and comprehend things, including themselves (Burston and Frie 2006; Martin, Sugarman, and Thompson 2003). Psychology, on this view, must always consider the feeling, desiring agent within a shared, practical lifeworld.

The contemporary perspective of methodological hermeneutics draws directly on Dilthey's criticism of the naturalistic framework in psychology. In contrast to objectivist social science, methodological hermeneutics "does not strive for decontextualized facts, but emphasizes meanings as experienced by individuals whose activities are rooted in given sociohistorical settings. The hermeneutic approach insists upon the inseparability of fact and value, detail and context, and observation and theory" (Messer, Sass, and Woolfolk 1988, xiii–xiv). As such, the primary difficulty with reductive strategies in psychology—be they behavioral, computational, or biological—is that they distinguish psychological phenomena from their sociocultural contexts, and in the process cannot find their way back to the lived experience of the human subjects they are studying.

From a hermeneutic perspective, human behavior can never be fully analyzed apart from the contexts in which it emerges. If the study of psychology is understood as making sense of the world as it is experienced by human beings, then any analysis that does not sufficiently account for situational and cultural variables is necessarily incomplete. As humans, we are not only constituted atomistically, but relationally and socioculturally. And as social beings, our thoughts, feelings, desires, and actions take place in expressly social contexts. These contexts must therefore be included in any psychological analysis.

The Postmodern Critique

The focus on social and cultural contexts as explanations for human behavior is a central facet of postmodern psychology. Although psychologists have come rather late to postmodernism, its impact on theory and practice is noteworthy. In this section, I consider the challenge of postmodernism for a theory of situated agency. Because the deconstructionist impulse has been particularly significant for how the self and agency are conceptualized, I will examine these developments in some detail.

Psychologists who identify with postmodernism are critical of the broadly objectivist traditions in Western psychology and take issue with the traditional focus on the individual mind. From a postmodern perspective, persons are shaped and determined by their contexts, and their identities are culturally constructed. Such terms as *context* and *construct* are most often identified with social constructionism. Among postmodernists, social constructionist psychologists have argued for an almost exclusive emphasis on the formative effect of social and cultural experience on the person. Indeed, for more radical versions of postmodernism, the issue is not whether psychology is a science, but whether psychology is right to be concerned with the study of the individual psyche. Thus, Kenneth Gergen (1985, 271) notes that the aim of social constructionists is to shift the "explanatory locus of human action . . . from the interior region of the mind to the processes and structure of human interaction." More pointedly, he argues that "under postmodernism, processes of individual reason, intention, moral decision making and the like—all central to the ideology of individualism—lose their status as realities" (p. 241).

Just as the importance of biological forces cannot be denied, there can be little argument with the notion that social and cultural processes form the contexts in which human development and experience unfold. Culture infuses the person through the social practices of the everyday world, shaping and forming in the most fundamental ways how persons conceive of the world and their place in it. Postmodern psychologists recognize that their work is unalterably affected by the cultures, societies, and times in which they live. Insights, generalizations, and understandings all arise within specific contexts and are necessarily incomplete and limited. Most researchers and practitioners resonate with such themes of difference, plurality, and irregularity. In fact, they are rather refreshing changes from past adherence to sameness and strict rationality. By challenging the assumptions they hold, many psychologists have now come to understand human experience as a dynamic process that can be seen from multiple perspectives.

Postmodernism in psychology is made up of a diversity of viewpoints, but in the main is a reaction to the modernist conception of the human subject. When René Descartes pronounced the autonomy of the introspective, thinking self, in his formulation "I think, therefore I am," he ushered in the age of modern philosophy. Although the term *self* can have many meanings, postmodernists generally distinguish between the modern and postmodern self. The former is identified with a belief in the possibility of autonomy and self-mastery, which is achieved through rational decision making and results in a sense of certainty and consistency. The postmodern self, by contrast, is fluid, dispersed, and multiple. It is a reflection of the fragmented postmodern culture in which we live, which lacks any continuity or solid structure. Because agency is closely linked to the concept of the subject, or selfhood, the postmodern critique of agency is based on the rejection of those notions—autonomy, self-transparency, rationality, and individuality—that define the isolated Cartesian mind.

Postmodernists seek to deconstruct the belief that consciousness is unified and transparent to itself. Drawing on psychoanalysis, they argue that people are fundamentally opaque to themselves, and that their motives for action may be unknown and conflictual, thus undermining the notion of free will. Postmodernists similarly challenge the Kantian view of persons as self-determining, rational self-legislators. Feminist and diversity critiques take issue with the notion of free will, because they see it not as a political ideal, but as imposing a universal and hegemonic identity on others. They argue that the ideals of autonomy, individuality, and universality on which traditional theories of agency are based, mask a hegemony of reason, masculinity, and racial discrimination. Agency is not simply an instrument of individual self-expression, but a representation of active and passive gender positions between men and women, and dominant and subordinate positions between different racial and socioeconomic groups.

Issues of power and domination are also central to the poststructuralist critique of the asymmetrical and inegalitarian features of modern society. This perspective owes much to Michel Foucault's model of the social field, constituted by myriad shifting relations, and multiple centers of power confronting multiple centers of resistance. Foucault analyzes the way the person is constructed within dominant discourses and becomes an "effect" of "regimes" of ideology, power, and knowledge. In the broad poststructuralist argument, subjects are forced to take up diverse subject positions in discourses over which they have no control. Because they are unable to bind these heterogeneous, often contradictory positions together, they are fundamentally split and incapable of assuming the agentic stand of the unified subject.

Postmodernism clearly alerts us to the need to develop a conception of agency that can account for the differentiated configurations of social, cultural, and historical contexts. Yet the postmodern depiction of the idealized, autonomous Western self is itself open to question. While conceptions of the self that rest on Cartesian and Kantian assumptions may succumb to sweeping generalizations about the human subject as self-transparent and capable of self-mastery, neither the history of philosophy nor people's representations of themselves in the stream of everyday life conform to the model of the subject as unified and integral. Indeed, closer examination demonstrates that there is no single overarching conception of subject.

The reconceptualization of agency requires a different view of the subject, one that is other-directed, fluid, and necessarily incomplete. This view finds its basis in a tradition of European "continental" philosophers who took issue with Descartes, but often go unacknowledged by later postmodern critics. Beginning with early German Romanticism, F. W. J. Schelling and Novalis (Friedrich von Hardenberg) argued that the thinking self that forms the basis of the Cartesian tradition fails to account for prereflective experience on which reflective self-knowledge necessarily depends. Heinrich Jacobi's philosophy of dialogue and G. W. F. Hegel's theory of mutual recognition directly oppose the isolated nature of the Cartesian subject, claiming that there can be no I without an Other. Self-consciousness develops only as a result of recognition by another person in a reciprocal process of interaction. Similarly, the Kantian idea of self-mastery, based on reason and moral responsibility, is directly challenged in the nineteenth-century philosophy of Arthur Schopenhauer and Friedrich Nietzsche; their critique anticipates and forms the basis for Freud's project of psychoanalysis.

Given this alternative reading of the self in modern philosophy, it is possible to ask whether the postmodern critique unnecessarily conflates agency with the unified and self-transparent Cartesian subject. As the contributors to this book will assert, psychological agency need not be equated with individuality and rationalism, or indeed with patriarchy and colonialism. The identification of agency with autonomy is a case in point. According to traditional political and philosophical theories of autonomy, individuals would be able, at least in principle, to exercise their free will outside of all contexts. In contrast to this idealized, disengaged subject, situated agents can reason and act in novel ways only against the background of the contexts in which they are embedded. As a number of feminist political theorists have asserted (Gardiner 1995; Mackenzie and Stoljar 2000), the notions of agency and autonomy need to be reconfigured to take into account our fundamentally intersubjective and contextualized nature. Mackenzie and Stoljar (2000) coin the term *relational autonomy* and suggest that postmodern and feminist critiques be employed in the recasting of agency. Their point is that agency and autonomy emerge within the social contexts that make action possible to begin with and, as such, are necessarily relational in nature.

Postmodernism can aid in the development of a notion of agency that can account for difference and otherness, yet the postmodern critique runs into problems when social contexts are seen as the only appropriate level of analysis. If contexts are used not only to describe but also to explain the nature of human action, we run the risk of reducing meaning to a one-sided causal pattern between the context (cause) and the action (effect). Because persons are more than living enactments of their contexts, the analysis of contexts must also account for the role of agency in the construction of personal meaning. This construction of meaning occurs despite the continual fragmentation and dislocation of human experience. Indeed, I believe that agency must be reconceptualized to account for the way experience is characterized by shifts between centering and decentering, integration and disintegration.

The postmodern concepts of multiplicity, fragmentation, and difference, while important, need to be linked with an understanding of the nature of reflexivity, meaning making, and responsibility. Without such an appreciation, the focus on multiplicity of selves and the fragmentation of identity has the potential to overlook the psychological and social harm these experiences can carry. As Anthony Elliott (2004, xix) suggests, "The politics of difference is a risky undertaking—both at the level of self-identity where otherness is located as regards the psyche and interpersonal relationships, and at the level of radical politics, where otherness is addressed in terms of the whole society. Too much toleration for difference and you run the risk of fragmentation; too little and you are left with a spurious (modernist) homogeneity."

This tension is clearly evident in the poststructuralist analysis of the self. According to Foucault, theories of self derive from the social and cultural practices specific to a historical epoch and currents of power whose interest it is to define the self in ideological terms. This Foucaultian perspective demonstrates issues of power and repression involved in all human experience. Although a resourceful subversion of the dominant value system, it is problematic when it comes to the question of individual action. The uncovering of ideology, discourse, or power confronts the problem of accounting for potential change. That is, if humans arrive at beliefs within an ideology, do they not also have the capacity to modify that ideology? For the Marxist critic Terry Eagleton, this points to the need for a coherent theory of agency. As Eagleton (1991, 198) observes, "A certain provisional stability of identity is essential not only for psychological well-being but for revolutionary political agency." Without a coherent notion of agency, which points to the potential to see and act in ways that are different, new, and fresh, it is difficult to account for the nature of change, whether in the therapeutic setting or in wider sociopolitical contexts.

To be sure, neither postmodernism in general, nor Foucault's work in particular, is monolithic in scope. Despite Foucault's outright rejection of Enlightenment humanism, he seems to reintroduce a theory of agency late in his work, giving some observers reason to interpret altogether different versions of Foucault (see Dews 1987 and Sawicki 1991). While there is admittedly an ambivalence in the postmodern perspective on agency, for Eagleton agency is undeniably central to any theory of human behavior, whether political or psychological—and one might well ask whether politics and psychology ever can or should be separated from one another. From his standpoint, Eagleton (1991, 198) charges that radical postmodernism contains "no adequate theory of such agency, since the subject would now seem no more than the decentered effect of the semiotic process; and its valuable attention to the split, precarious, pluralistic nature of all identity slides at its worst into an irresponsible hymning of the virtues of schizophrenia." In other words, to assume that persons have no voices other than the prevailing discourses in which they exist not only dismantles agency but potentially undermines the possibility of psychological, social, and political change. As Eagleton concludes, "The Left, now more than ever, has need of strong ethical and even anthropological foundations." Without "an adequate theory of political agency . . . postmodernism is in the end part of the problem rather than the solution" (Eagleton 1996, 135).

To hold the postmodern perspective up for review is not to deny its significance. I am arguing that in spite of the subordination of the subject to organizing structures and discourses that are either outside of our awareness or beyond our control, it remains vital that we retain the notion of an experiencing person with a reflective capacity. Ironically, postmodernists and their critics (usually referred to as humanists) each accuse the other of determinism. The postmodernist asserts that the humanist ignores the effect that the forces of fragmentation have on human action, while the humanist argues that the postmodernist focuses only on discourses and therefore disregards the role of the human agent (Gardiner 1995, 9). In fact, this dichotomous construal illustrates the challenges involved in accounting for agency.

The objective, in my view, is to keep in sight the situational and context-bound reflective capabilities of the psychological agent. By imagining and then reorienting one's behavior, we have the potential to create possibilities for new experience, and thus affect and possibly transform our contexts. In contrast to the static, disengaged self on which the notion of free will is based, I suggest that we think of agency, like the self, as a fluid, dynamic process that is fundamentally embedded in ever-changing biological and sociocultural contexts.

Once contexts are viewed as fundamental to, but not entirely determinative of the person, there is space to consider how action takes place. Activity is a necessary, indeed essential facet of all human experience, but it is neither strictly the product of structures and practices nor the subject. As Holland et al. (1998) suggest in their anthropological study of agency, action is derived from the ways humans replicate, use, or respond to the contexts and cultures in which they exist. The possibility for change and transformation arises because of the human ability to act within traditions in ways that are potentially new and different. In other words, social and cultural discourses both position people and provide them with the resources to respond to the myriad situations in which they find themselves. Our contexts enable our agential capacity, yet our agency, however personal or private it may feel, can never occur outside of these contexts. Whenever the locus of action is found exclusively in contexts *or* in agents, we become mired in the binary thinking characteristic of Cartesian modernism.

Professionalism in Clinical Psychology

While reductionisms of any kind are harmful to achieving an understanding of lived experience, the contemporary changes to clinical psychology also pose serious challenges for understanding agency. The practice of psychotherapy, for example, is rapidly being transformed as a result of a number of powerful factors—pressures from insurance companies, the pervasive drive toward medication, and a general indifference to the complexity of psychological change and development. Whereas psychotherapy once provided a lens through which social and political forces at work in individual and group experience could be critically examined, the growing technocratic culture of therapy seems to overlook the need for preserving a space for uniqueness and critical reflection.

A major part of this transformation is the increasing zeal for technical precision and skill. Indeed, clinical psychology is often conceptualized as a purely technical undertaking. Psychotherapy, however, is not only a learned technique. It rests on ideas, concepts, and theories that provide the foundation for appreciating the nature of human experience (Burston and Frie 2006). Within this rapidly changing clinical environment, the risk is that our inquiries become less a matter of direct human encounter than of technical correctness.

The technical disposition is part of a larger drive to achieve objectifiable results in psychotherapy. This has led to the growth of empirically validated therapies and the widespread reliance on manualized, or "scripted," treatment protocols. While empirically supported treatments demonstrate the reduction of symptoms in specific disorders, the focus on objectivity tends to overlook the fact that therapy is a relationship between two unique human beings—and as such, its progression and outcome are not always predictable.

The objectivist approach in psychotherapy also relies on a normative conception of mental health that is derived from the medical model. Broadly stated, mental health is equated with the absence of symptoms and dependent on one's rational self-knowledge and self-reliance. Inherent in the medical model is a rationalist theory of agency that is based on Kantian ideas and associates a mental disorder with a dysfunction of agency. This perspective is formulated by the contemporary Kantians, Jeanette Kennett and Steve Matthews (2003, 306):

> It is a fundamental requirement of both moral and social life that persons have the capacity to undertake and complete projects and plans of varying importance, participate in social relationships, and occupy social roles in the service of a variety of institutional ends. We argue that the development and exercise of these capacities requires significantly unified agency. If this is so, then psychiatric disorders that have a disunifying effect should be seen as disvaluable to the extent that they deny persons the goods bestowed by agential capacities.

This Kantian perspective seeks to underscore the value of persons as autonomous agents. In discussing the function of agency in psychiatric patients, Kennett and Matthews argue that psychiatric disorders deny persons the goods bestowed by agential capacities. They define these goods as the ability "to make, shape, and revise plans in light of practical principles, to carry them out, to engage in a variety of both short- and long-term projects and commitments.

Thus autonomous agency requires both the capacity for competent deliberation and capacity for self-control over time" (p. 308). Their definition of autonomous agency relies on a strong rationalist component according to which psychiatrically disordered patients experience a dysfunction in their agential capacities for deliberation and self-control. In order to return to health, patients are viewed as needing therapy to restore "unified agency."

This rationalist conceptualization of agency rests on a number of questionable assumptions about the nature and function of agency in the therapeutic setting. First, the emphasis on the autonomous capacity of agency overlooks the fact that agency, like therapy, always takes place within specific social and cultural contexts and so is relationally generated. Second, the rationalist conception of agency runs into the difficulty of explaining change in patients who may never have met the criteria for "autonomous agency" to begin with. I will address both of these issues in turn.

In the medical model of psychotherapy, the therapist's role tends to be analogous to the scientist who is capable of viewing the patient's mind and behavior with objective detachment. This approach is often referred to as a "one-person" psychology because it discounts the role of the therapist's subjectivity in the therapeutic interaction. In contrast, many of today's clinicians regard therapy as a dialogical endeavor that always involves two people. Rather than simply offering advice or insight, the therapist works with the patient. Indeed, throughout the process of therapy, the therapist is not simply "treating" the patient but sharing in the experience of the patient.

Exploring patients' difficulties in terms of their intersubjective meanings and sociocultural roots and ramifications is quite different from strict symptom remediation, which, as we have seen, relies on a rational conception of autonomous agency. In the intersubjective approach to therapy I am describing, therapist and patient form an indissoluble dyad, and it is the relationship between them that becomes the domain of therapeutic inquiry. Phenomena that are the traditional focus of psychotherapeutic investigation are not understood as isolated biological or intrapsychic events, but as having been formed in an intersubjective field of existence. The role of therapy is to reach an understanding of such phenomena as they emerge in the therapeutic interaction.

Therapy thus rests on the assumption that relatedness is central to self-understanding and a sense of well-being. The patient's experiences are not viewed as isolated or autonomous processes that are biologically derivative or behaviorally determined, but are seen as having been formed in ongoing intersubjective experiences. On this view, agency is not an autonomous event that can be restored through rational self-engagement. Agency is never simply the work of the intellect, nor is it strictly a solitary, private affair. On the contrary, the process of therapeutic action illustrates that psychological agency is always situational in nature.

Within the clinical setting, agency exists and comes to be in the presence of the Other. And it is often precisely the response of the other person that makes agency tangible for patients and therapists alike. As Jessica Benjamin (1988, 12) suggests, the process of recognition "allows the self to realize its agency and authorship in a tangible way." This response may be nonverbal and not immediately open to articulation, yet it is no less significant. Within the complexity of the therapeutic relationship, the articulation of recognition and response occurs over time, enabling implicit interaction to become explicit. The emergence of agency is rarely a matter simply of choice, just as therapeutic action is never strictly linear—indeed, it might better be described as a nonlinear process.

Change is based on an openness to new possibilities of being. When we come to understand ourselves as agents in our world, it becomes possible for us to imagine making different choices, and to relate to others and act in different ways. An aim of therapy is to become aware of this shifting horizon of understanding (Gadamer 1995), so that new ways of feeling, thinking, and being may emerge, and meanings that were previously "prereflective" or unformulated can become discursively elaborated. The assumption of agency is an important part of this intersubjective process.

Probably the strongest argument against autonomous agency, however, concerns those persons lack a sense of themselves as agents to begin with. Indeed, many persons may experience feelings and thoughts as happening to them, rather than as generated by them. If agency is elevated to the ontological core of psychological life, it becomes difficult to account for experiential states in which the sense of agency has atrophied or is uncertain as a result of developmental interferences and derailments (Stolorow and Atwood 1992). In cases where there is little or no sense of agency to begin with, it is hard to assume that the sense of agency experienced by the patient on the completion of therapy actually facilitated the integration of experiences during the course of the therapy and was there, although disclaimed, all along (Mitchell 1993).

The problem with many accounts of agency in the therapeutic setting is that they are reduced to the riddle of whether agency actually facilitates change, or whether agency is itself a consequence of that change. This binary framework relies on an oversimplified view of both concepts—agency and change—thus reducing their interaction to a matter of cause and effect. If we see agential experience much the same way we tend to view self-experience—as malleable and fluid, generated by the complexity of psychic life and by continual shifts in our sociocultural contexts—then it is possible to avoid static definitions that reduce agency to developmental or sociocultural determinants.

The primary issue, in my view, is to acknowledge the relevance and possibility of psychological agency for the process of therapeutic change, without reverting to a false conception of an autonomous agent. The continual embeddedness of our sense of agency in a nexus of intersubjective relatedness implies that agency cannot be equated with the autonomous, rational subject. From the perspective of our situated, intersubjective nature, the notion of autonomous agency is illusory because it constitutes an essential denial of our fundamental contextuality.

Psychotherapy, on this view, provides the opportunity to elucidate the meaning of distress and suffering, and to realize the reflective capacity of the subject within the constraints imposed by psychological development and everyday life. Indeed, psychological inquiry and practice cannot stand apart from the everyday world of human activity. A wider appreciation of human experience as "situated" in multiple sociocultural contexts is necessary so that the problems that patients present in therapy are not construed in narrow psychological terms.

Psychoanalytic Skepticism

Whereas professional psychology tends to rely on an overly robust conception of agency, according to which symptom relief is dependent on the patient's capacity for autonomous, rational agency, psychoanalysis provides a more variable picture of human experience. In fact, from its inception, psychoanalysis sought to show that motivation for behavior is multidetermined, often hidden, and formed by interpersonal relationships over the course of human development. Not surprisingly, psychoanalysis has historically demonstrated an outright skepticism toward agency in the clinical setting. This skeptical stance, I suggest, bears closer scrutiny, because it provides an important alternative perspective for understanding the nature of agency. In this section I will explore the place of agency within the two major and contrasting historical paradigms in psychoanalysis: the intrapsychic perspective of Freud and the interpersonal perspective of Harry Stack Sullivan (Greenberg and Mitchell 1983). I demonstrate the limits of conceptualizing agency exclusively from an intrapsychic or an interpersonal perspective and point to the salience of alternative models of research and practice, in order to account for the embodied, situated nature of agency.

Freud's so-called discovery of the unconscious was a direct response to the Enlightenment tradition of Cartesian thought: the heralding of reason over the emotions. While Descartes inaugurated the modern era of philosophical and scientific thinking, he left us with a number of intractable problems, perhaps the best known of which is the division between reason and emotion, or mind and body. Today, it is difficult to imagine that any practicing clinician could believe in this traditional division. But how emotion becomes a source of knowledge remains a central problem for psychology and related disciplines, and as I will suggest below, is directly related to the process of agency.

As a representative of the Enlightenment era, Freud believed that the power of reason could be used to strengthen the conscious mind. At the same time, Freud sought to do justice to the underside of reason, namely, the unconscious. By demonstrating the inevitability of distortion in our thinking, Freud presented a more variable picture of the human mind than his Enlightenment predecessors. His conception of the mind combined rationalism with irrationalism. The importance of Freud's unconscious cannot be underestimated. The radicality of Freud's project lay in its assertion that the capacity to reason is undermined by unconscious, instinctual forces. In the process, Freud subverted the Enlightenment belief that reason enables us to be conscious agents of all our actions: we are never truly masters in our own house. In taking this stand, Freud was lending scientific credence to a whole tradition of German Romantic and post-Romantic philosophy from Schelling through Nietzsche.

The tension between these two seemingly oppositional forces—rationalism and irrationalism—is evident in two of Freud's most famous dictums. Freud remarks that that "Where id was, there shall ego become" (Freud 1933, 111), yet also states that "The ego is not master in its own house" (Freud 1917, 143). The former statement is believed to demonstrate Freud's loyalty to the Enlightenment and forms the cornerstone of ego psychology. The latter statement is often used by proponents of postmodernism, who seek to undermine the Enlightenment view of the ego as the center of all action and motivation. The notion that the ego is a passive effect of forces outside of its control would seem to be borne out by the following statement: "Thus in relation to the id [the ego] is like a man on horseback, who has to hold in check the superior strength of the horse" (Freud 1923, 25).

I would argue that Freud's aim is to show the ways human nature is essentially dialectical—that is, determined both by reason and by the instincts. From a traditional ego psychological perspective, the purpose of psychoanalysis is to strengthen the ego. Because psychoanalysis seeks to heal splits and to restore and enlarge the ego to the greatest possible extent, agency is most often identified with the ego. As Freud (1919, 161) states, "In actual fact, indeed, the neurotic patient presents us with a torn mind, divided by resistances. As we analyze it and remove the resistances, it grows together;

the greater unity which we call his ego fits into itself all the instinctual impulses which before had been split off and held apart from it." On this view, however, it seems that Freud attributes agency to the psychic apparatus, not to the person. Indeed, I would argue that Freud has less interest in the person per se than in showing how the psychic apparatus functions. As a result, it is not always clear who is acting: the apparatus or the person. Psychological agency, in Freud's project, is curiously depersonalized.

The conceptual status of agency in the history of interpersonal psychoanalysis is similarly uncertain. Sullivan, not wishing to take on the metatheoretical rhetoric of Freud, was less interested in creating structure within the person than in showing how the person relates to and is constituted by her environment. Sullivan questions whether the reified explanatory concepts like the id, ego, and superego actually contribute to our understanding of human experience, which he sees as dynamic in nature. He relegates biological drives or instincts to a much more limited role, and emphasizes the importance of interpersonal connectedness. As Sullivan (1950b, 302) states, "Everything that can be found in the human mind has been put there by interpersonal relations, excepting only the capabilities to receive and elaborate the relevant experiences. This statement is intended to be the antithesis of any document of human instincts."

Drawing on the sociology of George Herbert Mead, Sullivan argues that the self is always relationally generated and maintained. According to Sullivan, the content of consciousness is socially derived and gives rise to an illusory sense of self. He maintains that "no such thing as the durable, unique, individual personality is ever clearly justified. For all I know, every human being has as many personalities as he has interpersonal relations" (Sullivan 1950a, 221). Sullivan defines the human being as the total of her relations with others and makes possible the development of a theory of "multiple selves." He recommends that clinicians give up their attempt to define a unique individual self and instead try to grasp what is going on at any particular time in the interpersonal field.

As such, the Sullivanian tradition of interpersonal psychoanalysis has limited interest in the concept of agency. In similar fashion the contemporary postmodern theory of multiple self-states makes it difficult to address the issue of agency with any philosophical consistency. In Sullivan's (1953, 191) words, which leave no doubt about his position on agency: "I know of no evidence of a force or power that may be called a *will*." Yet, clearly the notion of agency *is* important for therapy, and indeed, it is difficult to conceive of continuity of experience, or the possibility of choice, without a concept of agency, however minimal.

The problem, as Sullivan's comments on the "unique, individual personality" illustrate, is that all too often the notion of agency is linked to the solitary, rational Cartesian mind, along the lines of: I think, *I choose*, therefore I am. And it is precisely the rejection of the solitary, rational mind that leads many psychoanalysts to neglect the relevance of agency as a clinical and theoretical concept. However, agency is never simply an isolated act of choice, but a complex process of reflection, informed by personal history and fundamentally embedded in biological and sociocultural contexts. As a result, the singular focus on either the internal, intrapsychic dimension or, conversely, on the interpersonal, social dimension, will not provide a satisfactory account of agency. To appreciate agency as a continually unfolding, contextualized and affective process, it is necessary to turn to other sources.

A Theory of Situated Agency

The complexity of factors that constitute the ground of human experience implies that agency is always multidetermined. We require a pluralistic epistemology that combines first- and second-person perspectives of philosophy and psychotherapy with the third-person perspective of neuroscience (Modell 2003). While reflective self-knowledge is important to the discursive expression of agency, our agential capacities can best be described as emergent, embodied, and experiential. This process always evolves within an intersubjective field and cannot be understood as the function of a disengaged, rational mind. In this final section, I will propose a theory of situated agency that draws from multiple perspectives. Although the ideas I develop here are only briefly elaborated, they will be discussed in the individual chapters of this book.

The traditional separation of thought from action in psychology has made the conceptualization of agency problematic. The history of psychological theorizing over the past century has been persistently marked by this dualism. By viewing agency as fundamentally embodied and active, I believe we can begin to bridge the divide between thinking and action. Much recent physiological and neuroscientific research argues for the basic involvement of the body in all human experience. The process of reflective thought is fundamentally dependent on our embodied, affective interaction with the world around us. Indeed, it is precisely our engagement in the everyday world of practical activity (Giddens 1984) that demonstrates that agency is not an isolated, cognitive process.

In a remarkable confluence of views, philosophers, neuroscientists, and psychoanalytic researchers alike argue that the foundation of our capacity for self-reflexivity lies in our bodily sensations. According to Merleau-Ponty (1962, 3), the mind can only be understood in terms of the body: "The perceiving mind is an incarnated body." His philosophy seeks to undercut the Cartesian distinction between mind and body by arguing that the subject essentially *is* a body. Our bodies continually provide a sense of the situations and contexts in which we exist and interact. In a manner akin to Merleau-Ponty, the linguists George Lakoff and Mark Johnson (1999) insist that the body's preconceptual meaning structure provides the possibility of human thinking. They show that our conceptualization of the world and ourselves is intrinsically linked to our sensorimotor makeup. The body's preconceptual meaning structure also provides the basis for primary metaphors of space and time with which we construct our subjective lives. A similar perspective can be found in the work of the neuroscientist Antonio Damasio (1994, xvi), who argues that the body is a "ground reference" for understanding the world around us:

> The body, as represented in the brain, may constitute the indispensable frame of reference for the neural processes that we experience as the mind; that our very organism rather than some absolute external reality is used as the ground reference for the constructions we make of the world around us and for the construction of the ever-present sense of subjectivity that is part and parcel of our experiences; that our most refined thoughts and best actions, our greatest joys and deepest sorrows, use the body as a yardstick. Surprising as it may sound, the mind exists in and for an integrated organism; our minds would not be the way they are if it were not for the interplay of body and brain during evolution, during individual development, and at the current moment. The mind had to be first about the body, or it could not have been.

Our bodies, on this view, form the basis of affective experience and enable reflective cognitive processes to take place. Contrary to the traditional division of mind and body, these writers describe the fundamental involvement of the body in all human action.

The strict association of agency with reflective, rational thought thus overlooks the fact that reflection is only possible as a result of our prereflective bodily sensations. Our bodily sensations are interactive, akin to affective antennae that make possible our reflective thought and action. Without them we are like a ship without a rudder. A case cited by Damasio (1994) illustrates the way affectivity is vital to the process of agency. Damasio describes a man who suffered extensive brain damage, so that the frontal lobe area of his brain was essentially dissociated from his emotions. While the patient's intellect was apparently intact, he showed an extensive affective flattening. His memory and intelligence were functional but he lacked the capacity to make discriminate judgments because he was not guided by feelings. As a result, he made disastrous decisions. In striking contrast to his previously sound judgment, he could no longer judge future expectations. His ability to reflexively act, to be an agent and choose a course of action, was profoundly restricted. Damasio's case illustration suggests that the process of agency be seen as fundamentally embodied, dependent on our emotions.

From this perspective, we might conclude that the intellect and reflection are a *necessary* but not *sufficient* condition for psychological agency. While the definition of agency in terms of rational, self-knowledge adheres to the Cartesian doctrine of first-person authority, which claims direct introspective access to intentional mind states, I have suggested that agency in the therapeutic setting is more usefully seen as an affective, developmental capacity that is only gradually elaborated. This capacity is intersubjective in nature and related to the response of the other, whether verbal or nonverbal, direct or indirect.

Recent studies of therapeutic interaction, informed by infant research and cognitive science, have revealed the way humans relate to each other not simply on the level of reflective self-knowledge, but at a more primary prereflective level, which is related to bodily sensing. Daniel Stern, a psychoanalytic researcher, refers to this ongoing and ever-present form of human interaction as "implicit relational knowing," and describes it as the domain of knowledge and representation that is "nonsymbolized" and "nonconscious." Rather than being a cognitive process, implicit relatedness is an active, embodied perceptual process. As Stern (2004, 242) states, "Knowledge often implies consciousness knowledge. Implicit relational knowing is nonconscious . . . it has never, as yet, needed to be put into words and may never need to be. It is nonconscious in the sense of never becoming reflectively conscious. The vast majority of all we 'know' about how to be with others resides in implicit relational knowing." Implicit relational knowing has its origins early in infancy, prior to symbolic communication, when interactions between the infant and caregiver take place through the recognition and response to nonverbal affective cues.

Not surprisingly, then, the sense of agency emerges developmentally from the affective relationship between infant and primary caregiver. Indeed, mental agency needs to be understood not as a given, but as a capacity that develops over time. According to Stern (1985), a sense of emergent agency is already evident from birth, and comes to be through affective interaction with the parent. This interaction takes the form of "affective mirroring," by virtue of which infants not only begin to understand what they feel by seeing it reflected in the caregiver, they see that they have the potential to control or modulate those feelings. The capacity for affect regulation is crucial for the child to be able to interpret her own mental states as well as those of others.

By age four or five the child is able to realize her own sense of self—the so-called autobiographical sense—through the process of mentalization, which involves both a self-reflective and an interpersonal component (Fonagy and Target 1998). Thus, the ability to understand others as intentional agents, and in turn to develop our own sense of ourselves as agents, far from being dependent simply on our cognitive, linguistic abilities, is embedded in the relational and developmental nature of our interactions with the world.

In their study of infant development and mentalization, Fonagy et al. (2002) trace the development of the young child's emerging understanding of the self and others as agents in its environment. They delineate five levels of agency of which the developing human infant acquires a progressive understanding: physical, social, teleological, intentional, and representational, ranging from early infancy through four to five years of age. Their studies suggest that the mature understanding of the self as a mental agent is likely to be the product of complex developmental processes. When these developmental processes are derailed or when pathological forms of attachment occur, then not only may a sense of agency be forestalled, it may also be pathological.

A developmental perspective can help us appreciate that the capacity to become an agent is both enabled and inhibited by the intersubjective and discursive fields in which we live. In other words, it is possible for a person to have a "healthy" as well as "pathological" sense of agency.[2] A healthy sense of agency can potentially be understood in terms of a person's relational engagement with the other and the situational contexts in which she finds herself. By relating to the other person it becomes possible to resolve problems in living through reflective action. A "pathological" sense of agency can be described in terms of a constriction of the relational potential for interaction and dialogue with others. As a result of this constriction, subsequent behaviors may impact negatively on the person and her attempts to deal with others and her contexts.

By making a direct link between action and relational engagement, I am suggesting that agency does not occur in a vacuum but is always and already emergent in the intersubjective field of our experience. The ability to make creative choices that can affect life experience is dependent on an openness to new possibilities of relating to ourselves, to others, and to the world around us. Thus, the potential for agency is shaped throughout life as our experiences are learned and transformed by us in intersubjective contexts that range on multiple levels from the family, to organizations, institutions, and the nation-state (Gardiner 1995).

As I have suggested, this view of agency as fundamentally contextualized is indebted to the hermeneutic perspective. This broad tradition owes much to the ideas of Martin Heidegger (1996) and Hans-Georg Gadamer (1995). In his early philosophy, for example, Heidegger seeks to overcome naturalism and determinism in his ontological account of existence. Heidegger rejects the Cartesian view of the subject, arguing that existence manifests itself as "being-in-the-world." Accordingly, the person is not simply *of* a particular sociocultural context, and this context does not *only* form the background for activity. The embeddedness of the person in sociocultural contexts is so profound as to render any absolute distinction of action from context nonsensical. We are "always and already in the world" in such a way that there is no possibility of separating the self and world. From this perspective, we can never exist outside of our world of experience. We find ourselves "thrown" into a world we neither create nor control. Yet it is up to each of us to take up the possibilities of self-understanding into which we are thrown and shape them into lives that are our own. In other words, the capacity for agency is dependent upon our being-in-the-world. As self-interpreting beings, persons are always contributors to the contexts in which they exist and participate.

The hermeneutic tradition suggests that there is no psychological experience that is not constituted by the sociocultural and interpretive contexts in which we find ourselves. Our experience is always contingent on the context that constitutes our personhood by way of interpretations and practices. In his elaboration of the hermeneutic position, Charles Taylor (1989, 30) describes a human agent who exists in a space of questions: "These are the questions to which our framework-definitions are answers, providing the horizon within which we know where we stand, and what meanings things have for us." This perspective throws up a strong challenge to the image of an agent free from all frameworks, who, according to Taylor, would be "a person in the grip of an appalling identity crisis. Such a person wouldn't know where he stood on issues of fundamental importance, would have no orientation in these issues whatsoever . . . a person without a framework altogether would be outside our space of interlocution" (p. 31). The hermeneutic conceptualization of agency seeks to move beyond the objectivist view of reality and emphasizes both our situated psychological existence and the role of the interpreting agent.

Up to this point I have referred primarily to the "personal" nature of our agential capacity. I want now to focus more specifically on the psychological nature of agency. Whereas the hermeneutic perspective demonstrates the way we are always and already embedded in the sociocultural contexts in which we participate, I believe a contemporary psychodynamic or psychoanalytic perspective can help us elucidate the importance of the affective dimension of experience. The approach I am espousing is not concerned with the individualistic and Cartesian intrapsychic structures identified by

Freud and classical psychoanalysis, but with affective processes, often prereflective and prediscursive in form, that emerge at the nexus of personal, interpersonal, and sociocultural dimensions of experience.

Although psychoanalysis often continues to be perceived as a monolithic entity, characterized by an exclusive set of Cartesian ideas and beliefs associated with Freud and his followers, the dispersion and transformation of analytic theory, practice, and research over time have created a broad and rich contemporary clinical tradition with links to such disciplines as the neurosciences (Modell 2003), philosophy (Frie 1997; Mills 2003; Stolorow, Atwood, and Orange 2002), sociology (Elliott 2004), anthropology (Molin 2004), and others. The contributors to this book who are practicing psychoanalysts, in addition to being clinical psychologists or psychiatrists, identify themselves within this contemporary "revisionist" analytic and interdisciplinary sensibility. Thus, the term *psychoanalysis* as it is used here refers not to the analysis of "interior processes" of isolated individual minds, but to the understanding of human experience as fundamentally intersubjective and context-bound.

An orientation attuned to the ambiguity of psychological experience helps us shed light on the shifting nature of psychic life between the prereflective and reflective, and prediscursive and discursive dimensions of experience. Reflectiveness, as we have seen, is not only a realm of cognitive, discursive intersubjectivity. Rather, reflectiveness presupposes the creative and affective dimensions of imagination, wishes, needs, and desires—and psychoanalysis can help us understand and appreciate the emergent, affective processes on which our reflective capabilities depend. As the philosopher and psychoanalyst Cornelius Castoriadis (1997, 127–128) states, "What is most human is not rationality but the uncontrolled and uncontrollable surge of creative radical imagination in and through the flux of representations, affects, and desires."

While psychological experience cannot easily be distinguished from the contexts in which we exist—lest we fall back on the binary separation between an internal, introspective self and the external object world—it is important to account for ways in which our psychological being affects our situatedness. The point is that the psychological is not simply reducible to the cultural surround, but has a crucial function in the shaping and constituting of human life and society. As Nancy Chodorow (1999, 174) suggests from her interdisciplinary perspective of sociology and psychoanalysis,

> Each of us creates psychological meaning throughout life. This individual psychological meaning is an equal constituent of any person's experience of cultural meaning. . . . If the meanings of particular feelings and the experience of self, personhood, tribe, group, class, or nation, gender, or sexuality are important and culturally charged, it is

also because they are individually charged, through those interpersonal processes and emotional contexts, verbal and nonverbal, in which they are given meaning, and as individuals throughout life bestow on them their own set of personal meanings in addition to experiencing the rich, polysemic meanings of culture.

It is not enough, however, to talk of "interaction" between personal psychological meaning and culture. Rather, the person is communally forged (Martin 2007), through her participation in the relational practices of social and cultural contexts. There is no person, and no agency, outside of the biophysical and sociocultural contexts in which we exist. Yet neither can the person, or agency, be wholly reduced to these contexts.

I believe that a contemporary psychoanalytic perspective can provide the means to document psychological processes, such as agency, which create personal meaning in addition to culture, language, and power relations. Following Chodorow (1999), I see this agential process of making meaning as infusing culture with personal and psychological significance at the same time that it potentially changes and transforms the discourses and traditions in which we participate. The person is not simply inscribed into a given reality or context. The world exists for us because we participate in it and invest it with meaning of a personal, psychological nature.

Chapter Outline

Part I: Theoretical Contexts

The initial group of chapters seek to counter the Cartesian distinction between thought and action, which rests on assumptions about first person authority and an internal, isolated mind. The chapters address the problem of psychological agency from neuroscientific, philosophical, and sociopolitical perspectives. Agency is viewed as situated rather than scientifically distinct, decontextualized, neutral, or predictive. The authors develop a concept of agency that arises out of biology, society, and culture, but that cannot be entirely reduced back to these origins. Human existence, in their view, is dependent on biophysical and sociocultural realities, but agency is not wholly determined by these levels of reality. The chapters seek to account for how contexts operate in persons and how persons operate in contexts, each creating the other in a seamless web.

In the first chapter, "The Agency of the Self and the Brain's Illusions," Arnold Modell develops the parallels between contemporary neuroscience and certain forms of psychoanalysis. The interaction of these two disciplines, according to Modell, can provide a way to appreciate and understand biophysical theories of human action without reducing the human being to a series of brain functions or responses to stimuli. Although neuroscience has confirmed that our sense of agency may be an illusion, Modell argues that it is a necessary illusion, which can be impaired or enhanced. He suggests that while the experience of emotional trauma may impair our sense of agency, psychological treatment can augment the self-as-agent. Agency is enlarged through the creation of new meaning and is related to the recontextualization of the memories and feelings of past experience in the therapeutic process.

In the second chapter, "Becoming Agents: Hegel, Nietzsche, and Psychoanalysis," Elliott L. Jurist employs the philosophical positions of Hegel and Nietzsche to develop the outline of a psychoanalytic theory of agency. Although these two thinkers are often characterized as opponents—Hegel as the advocate of the Enlightenment, Nietzsche as challenging the Enlightenment—Jurist suggests that the truth is considerably more complex. Hegel celebrates rationality as the key to human agency, but he also affirms a psychological approach: emphasizing the importance of intersubjectivity and appreciating the inevitability of failure as part of the search for well-being. Nietzsche draws attention to the theme of irrationality, but he also relies on a psychological approach: claiming that we need to embrace rather than deny our narcissism, our bodies, our affects and instincts. While Hegel and Nietzsche do not agree, Jurist suggests that their views can be accommodated and incorporated into a theoretically coherent and clinically relevant theory of psychological agency.

In the third chapter, "Understanding Persons as Relational Agents: The Philosophy of John Macmurray and Its Implications for Psychology," Jeff Sugarman presents the view that persons are distinguished by a human agency whose nature takes shape through its immersion and participation in communal relations with others. In articulating this viewpoint, Sugarman elaborates the work of the twentieth-century Scottish philosopher John Macmurray, and draws parallels with recent social philosophy, psychotherapy, and psychoanalysis. Macmurry argues that the individual is not only an intentional agent who chooses and constructs experience through action, but is also a person who exists, from birth, in dynamic interaction with other persons, and whose particular kind of self-conscious agency arises as a consequence of embeddedness in human relations. Personal existence, in Macmurray's view, is a relational becoming, an ongoing agentic activity in which we are constituted mutually with each other as persons. Building on Macmurray's ideas, Sugarman considers the relevance of this relational conception of agency for the therapeutic setting and within a wider, social and political realm. He concludes that agentic and relational personhood should assume a central role in any adequate conception of human psychology.

Part II: Clinical and Developmental Contexts

Psychologists often presuppose that human action and experience are determined by biophysical and sociocultural causes and, at the same time, regard everyday choices, actions, and experiences as significant and influential (Martin, Sugarman, and Thompson 2003). Clinical psychologists, in particular, tend to take human agency for granted, because they assume that their clients are capable of making choices and of actively initiating change in ways that can transform their lives. As the second group of chapters suggest, the practice of psychotherapy requires a less unified, more malleable notion of agency. The process of agency is not a product of the individual mind, nor does agency refer strictly to intentions and choices. Rather, agency is a developmentally emergent process that is evidenced in the flow of human action. Using clinical examples and drawing on a variety of intersubjective and developmental perspectives, the authors present a conceptualization of agency that can account for the complexity of psychological experience. They eschew rationalist conceptions of autonomous agency and instead emphasize the fundamentally relational nature of our agential capacity.

In the fourth chapter, "Perspectival Selves and Agents: Agency within Sociality," Jack Martin suggests that when agency is understood as a particular kind of self-determination, its developmental emergence goes hand in hand with the emergence of selfhood. Drawing on the sociology of George Herbert Mead, Martin argues that selfhood arises from taking the perspectives of others and the broader society, and applying them to one's own person and activities. He presents a detailed sketch of the development of this perspectival self during ontogenesis. Martin incorporates ideas and findings from pragmatic, hermeneutic, sociocultural, and developmental scholarship in psychology and philosophy. The relevance of this approach to agency is illustrated by using a clinical case example from psychotherapy. Particular emphasis is placed on perspective taking, self-interpretation, and self-reactivity. Martin argues that these uniquely human capabilities enable a self-determining agency that is conditional, but constantly emergent across the life course of human beings.

In the fifth chapter, "Agency and Its Clinical Phenomenology," Jill Gentile argues that psychological agency arises at the cross-section of three dimensions of experience: the individual, the intersubjective, and the Third. In this interplay, transformations of personal experience emerge in tandem with transformations of our intersubjective relations and with semiotic empowerment. It is particularly the process of semiotic empowerment—the capacity to use signs to communicate our desires and intentions, and to interpret the communications of others—that for Gentile is inseparably linked to a phenomenological trajectory of meaning creation. From a clinical perspective, she describes the "clinical impasse" as a semiotic confinement in which there is no space for interpretation or reflection and in which a phenomenology of "perverse agency" predominates. Using clinical case examples, she describes how the opening of a space for interpretation allows for the emergence of increased semiotic empowerment and an experience of personal agency. Clinical markers of early transformations in the phenomenology of personal agency, as patients first begin to experience themselves as agents of meaning making, are described.

In the sixth chapter, "Agency as Fluid Process: Clinical and Theoretical Considerations," Pascal Sauvayre addresses the incompatibility of the claims of freedom and determination for understanding agency within clinical contexts. Sauvayre argues that agency arises in the activity of the self in the flow of experience. He uses a clinical case example to illustrate the ways agency is an inherently fluid rather than static process. Attempts to solve the philosophical debate between freedom and determination run into an impasse when they view agency and experience as static concepts. Sauvayre suggests that a different type of reflection, exemplified in the philosophical work of Bergson and Merleau-Ponty, overcomes the limitations of the traditional freedom-versus-determinism debate, and allows for the elaboration of agency as a fluid, dynamic, and essential psychological process.

In the seventh chapter, "Dimensions of Agency and the Process of Coparticipant Inquiry," John Fiscalini articulates the role of agency as a guiding clinical principle within the paradigm of coparticipant inquiry. This perspective integrates and moves beyond the individualistic (one-person) psychology of classical psychoanalysis and the interpersonal (two-person) paradigm of participant observation. The clinical dialectics of the interpersonal and personal dimensions of a multidimensional conception of the self are elaborated to account for the complexity of self-experience. With the use of a clinical case example, the therapeutic importance of psychological agency is elaborated, as are the curative roles of personal responsibility and interpersonal responsiveness. Agency is contextualized within the paradoxical nature of the human psyche—that humans are all uniquely individual while simultaneously communally connected.

Part III: Social and Cultural Contexts

Psychological approaches to agency often overlook the larger contexts not only of cultural beliefs and values, but also of the distribution of power and other resources that shape human efficacy. Agency occurs within social and cultural contexts that always frame it in particular ways. Yet agency can have varied meanings and take different forms in specfic contexts, or among different groups of people. Closer examination of race, ethnicity, gender, social class, and other factors also reveals the ways subordinate status often shapes opportunities for agency. These factors limit as well as determine questions of choice and action, and the authors of this third group of chapters suggest that it is not only possible but necessary to respond to these limits. Thus, the final chapters consider the diverse ways of responding to the possibilities and constraints created by sociocultural contexts. In the process, the authors seek to describe the diversity of agency across different contexts.

In the eighth chapter, "Psychological Agency: A Necessarily Human Concept," Adelbert Jenkins argues that a developed conception of psychological agency is an essential component of the effort to understand the contextualized nature of human individuality. Jenkins focuses on the capacity for the imaginative construction of meaning as a psychologically and socioculturally adaptive tool. He grounds his view of agency in the "logical learning theory" of Joseph Rychlak, and takes issue with recent trends in social science scholarship that discount the importance of psychological agency. Jenkins illustrates the significance of the agency framework by presenting a discussion of its relevance to two subject domains: those of psychotherapy and multicultural psychology. With respect to the first topic he suggests that the agency concept indicates ways psychotherapy works by opening a client's imaginative and experiential capacities to more fruitful alternatives for engaging their circumstances. With regard to psychological issues among people of color, Jenkins argues that their survival in the United States has depended historically on their ability to reconceptualize the negative images and situations presented to them. This use of agency, he suggests, has enabled ethnic minorities to find their own sense of worth and personhood. Jenkins thus argues that the person is an active agent who chooses from among the possibilities for conceiving situations and in so doing is crucially responsible for influencing the direction of her life.

In the ninth chapter, "Sexual Agency in Women: Beyond Romance," Linda Pollock argues that despite the fact that sexualized images of women are ubiquitous, and despite the fact that women are more sexually expressive today than in the past, women's sexual desire continues to be obscured and silenced. In Western culture sexual desire is traditionally a male province, associated with domination and aggression, and a factor that perpetuates the oppression and control of women. Pollock focuses on young women, especially adolescent women, who tend to be most vulnerable to our culture's misogynist assumptions. Under pressure from consumer-driven culture, adolescent women find themselves in the paradoxical position of striving to be attractive to men while protecting themselves from men. Basic to any resolution of this paradox is the development of a healthy sense of sexual agency, a woman's ability to take responsibility and make choices about her own sexual behavior. To understand better the psychological forces at work in adolescent women struggling to define their sexuality on their own terms, Pollock elaborates a model of human development that draws on the work of Robert Kegan and offers insight into the psychological underpinnings of sexual agency.

In the final chapter, "Navigating Cultural Contexts: Agency and Biculturalism," Roger Frie examines the problem of psychological agency within the context of biculturalism. Two perspectives on agency are counterpoised; each is relevant for understanding the experience of biculturalism. On the one hand, I argue that agency is understood as a cultural phenomenon, in which action and choice depend on cultural processes for their realization. On the other hand, I argue that an overarching emphasis on cultural contexts tends to overlook the place of agency in the construction of personal meaning. In bicultural experience, agency plays a key role in the psychological functioning of individuals across cultures, enabling them to navigate and make sense of multiple identities. When the role of the person as agent is overlooked or downplayed, it is difficult to understand the person's capacity for reflectivity despite the demands and constraints of their cultural contexts. Using a clinical case example, I argue that the current emphasis on social context and cultural categories, though important, often underestimates the idiosyncratic backgrounds and needs of the individual person. Although the person is culturally formed, she retains the potential to respond to her sociocultural contexts. Over time, the shape of this conversation constitutes who we are as persons.

Notes

1. In maintaining that the distinction between naturalism and postmodernism constitutes a serious challenge to the conceptualization of agency, I am drawing on a rich intellectual tradition. This tradition includes, among others, the following key works: first and foremost, Charles Taylor, *Sources of the Self: The Making of Modern Identity* (1989), which forms the background against which much current theorizing about agency in psychology takes place; Richard Bernstein, *Beyond Objectivism and Relativism: Science, Hermeneutics, and Practice* (1983), which argues for an understanding of the intersubjective and communal nature of rationality; and Jack Martin, Jeff Sugarman, and Janice Thompson, *Psychology and the Question of Agency* (2003), whose work has helped to reinvigorate the discussion of agency in contemporary psychology. Employing a hermeneutic perspective, Martin, Sugarman, and Thompson provide an analysis of a wide range of historical and contemporary approaches to

agency in psychological theory, practice, and research. It is their notion of agency as a thoroughly contexualized yet "emergent" phenomena that has been particularly useful to my own thinking on the subject.

2. Given the normative implications of such terms as *healthy* and *pathological,* it is important to note that I am using them here simply to illustrate that the development of agency can take different clinical forms. Such terms, in my view, are best understood as "fluid descriptors" of behavior, and always need to be understood against a background of the ever-changing historical and sociocultural contexts and norms in which we live.

References

Benjamin, J. 1988. *The bonds of love: Psychoanalysis, feminism and the problem of domination.* London: Virago.

Bernstein, R. 1983. *Beyond objectivism and relativism: Science, hermeneutics and practice.* Philadelphia: University of Pennsylvania Press.

Burston, D., and Frie, R. 2006. *Psychotherapy as a human science.* Pittsburgh: Duquesne University Press.

Castoriadis, C. 1997. *World in fragments: Writings on politics, society, psychoanalysis, and the imagination.* Ed. and trans. David Ames Curtis. Stanford, Calif.: Stanford University Press.

Chodorow, N. 1999. *The power of feelings: Personal meaning in psychoanalysis, gender, and culture.* New Haven, Conn.: Yale University Press.

Damasio, A. 1994. *Descartes' error: Emotion, reason, and the human brain.* New York: Avon Books.

Dews. P. 1987. *Logics of disintegration: Post-structuralist thought and the claims of critical theory.* London: Verso.

Dilthey, W. 1977. *Descriptive psychology and historical understanding* Trans. R. M. Zaner and K. L. Heiges. The Hague: Martinus Nijhoff. (Originally published in 1894 and 1927.)

Eagleton, T. 1991. *Ideology: An introduction.* London: Verso.

Eagleton, T. 1996. *The illusions of postmodernism.* Oxford: Blackwell.

Elliott, A. 2004. *Subject to ourselves: Social theory, psychoanalysis, and postmodernity.* Boulder, Colo.: Paradigm.

Fonagy, P., Gergely, G., Jurist, E., and Target, M. 2005. *Affect regulation, mentalization and the development of self.* New York: Other Press.

Fonagy, P., and Target, M. 1998. Mentalization and the changing aims of child psychoanalysis. *Psychoanalytic Dialogues* 8:87–114.

Freud, S. 1917. A difficulty in the path of psychoanalysis. In *The standard edition of the complete psychological works of Sigmund Freud*, vol. 17. London: Vintage, 2001.

Freud, S. 1919. Lines of advance in psycho-analytic therapy. In *The standard edition of the complete psychological works of Sigmund Freud*, vol. 17. London: Vintage, 2001.

Freud, S. 1923. The Ego and the Id. In *The standard edition of the complete psychological works of Sigmund Freud*, vol. 19. London: Vintage, 2001.

Freud, S. 1933. New introductory lectures. In *The standard edition of the complete psychological works of Sigmund Freud*, vol. 22. London: Vintage, 2001.

Frie, R. 1997. *Subjectivity and intersubjectivity in philosophy and psychoanalysis*. Lanham, Md.: Rowman and Littlefield.

Gadamer, H.-G. 1995. *Truth and method*. Trans. J. Weinsheimer and D. G. Marshall. 2nd ed. New York: Continuum. (Originally published in 1960.)

Gardiner, J. K., ed. 1995. *Provoking agents: Gender and agency in theory and practice*. Champaign: University of Illinois Press.

Gergen, K. 1985. The social constructionist movement in modern psychology. *American Psychologist* 40:266–275.

Gergen, K. 1991. *The saturated self*. New York: Basic Books.

Giddens, A. 1984 *The constitution of society: Outline of the theory of structuration*. Berkeley, CA: University of California Press.

Greenberg, J., and Mitchell, S. A. 1983. *Object relations in psychoanalytic theory*. Cambridge, Mass.: Harvard University Press.

Heidegger, M. 1996. *Being and time*. Trans. J. Stambaugh. Albany: SUNY Press. (Originally published in 1927.)

Holland, D., Lachicotte, W., Skinner, D., and Cain, C. 1998. *Identity and agency in cultural worlds*. Cambridge, Mass.: Harvard University Press.

Kennett, J., and Matthews, S. 2003. The unity and disunity of agency. *Philosophy, Psychiatry, and Psychology* 10:305–312.

Lakoff, G., and Johnson, M. 1999. *Philosophy in the flesh: The embodied mind and its challenge to Western thought*. New York: Perseus Press.

Mackenzie, C., and Stoljar, N., eds. 2000. *Relational autonomy: Feminist perspectives on autonomy, agency, and the social self*. Oxford: Oxford University Press.

Martin, J. 2007 The selves of educational psychology: Conceptions, contexts, and critical considerations. *Educational Psychologist* 42:79–89.

Martin, J., Sugarman, J., and Thompson, J. 2003. *Psychology and the question of agency*. Albany: SUNY Press.

Merleau-Ponty, M. 1962. *The primacy of perception*. Evanston, Ill.: Northwestern University Press.

Messer, S. B., Sass, L. A., and Woolfolk, R. L., eds. 1988. *Hermeneutics and psychological theory: Interpretive perspectives on personality, psychotherapy, and psychopathology*. New Brunswick, N.J.: Rutgers University Press.

Mills, J. 2003. The unconscious abyss: Hegel's anticipation of psychoanalysis. Albany, NY: SUNY Press.

Mitchell, S. A. 1993. *Hope and dread in psychoanalysis*. New York: Basic Books.

Modell, A. 2003. *Imagination and the meaningful brain*. Cambridge, Mass.: The MIT Press.

Molino, A., ed. 2004. *Culture, subject, psyche: Dialogues in psychoanalysis and anthropology*. Middletown, Conn.: Wesleyan University Press.

Sawicki, J. 1991. *Disciplining Foucault: Feminism, power, and the body*. London: Routledge.

Stern, D. 1985. *The interpersonal world of the infant: A view from psychoanalysis and developmental psychology*. New York: Basic Books.

Stern, D. 2004. *The present moment: In psychotherapy and everyday life*. New York: Norton.

Stolorow, R., and Atwood, G. 1992. *Contexts of being: The intersubjective foundations of psychological life*. Hillsdale, N.J.: Analytic Press.

Stolorow, R., Atwood, G., and Orange, D. 2002. *Worlds of experience: Interweaving philosophical and clinical dimensions in psychoanalysis*. New York: Basic Books.

Sullivan, H. S. 1950a. The illusion of personal individuality. In *The fusion of psychiatry and social science*, 198–226. New York: Norton.

Sullivan, H. S. 1950b. Tensions interpersonal and international. In H. Cantril, ed., *Tensions that cause war*. Urbana: University of Illinois Press.

Sullivan, H. S. 1953. *Conceptions of modern psychiatry*. New York: Norton.

Taylor, C. 1989. *Sources of the self: The making of the modern identity*. Cambridge, Mass.: Harvard University Press.

I Theoretical Contexts

1 The Agency of the Self and the Brain's Illusions

Arnold Modell

Our feelings arise from within our bodies without our bidding, and are therefore beyond our control. This fact, that we do not control our feelings, is an aspect of human nature that has been noted since antiquity. This then raises the question, if we do not control our feelings, to what extent we are free, and as a corollary, to what extent are we responsible for our actions?

If we are not free but in bondage to our feelings, our sense of agency is an illusion. Contemporary neuroscience appears to have confirmed this assumption. Although our feeling of agency is an illusion, it is a *necessary* illusion, an illusion that can be enhanced or impaired. Emotional trauma can permanently impair our feeling of agency. On the other hand, one of the aims of psychoanalysis as well as other forms of psychological treatment is to further self-actualization, to enhance and enlarge the sense of agency. I will suggest that psychological treatment may augment the sense of agency of the self by recontextualizing the memories and feelings of past experience. Agency is enlarged through the creation of new meanings. If successful, this recontextualization promotes a more coherent narrative of the self. Although neuroscience has shown that conscious will is an illusion, science has also shown that creating illusions is what the brain does.

The source of our feelings, what we now attribute to an unconscious neural process, the ancient Greeks attributed to an interfering God. In the *Iliad,* Agamemnon states regarding his fury at Achilles, which proved catastrophic: "I am not to blame, Zeus and Fate are the ones that drove this savage madness in my heart" (quoted in Lear 2005). The *Iliad* therefore recognized the problem of agency of the self: to what extent are we in control of our soul? This question has been examined since the beginning of psychological thought. Plato viewed the problem of agency as a dialogue between the "passions of the body" and the immortal soul. In *The Laws,* Plato suggested that humans may merely be puppets: "Whether the gods made us simply as a plaything or for some serious purpose one cannot tell; all we know is that the creature is on a string, and its hopes and fears, pleasures and pains, jerk it about and make it dance" (quoted in Dodds 1951). Later Greek philosophers recognized the source of agency to be internal and not God driven, because they observed a fundamental conflict between the passions and the controlling influence of reason. Some Greek philosophers believed that emotions are unreasoning movements that push the person around like gusts of wind. Much later, Spinoza described the passions as a form of human bondage. Moreover: "Freedom of the individual is the sole independent value to which all creatures pursue by nature." Spinoza viewed self-actualization as the ultimate sign of freedom, suggesting that freedom from bondage can be found in the use of the imagination when combined with reason (Hampshire 2005). Spinoza anticipated my thesis that the self becomes free through the creation of new meanings. There are echoes of Spinoza in Freud's famous aphorism regarding the aim of psychoanalysis: "Where id was ego shall be," or in a more recent paraphrase, "Where it was I shall be." The aim of psychoanalysis is to extend the agency of the self, through the expansion of personal awareness and conscious intention over the impersonal id.

When Freud demonstrated that consciousness occupies a much smaller part of mental life than had been believed, he was by implication referring to our sense of agency. He famously declared that "human megalomania will have suffered its third [after Copernicus and Darwin] and most wounding blow from the psychological research at the present time which seeks to prove to the ego that it is not even master in his own house" (Freud 1917, 143). In *The Ego and the Id*, Freud (1923, 25) used the metaphor of horse and rider to describe the ego's relationship to the unconscious forces of the id: "The relation to the id is like a man on horseback, who has to hold in check the superior strength of the horse; with this difference, the rider tries to do so with his own strength while the ego uses borrowed forces. The analogy may be carried a little further. Often a rider if he is not to be parted from his horse, is obliged to guide it where it wants to go." Parenthetically, the editors of the Standard Edition note that Freud may have been influenced in his choice of metaphor by an old joke: a friend sees Sammy riding in the park one Sunday and inquires where he is going. Sammy replies, "I don't know, ask the horse."

Agency and the Ambiguity of the Ownership of Feelings

Agency means causality, and strictly speaking, we are never the cause of our feelings but only responsible for their interpretation. If agency implies causality, ownership implies a recognition that I am the one that is having the feeling (Gallagher 2000). But we can never be quite sure whether our feelings originate in our own bodies or have been secondarily placed within us. We do not question that we are the one experiencing the feeling, but we remain uncertain as to how the feeling got there. Feelings have what William James described as an ambiguity of place. Inasmuch as feelings are unconsciously communicated, what we feel may be in response to an unconscious perception of feelings that originate in other minds and are directed toward us by the Other. Our feelings belong to us because they are part of our body, but because our feelings respond to the feelings of the Other, like Agamemnon we can say we are not to blame.

It is now established that our response to the affective state of the Other is a biological given. Since infancy we have empathically responded to the feeling state of the Other. Is my depressed mood sui generis or the result of contagion, a response to the Other's depression? Psychoanalysts are aware of this problem daily, because they need to sort out whether the primary source of their feeling state is a private matter that has nothing to do with their patient, or whether their feeling state is a conjoined response to feelings originating in the mind of the patient. Regarding the origin of feelings, a threefold distinction may be useful: feelings that are entirely generated from within; feelings that are conjoined through empathy; and feelings that are "placed" there by the Other and are alien to our own sense of self, an example of which would be projective identification.

Agency Marking the Awareness of Self

We believe that the child's discovery of their sense of agency promotes and reinforces their awareness that the self is an entity in the world, an entity that has an effect on inanimate objects and also persons. As an entity in the world we need to know that we can evoke a response in the Other. Children of depressed mothers, mothers who do not respond to them, experience a loss of agency. On the other hand, a feeling of agency enhances consciousness of self. This awareness can be the source of immense pleasure. The noted Australian physiologist Derek Denton (1993, 68) provided the following remembrance:

> This instance in my own childhood at about age 3, is still dramatically clear. My father owned a factory, and one day brought home a couple of hundred or so small wooden blocks of various shapes. In those days, ocean liners were preeminent, and I had obviously seen pictures of them. For two or three days I must have worked in the garden in Tasmania intent on building my liner, but the final moment when I put the gangplank across is a vivid recollection. It was a sense of real joy at something I had done or had

made. I recall exactly where the sun was and the scene including the light and shadow across a tree fern nearby, and the exact positions of buildings, doorways and so forth. I suspect the satisfaction has something to do with the sense of self.

Denton's observation that this has something to do with the sense of self is an understatement. The vividness of his memory marks nothing less than the full-grown birth of his sense of self. And I suspect that the persistence he demonstrated in constructing his ship at the age of three represented a character trait that contributed to his later eminence.

Our first feeling of agency, in infancy and early childhood, has its source in the body, our feelings of the action of our muscles and tendons in their interaction with the world. Let us imagine an infant lying on her back with a mobile suspended overhead. Her feet at first move in a random uncontrolled manner, then one day she accidentally kicks against the mobile and sees that it moves. She repeats the action and gradually she learns that she can control the movement of her feet and, in turn, her feet can alter an object in the real world. What she wills has an effect not only on her body but also in the world. She can make things happen. This discovery of effectiveness is a source of joy. Experiencing a sense of the expanding agency of the self remains pleasurable throughout our lives, affirming that the agency of the self contributes to a feeling of vitality. Robert White (1963) spoke of this as *effectance*, the pleasure of observing that our actions have consequences in the world. If our earliest sense of self is reinforced through motor action, the loss of such agency can prove devastating to one's sense of self.

An Example of the Loss of Motor Agency and Its Consequences

An account of the loss of motor agency was provided by the neurologist Oliver Sacks in his book *A Leg to Stand On* (1984). Sacks tells us that he encountered a bull when climbing a mountain in Norway. Fearing attack, he ran down the mountain and suffered an injury that seriously damaged the muscles and nerves of his leg. He lost all sense of proprioception in that leg; he lost an unconscious affirmation that the leg existed as an object in the world. His leg was there, it was not missing, he could see it and therefore infer that it was there, but he could not move it or feel it. He described this loss of proprioception as follows:

One may be said to own or possess one's body—at least as limbs and movable parts—by virtue of a constant flowing of incoming information, arising ceaselessly, throughout life, from the muscles, joints and tendons. One has oneself, one is oneself, because the body knows itself, confirms itself, at all times, by this sixth sense. . . . The more

I gazed at the cylinder of chalk (the cast), the more alien and incomprehensible it appeared to me. I could no longer feel it as mine, as part of me. It seemed to bear no relation whatever to me. It was absolutely not me—and yet, impossibly, it was attached to me—and even more impossibly, continuous with me. (pp. 50–51)

Sacks further states after the cast was removed:

The day before touching it I had at least touched something . . . whereas today I touched nothing at all. The flesh underneath my fingers no longer seems like flesh. It no longer seemed like material or matter. It no longer resembled anything. The more I gazed at it and handled it, the less it was there, the more it became Nothing and Nowhere. Unalive, unreal it was no part of me—no part of my body, or anything else. It didn't "go" anywhere. It had no place in the world. I lost the inner image, or representation, of the leg. It was a disturbance, an obliteration of its representation in the brain—of this part of the body image. (p. 52)

Sacks goes on to describe his gradual recovery and his regaining of a sense of agency. Initially he felt that his leg did not belong to him when it refused to obey orders. In Sacks's account, "When I awoke I had an odd impulse to flex my leg—and in that self-same moment immediately did so! Here was a movement previously impossible. I had thought it and done it. The idea, the impulse, the action were all one. The power of moving, the idea of moving, the impulse to move would suddenly come to me—and then suddenly go" (p. 54). What was central in this process of gaining control of movement was the awareness of the self. In his words, "These flashes of involuntary spontaneous unbidden movements involve me: they weren't just muscle jumping but *me* remembering: they involve me and my mind no less than my body" (p. 54).

The Recontextualizing of Proprioception

When Oliver Sacks lost proprioceptive sensations in his leg he essentially lost a sense of ownership of that leg. That leg did not belong to him. As he showed, the sense of ownership referred not only to his body but also to his self. It would appear that the bodily self requires updating through constant sensory inputs. In the absence of such inputs the self loses both a sense of ownership and a sense of agency. The phenomenon of phantom limbs also illustrates this observation. If a limb is lost through amputation, the brain can reconstruct the body image to create an illusionary limb. The brain can construct the illusion of coherence of the body image irrespective of the actual state of the body. The neurologist V. S. Ramachandran (1998) reports that 70 percent of those who suffer from phantom limbs experience pain, and the pain may persist for as long as twenty-five years after the injury. Ramachandran has shown that there is evidence that this pain is not the product of irritated peripheral nerves but is an illusion created centrally by the brain. Phantom limbs are not only just there, but can be experienced as if they respond to the will and perform specific acts. Some phantom limbs can be experienced as if they are performing customary motor acts of everyday life such as waving goodbye or reaching for a cup. It would seem that the brain, in the absence of sensory inputs, creates the illusion not only of sensory inputs but also of an ensemble of motor actions. Phantom limbs have even been observed in individuals who have been born without limbs (Bruggeret al. 2000). In these individuals, the brain creates the illusion of missing sensations entirely from within, because such individuals have no memory of having had limbs.

To summarize, phantom limbs attest to the brain's capacity to create illusions in the absence of sensory inputs. The brain can emulate the reality of a portion of the body in the absence of sensation; this is analogous to a dream state.

The Recontextualization of Memory and Feelings

We know that without proprioceptive feelings, we do not believe that we are the agent of motor actions, as Sacks (1984) described. This feeling in our limbs in turn is experienced in the context of a stream of sensory inputs that contribute to the image of our body as a whole, as a separate entity in the world. The image of the body as a whole serves as a background condition. The motor act is the foreground, a figure against the background of the body as a complete entity, so that our motor actions are always felt within the context of that entity, a foundational source of self feelings.

Is there an analogous process with regard to mental agency? Mental agency is more difficult to define than physical agency. I think of mental agency as the pleasure of using one's mind in the service of self-actualization. Mental agency is the awareness that one is the author of one's thoughts. The expansion of mental agency is an implicit aim of psychoanalysis, as expressed in Freud's (1933, 111) aphorism: "Where id was there shall ego be." Mental agency means replacing inanimate, involuntary forces with the "I." This term refers to what Spinoza described as the use of the imagination combined with reason as a path to freedom (Hampshire 2005).

I will suggest that analogous to the stream of sensory inputs necessary for the experience of the bodily self, the intactness of the psychological self requires a continual recontextualization of memory and feelings. The evidence for this assertion comes from the observation of the loss of agency resulting from psychological trauma where defensive processes such as repression and dissociation prevent recontextualization. When Freud believed in the traumatic origin of hysteria, he asserted that it was not the traumatic event in itself that caused the symptoms of hysteria; it was the subsequent *memory* of the trauma, with its displaced web of associated meanings, that was the determining factor. As the body image needs to be updated so does memory. Psychological trauma can prevent this process of recontextualization with a subsequent hiatus in the sense of self. It is vital for the sense of agency that new meanings be created. That the memory of trauma needs to be transformed through such a recontextualization was intuited by Freud well over a hundred years ago. Freud described the process of *Nachträglichkeit,* that memory is retranscribed in accordance with later experience. He defined psychopathology as a failure of translation or retranscription. For example, if a sexual trauma in childhood occurred at a certain age, say X, the memory and its associated meanings need to be reinterpreted at age Y, and then again at age Z. The unconscious defenses instituted in response to trauma, such as repression and dissociation, prevent this reinterpretation of memory and feeling. Defenses such as dissociation can be looked on as an attack on the holism of meaning. To interpret the meaning of past experience, memory must be available and also must be felt. If one is disassociated, one is not there to feel.

We cannot control what we feel any more than we can control our heartbeat. Our feelings simply happen to us. What we can control, at least potentially, is our *interpretation* of those feelings. Our sense of agency is linked to the degree of freedom we can bring to this act of interpretation, which in turn is dependent, as I have noted, on the availability of emotional memory. We believe that relational trauma experienced in childhood has a continuing effect because unconscious metaphorical correspondences between past and present will control the interpretation of current experience. Our imagination is no longer free (Modell 2003). Imagination, which includes our expectations of the future, is constricted by traumatic experience and is therefore not free but directed and stereotyped. Trauma becomes imprinted on our imagination and controls our expectations of the future. The past simulates the future.

Consider this example: When this woman was a girl, she had a loving relationship with her father that was irrevocably lost when he became brain damaged as a result of an industrial accident. As an adult, she was compulsively driven to uncover defects in men, almost as if it were a matter of her survival. These presumed defects were then selectively perceived to the exclusion of whatever other virtues might be present. For example, on one occasion she noted that her husband was driving slowly, overly cautiously, and, in her judgment, incompetently. She then wondered whether he was developing brain damage or becoming precociously senile. She became enraged at him and then felt guilty because of the irrationality of her reaction. The intensity of rage frightened her. She thought she was going a bit crazy, as if she had momentarily fallen into a time warp. For driving with her husband recreated in her imagination a similar scene from childhood when she was a five-year-old girl sitting next to her father in the family car. As a result of his illness, her father was visually impaired and could barely see the road, and she was terrified that they would be killed.

The Feeling of Agency Requires an Intact Narrative of the Self

Crucial to the sense of agency of the self is the ability to construct a narrative of the self. When the memory of trauma cannot be recontextualized, there is an interruption of this narrative. Observation of victims of the Holocaust (Strous et al. 2005) provides striking confirmation. Strous and colleagues found that in the process of obtaining video testimony of the Holocaust, just by means of recounting the narrative of their lives, psychotically ill survivors were clinically benefited. In the recounting of their history, gaps in the narrative were restored.

The principle I have tried to illustrate is that our sense of agency is enhanced not only through physically embodied acts but also through the creation of new meaning. Parallel to children's mastery of their body, they also enhance their sense of agency through the use of the imagination. Using their imagination, they have the power to create alternative worlds. A lovely example of children's use of the imagination in play was offered by the great Dutch historian Johan Huizinga (1955, 8): "A father found his four-year-old son sitting at the front of a row of chairs, playing 'trains.'" When he kissed his son the boy said, "'Don't kiss the engine daddy, or the carriages won't think it's real.'" Imagination allows experience to be endowed with new meanings.

The Feeling of Agency Is an Illusion Created by the Brain

For millennia, philosophers have questioned whether human volition can be considered a causal agent. Kant (1998) famously declared that "freedom of the will" is one of only three metaphysical problems that lie beyond the powers of the human intellect. Philosophers have long suspected that the belief that our will is a causal agent is an illusion. This ancient problem of free will has recently become a subject of scientific inquiry (Libet, Freeman, and Sutherland 1999; Wegner 2002). Neuroscience appears to have confirmed that our feeling of agency is just that, merely a feeling, an illusion created by the brain. Daniel Wegner has written a book titled *The Illusion of Conscious Will,* where he provides evidence that a feeling of agency is no more than an illusion. But he acknowledges that it is a necessary illusion. According to Wegner (2005, 30),

> The creation of our sense of agency is critically important for a variety of personal and social processes, even if this perceived agent is not a cause of action. The experience of conscious will is fundamentally important because it provides a marker of our authorship—what might be called an authorship emotion. Each surge of will we sense in the operation of controlled processes provides a bodily reminder of what we think we have done. In this sense, the function of will is to identify our action with a feeling, allowing us to sense in a very basic way what we're likely to have done, and to distinguish such things from those caused by events in the world or by other people or agents.

Wegner's observation that a sense of agency is simply a feeling that distinguishes our actions from those of the Other was shown experimentally by an investigation using positron-emission tomography (PET) and functional magnetic resonance imagery (fMRI) (Farrer and Frith 2002; Farrer et al. 2003). These researchers demonstrated that when the subjects used a computer joystick to drive a circle along a given path and did not know whether they or the computer generated the action, different areas of the brain were activated when they believed themselves to be the source of action as compared to action attributed to the Other. When the subjects believed themselves to be the agent, the anterior insula was activated; the right inferior parietal lobe was activated when they attributed the action to another agent. These studies suggest that the feeling of agency is a matter of belief and that it has its own neural circuitry. The feeling of agency is just that, a feeling and nothing more. But it is a feeling that is necessary for our existence in the world. It is hard to imagine living in the world if we had no sense of our own effectiveness.

In a famous set of experiments, Benjamin Libet (1999) has demonstrated that unconscious neural activity precedes conscious intent. Libet's subjects were wired to an EEG and were asked to flex their wrists and indicate on a timing device, which measured fractions of seconds, when they were aware of their intention to act. Neural activity described as a "readiness potential" occurred approximately 500 milliseconds before the subjects were conscious of their intent to move their wrists. Conventional wisdom might have anticipated that conscious thought occurred at the same time as the correlated neural activity. But this was not the case. Unconscious intentionality expressed as a neural event preceded conscious intention, and therefore can be judged as causal. Libet (1999, 51) states that "the initiation of the freely voluntary act appears to begin in the brain unconsciously, well before the person consciously knows he wants to act."

Libet's experiments were confirmed by others and are now established as fact. This would appear to establish the primacy of unconscious thought. Parenthetically, it should be said that Libet himself does not believe that his experiments refute the existence of free will because a willed inhibition was not preceded by neural activity. He believes that conscious will can block or veto an unconscious process. Libet's experiments confirm Freud's assertion that "in psychoanalysis there was no choice first but to assert that mental processes are in themselves unconscious and to liken the perception of them by means of consciousness to the perception of the external world by means of the sense organs" (Freud 1915, 171).

In his book *Wider than the Sky* (2004), Gerald Edelman insists as does Freud that causality is not a property of consciousness. Causality can only be attributed to physical processes because the physical world is a closed space and there are no ghosts to activate the machine; there is no causality apart from a neurophysiological process. Consciousness in itself does not cause anything. Consciousness is knowing, not causing. Causality can only be attributed to electrical and chemical forces.

The Self Is Also an Illusion

The current view in neuroscience is that all of what the brain constructs is an illusion. *Illusion* has been defined as a false appearance, a belief that does not have correlates in the physical world. We see a red rose and inhale its fragrance, but the color red does not exist in the physical world, nor does its fragrance. Colors and odors are the brain's constructions. What exists in the physical world are only packets of energy, photons of varying wavelengths; there are no odors, only chemicals. We constantly attribute and project onto the world that which we construct internally. Our feeling that seeing red is a constant sensation despite alterations in the reflecting light is the consequence of an internal neural process. As the neurophysiologist Semir Zeki (1993, 227) says, "Surfaces are not endowed with codes or labels which allow the brain to analyze them passively with respect to color." Because our perception of the self is a construction of the brain—a construction that does not correspond to anything in the physical world—the self can be justifiably described as an illusion. The illusory nature of the self has been examined in great detail by the German philosopher Thomas Metzinger in his book *Being No One* (2003). According to Metzinger, we essentially imagine ourselves. But we should not depreciate or disparage the belief in illusions as false conceptions; if the self is an illusion, it is an illusion without which we cannot live. We have only to be reminded that the loss of the sense of self—which has been described as annihilation anxiety—is a form of anxiety so horrific that some have been known to commit suicide rather than reexperience this loss.

The self is very difficult to define because it has its origins in our body, in our relation to the Other, and in our culture. There is only one experience of self, but that self can be viewed, as I have just described, as a self-organizing neural construction, and also as a co-construction with the Other—the so-called relational self. This is a view of the self that has been adopted by contemporary psychoanalysis. Finally, the self can be understood as a construction of culture. The idea of the self in Western thought has been constantly evolving from classical antiquity to our own era (Seigel 2005). Western and Eastern cultures have very different views regarding individuality and self-actualization. These different construals of the self have been shown to influence cognition and emotion (Markus and Kitayama 1991). The self is therefore simultaneously a neural construction, a relational construction, and a cultural construction.

Time and the Illusion of the Self

We need to keep in mind that the experience of the self incorporates a fundamental paradox regarding the experience of time. Most people accept the distinction between physical and psychological time. The experience of time is very different from that of a clock that indicates equally divisible segments of time (Varela 1999). Psychological time can be expanded or compressed. The self entails a paradox involving time in that we maintain a feeling of continuity over time, yet experience a self that is constantly changing. This is the paradox that puzzled and fascinated William James (1890)—how does the self encompass a stable sense of identity over time within the ever-changing stream of self-consciousness? How does a momentary state of consciousness connect with the stored memories of previous selves and create the unity that we experience as identity? We remember a continuous narrative of the self, but it is a narrative, with many gaps and omissions, and further it is a narrative that is constantly altered. Nevertheless, we feel that we are of a sameness over time, we experience an unchanging core identity, we always feel, in health, "I am who I am."

James (1890) uses the following analogy to explain the continuity of the sense of self over time. He asks the reader to imagine a heard of cattle whose owner recognizes their "brand" as his own. These cattle go their own way; the herd's unity is only a potential one until the owner arrives. The owner actively provides the coherence that underlies the sense of identity. But how does the owner impose this unity and coherence on the herd? Consciousness is ever changing; how does one establish a unity between past and present? James suggests that the "title" to the herd may be passed on from one to a succession of others (former selves). James recognizes that narrative memory consists of discrete "snapshots" of happenings. The question then is, how do these discrete "snapshots" result in a continuous sense of self? (Modell 1993).

A solution to the paradox that James's herdsman analogy attempts to solve might be found in current studies of consciousness, specifically the consciousness of vision. Discovering the neural correlates of consciousness has become the Holy Grail of contemporary neuroscience. Some view it as the most challenging problem in all of science. In a review of recent outstanding books on the neuroscience of consciousness, Sacks (2004) approaches the experience of time through the sensory portal of vision. In some cases of severe migraine, the sight of moving objects is not experienced as a continuity through time. Rather, motion appears to be frozen, as in a series of discrete snapshots. Sacks infers from this example of neuropathology that the experience of the visual continuity of motion is an illusion constructed by the brain. This process in the migraine patients went awry. Normally, the brain constructs the illusion of continuous motion in a manner analogous to a motion-picture film consisting of still snapshots. When these "stills" are accelerated, we see movies. Francis Crick and Cristof Koch (2003, 122) also claim that "conscious awareness (for vision) is a series of static snapshots with motion 'painted' on them." The river of consciousness or the stream of time is an illusion of continuity that the brain creates. Might we not infer that in similar fashion the brain creates the illusion of the continuity of the self? Had James known this, he would not have had to construct his elaborate cattle analogy.

The sense of coherence of the self, the feeling that we are a unified whole and not split or fragmented, is an ideal that we strive for but do not always achieve. At a neural level, however, the brain maintains the coherence of the body image, as attested by the existence of phantom limbs. The feeling of the coherence of the self is different from that of the feeling of continuity of the self in that the feeling of coherence refers to the present moment. The existence of phantom limbs shows that the brain fills in the gap of the missing limb in a manner analogous to the filling in of the blind spot on our retina. These are illusions of intactness and wholeness experienced in current time. All of this suggests that these illusions of the self are linked to our experience of time. As I noted earlier, the experience of self is fundamentally paradoxical; it is a paradox concerning time. We maintain a sense that we are the same person over time, yet our experience of self is constantly changing. It is for this reason that the philosopher David Hume (1961, 228) denied the existence of self: "Pain and pleasure, grief and joy, passions and sensations succeed each other, and never all exist at the same time. It cannot therefore be from any of these impressions, or from any other, that the idea of self is derived; and consequently there is no such idea."

But the self is also oriented toward future time; by means of our past memories we anticipate and predict the future. The feeling of agency of the self is the conscious element within the broader process of intentionality. Thomas Aquinas (1948) famously defined intentionality as the directing of action towards some *future* goal that is defined and chosen by the actor. The self simulates fears and desires in present time as a prediction of the future. We experience the present moment while predicting the future. It can be said that the self thickens the experience of time by extending the present moment to include predictions of the future (Modell 2002). Recontextualizing autobiographical memory may expand the sense of the passage of time while reinforcing our sense of agency and the continuity of the self.

Although our sense of agency is an illusion, as I have emphasized, it is an illusion that is necessary for living in the world. As William James (1890, 296–297) said, "The *fons et origo* of all reality . . . is ourselves. Our own reality, that sense of our own life which we at every moment possess is the ultimate of ultimates for our belief." It seems to me that James is saying that *we create what is real in accordance with our needs*. Our sense of agency feels real because we need it to be so.

References

Aquinas, S. T. 1948. *Summa Theologiae*. Allen, Tex.: Christian Classics. (Original work published 1264.)

Brugger, P. Kollias,S, Muri R.,Crelier G., Hepp-Reymind,M,Regard,M,. 2000. Beyond re-membering: Phantom sensations of congenitally absent limbs. *Proceedings National Academy of Science* 97:6167–6172.

Crick, F., and Koch, C. 2003. A framework for consciousness. *Nature Neuroscience* 6:119–126.

Denton, D. 1993. *The pinnacle of life*. San Francisco: Harper.

Dodds, E. R. 1951. *The Greeks and the irrational*. Berkeley: University of California Press.

Edelman, G. 2004. *Wider than the sky*. New Haven, Conn.: Yale University Press.

Farrer, C., Franck, Georgieff, M., Frith, C., Decety, J., Jeannerod, M. l. 2003. Modulating the experience of agency: A positron emission tomography study. *Neuroimage* 18:324–333.

Farrer, C., and Frith, C. 2002. Experiencing oneself versus another person as being the cause of action: The neural correlates of the experience of agency. *Neuroimage* 15: 96–603.

Freud, S. 1915. The unconscious. In *The standard edition of the complete psychological works of Sigmund Freud,* vol. 14. London: Vintage, 2001.

Freud, S. 1917. A difficulty in the path of psychoanalysis. In *The standard edition of the complete psychological works of Sigmund Freud,* vol. 17. London: Vintage, 2001.

Freud, S. 1923. *The Ego and the Id*. In *The standard edition of the complete psychological works of Sigmund Freud,* vol. 19. London: Vintage, 2001.

Freud, S. 1933. *New introductory lectures*. In *The standard edition of the complete psychological works of Sigmund Freud,* vol. 22. London: Vintage, 2001.

Gallagher, S. 2000. Philosophical conceptions of the self: Implications for cognitive science. *Trends in Cognitive Science* 4:14–21.

Hampshire, S. 2005. *Spinoza and spinozism*. Oxford: Oxford University Press.

Huizinga, J. 1955. *Homo ludens*. Boston: Beacon Press.

Hume, D. 1961. *A treatise of human nature*. New York: Doubleday. (Original work published 1748.)

James, W. 1890. *The principles of psychology*. New York: Dover.

Kant, I. 1998. *Critique of pure reason*. Cambridge: Cambridge University Press. (Original work published 1787.)

Lear, J. 2005. *Freud*. New York: Routledge.

Libet, B. 1999. Do we have free will? *Journal of Consciousness Studies* 6:47–57.

Libet, B., Freeman, A., and Sutherland K., eds. 1999. The volitional brain. *Journal of Consciousness Studies* 6:1–293.

Markus, H., and Kitayama, S. 1991. Culture and the self: Implications for cognition, emotion and motivation. *Psychological Review* 98:224–253.

Metzinger, T. 2003. *Being no one*. Cambridge, Mass.: MIT Press.

Modell, A. 1993. *The private self*. Cambridge, Mass.: Harvard University Press.

Modell, A. 2002. Intentionality and the experience of time. *Kronoscope 2*:21–39.

Modell, A. 2003. *Imagination and the meaningful brain*. Cambridge, Mass.: MIT Press.

Ramachandran, V. S. 1998. The perception of phantom limbs. *Brain* 121:1603–1630.

Sacks, O. 1984. *A leg to stand on*. New York: HarperCollins.

Sacks, O. 2004. In the river of consciousness. *New York Review of Books* 51:41–44.

Seigel, J. 2005. *The idea of the self*. Cambridge: Cambridge University Press.

Strous, R., et al. 2005. Video testimony of long-term hospitalized psychiatrically ill Holocaust survivors. *American Journal of Psychiatry 162*:2287–2294.

Varela, F. 1999. Present-time consciousness. *Journal of Consciousness Studies* 6:11–140.

Wegner, D. 2002. *The illusion of conscious will*. Cambridge, Mass.: MIT Press.

Wegner, D. 2005. Who is the controller of controlled processes? In R. Hassan, J. Uleman, and J. Bargh, eds., *The new unconscious*. New York: Oxford University Press.

White, R. 1963. Ego and reality in psychoanalytic theory. *Psychological Issues* 3:1–210.

Zeki, S. 1993. *A vision of the brain*. Oxford: Blackwell.

2 Becoming Agents: Hegel, Nietzsche, and Psychoanalysis

Elliot L. Jurist

Agency is a concept that can be as obscuring as illuminating. While it is a common term in philosophy and psychology, no consensus exists about what it really means. An agent, by etymological definition, is "one who acts," and may be contrasted with being a patient—that is, one who is acted on. An agent is someone who, on most accounts, acts freely and well. Yet, this does not tell us much, and it is important to be aware that these connotations of the term are not everyday ones. Indeed, the scholarly use of the term virtually is the opposite of many of the everyday associations that accompany the term—such as FBI agents, State Farm agents, and sports and other mega-deal-making agents, who are engaged in representing others, not themselves.

Originally, philosophers were drawn to the term *agency* in connection with the problem of free will. Being an agent is thus predicated on having one's own intentions, particularly the capacity to engage in second-order reflections on one's own desires and beliefs. For example, Taylor (1985) suggests that agents engage in "strong evaluations," which are distinguished by their "articulacy and depth" and which contribute to a sense of responsibility for oneself.

There is a large gap between thinkers who are inclined to think of agency in terms of the link between beliefs and action and philosophers who are seeking to capture something further—like self-understanding and self-realization. It is possible to distinguish what we might call a thin and thick sense of agency. The thin sense of agency denotes efficaciousness—success measured in terms of the commensurability of one's beliefs and actions. It has the merit of presuming less, but also meaning less. The thick sense of agency is in search of more—being a satisfied agent has a psychological dimension.

Efficacious agency is more abstract; it bears an affinity to the concept of personhood. Traditionally, being a person is defined as the locus of legal and theological responsibility; an underlying sense of identity is presumed. The identity of "persons" is a kind of generic category—its meaning fixed as much by how others regard one as by how one regards oneself. There is a vast philosophical literature on "personal identity" that focuses in detail on issues concerning continuity and reidentification.[1] Although personhood is sometimes represented as an achievement (which means that it is possible for some human beings to fail to be persons), the problems associated with this concept tend to presume that a person is a basic status that human beings possess. Personhood lacks the exemplary status that goes along with the concept of agency.[2]

The identity of "agents" is richer and more complex. At the risk of oversimplification, one might venture to say that agents have more interesting selves than persons do. Agents must have an investment in understanding themselves, and perhaps in addition, in pursuing the ideal of self-realization. Such a qualitative kind of goal ordinarily presupposes background values, which support and sustain the ideal. With the thick sense of agency, agency must be cultivated and thus exists on a continuum, rather than being a yes-no assessment. The thick conception of agency opens the door to tough issues about the distinction between private and public aspects of agency. It also forces us to ponder the universality of the concept. Nonetheless, *agency* is appealing as a term precisely because it is less ethnocentric than *selfhood*, which is predicated on an autonomous sense of self. All cultures have some notion of what is required for a desirable human life, but not all cultures share the Western view that the proper telos of development entails an individuated self.

Admittedly, the thick sense of agency coaxes us into the muddy waters of culture, which, in contrast, advocates of the thin sense have the good sense to try to avoid. In the end, however, the thin sense of agency is no freer of culture in its conception. One gains access to a certain range of problems with the thin sense of agency or personal identity, and these problems are well worth contemplating, but one does not thereby escape the factor of culture. The thick sense of agency depends on psychological considerations, that is, on the two senses of "becoming" invoked in the title of this chapter: that it must come into being and that it must be a desirable state. In this chapter, I ultimately defend a version of the thick sense of agency that is psychoanalytic. My approach is genealogical: a satisfying, contemporary understanding of agency depends on making sense out of where it has come from. More specifically, my focus is on exploring the concept of agency in the two towering figures of nineteenth-century philosophy, Hegel and Nietzsche, and on relating their work to the findings of psychoanalysis.

I Modern Agents

What it means to be an agent is transformed in modernity. It could be argued, in fact, that a crucial source of the concept of agency is the Enlightenment belief that humans are responsible for their own fate. In Kant's formulation, humans have the capacity to be agents because they are rational. This idea was adopted and modified in the early nineteenth century by German Idealists. Hegel follows Kant, but offers an expanded conception of rational agency, infusing it with *Bildung* and thus emphasizing the sense in which culture and cultivation are necessary aspects of agency. Later in the nineteenth century, Nietzsche challenges the conformism that is entailed by *Bildung*, yet he affirms a project of agency based on bodily experience and the acknowledgment of irrationality. As I have argued in *Beyond Hegel and Nietzsche: Philosophy, Culture, and Agency* (2000), Hegel and Nietzsche share a psychological approach to agency that features what I have termed "self-fathoming."

Self-fathoming develops from the modern notion that we have an obligation to determine meaning for ourselves. It emerges as an ideal once traditional culture no longer is seen as providing adequate values. Self-fathoming is based on but expands "reflection," the capacity to study our own mental processes actively that is vaunted in German Idealism. Self-fathoming is not simply about knowing oneself; it comes with the expectation of gravitating beyond knowledge to the realm of action. This requires a revision of the standard project of epistemology: life satisfaction, rather than knowledge itself becomes the aim of human agency.

Indeed, self-fathoming is not meaningful without the recognition that, along with its promise, modernity creates new kinds of anxiety, alienation, and self-division. A new kind of freedom becomes possible, but modernity also brings with it the threat of empty subjectivity and the loss of connection to nature and to society at large. Self-fathoming points to a project that is dynamic; it entails struggle and even failure. Self-fathoming is thus best conceived in terms of existing in a dialectical relation with self-deception. As we will see in the next section, Hegel presents a live drama of agency in the *Phenomenology of Spirit* (PhS), although he is strongly committed to the possibility of achieving integration—of the self within itself and between the self and others. Nietzsche is more skeptical about integration, and qualifies its meaning, because he considers modern self-division in terms of despair and sickness, not just alienation.

Self-fathoming is closely tied to what Taylor (1992) describes as "inwardness"—that is, the notion that we are defined by our interior life and ultimately by our sense of self. Taylor stresses that humans have not always thought of themselves in these terms. He moves on to offer a history of modern inwardness, which features two main components, "self-exploration" and "self--control." Although earlier manifestations of self-control are acknowledged in Greek philosophy, Taylor focuses on the specifically modern form of self-control that emerges from Descartes. Self-control as "self-objectification" means that one needs to seek distance in the name of attaining an objective first-person perspective on oneself.

Self-objectification and self-exploration are, in Taylor's account, at odds: "The one seeks to grasp us in the general categories of science, the other to allow our particularity to find expression" (p. 107). A chasm threatens to open up between a science of the self and an aesthetics of the self. As Taylor observes, self-objectification removes us from our own identity, whereas self-exploration directs us to it. Crucially, self-exploration is based on the assumption that "we don't already know who we are" (p. 105). This latter theme is prominent in Montaigne but emerges especially later in expressivism, where fulfillment and creativity are seen as the source of agency.

Expressivism represents a decisive moment in Taylor's historical account of agency.[3] *Expressivism*, a term that he takes over and develops from the work of Isaiah Berlin, captures the new mentality of the post-Enlightenment era, where the loss of external meaning results in the adoption of a heightened focus on inwardness. This transformation entails a turn away from humans as rational animals to an entirely new point of view: a person "comes to know himself as expressing and clarifying what he is and recognizing himself in this expression . . . self-awareness through expression" (Taylor 1975, 17). More specifically, Taylor explains that the pursuit of inwardness depends on the notion that one is lacking such determination beforehand. It is only through seeking determination that one can become individuated and fulfilled.

Taylor credits Herder with the idea that language is an "expression," not just a referential sign, as Enlightenment thinkers had maintained. This new notion of expression was linked to art and also to the idea that emotions have primacy in human life. Expressivism was born out of a spirit of affirming the human potential to create an integrated life.

Let us consider Taylor's understanding of expressivism in more detail. Four underlying demands of expressivism have been delineated: (1) the passionate wish for unity and wholeness, (2) the commitment to freedom, (3) the wish for union with nature, and (4) the wish for union with other people (Taylor 1975, 23–28). The first demand, unity/wholeness, arose as a protest against the tendency in the Enlightenment to dissect human nature, which fostered false dichotomies like soul and body or reason and feeling. The second demand, freedom, Taylor suggests, is claimed as the central value of humanity; it coincides with self-realization as the goal of human life. The third demand, union with nature, upholds the connection between the body and living nature and seeks communion. Finally, the fourth demand, union with others, seeks to attain a deeper bond of connection within the human community. Recalling the two trends of modern inwardness described previously, it is apparent that expressivism follows the trajectory of self-exploration, rather than self-control—especially insofar as self-control is understood as self-objectification.

Hegel's philosophy, according to Taylor, should be construed as an attempt to resolve and embrace both aspects of modern inwardness. In Taylor's (1989, 24–27) elaboration, Hegel adheres to the expressivist tradition in embracing unity/wholeness and being antidualist, in celebrating freedom as the principle of the modern world, in seeking union with nature, and especially in affirming union with others through *Sittlichkeit*. As a young man, Hegel was immersed in an intellectual atmosphere directed toward remaking not only art, but philosophy, as expressivistic. The influence of self-exploration can be found in Hegel's assertion that "Mind . . . is already mind at the outset, but it does not yet know that it is" (PM, #385). It can also be discerned in passages where Hegel defends the value of human emotion—like the suggestion that philosophers have propagated an "arbitrarily imposed" separation between thinking and feeling (PM, #471) or that the educated person feels more deeply than the undereducated one (PM, #448 (*Zusatz*)).

As Hegel developed his own philosophy, the influence of the modern philosophical tradition, especially Kant, deepened. Although Hegel offers an expanded version of rationality, he was in earnest about elevating philosophy to the status of science. He does not abandon the epistemological project of modern philosophy; as Speight (2001) has argued, he shifts its focus to be "corrigibilist"—that is, subject to retrospective revision. Hegel is sympathetic to self-objectification: he adopts it as part of a first-person perspective that aspires to be universal and impersonal. His allegiance to self-objectification can be discerned above all in his conviction that philosophy must seek justification for itself.

One cannot assimilate Hegel into the expressivist camp, therefore, without qualification. At the same time, it would be mistaken to emphasize his allegiance to self-objectification at the expense of acknowledging his investment in self-exploration. Hegel rejects the standard paradigm of epistemology: the goal of "actual knowing" replaces mere "love of knowledge" (PhS, 3). Hegel remained influenced by ancient Greek ideas about self-control as well as the modern idea of self-objectification, and he never abandoned the expectation that philosophy ought to be concerned about well-being.

It is not a part of Nietzsche's philosophical agenda to integrate self-objectification and self-exploration. While his commitment to self-exploration is evident, it is less clear what he thinks of self-objectification. Nietzsche has been portrayed as representing a radical modification of the version of expressivism that Hegel accepts (Taylor 1995). Whereas Hegel takes expressivism to mean that the self can be defined by self-expression, Nietzsche challenges this idea in the name of self-invention—that is, tipping the balance from "finding" to "making" (p. 117). Taylor reads Nietzsche as reveling in the aesthetics of existence, wherein the self becomes a work of art (p. 16); thus Nietzsche's allegiance to self-exploration as opposed to self-objectification is dramatized.

Let us consider where Nietzsche stands in relation to the four demands of expressivism. Nietzsche endorses antidualism, yet he is suspicious about the demand for unity/wholeness as unrealistic and ultimately as a fraudulent projection on our part. He embraces the demand for freedom in his conception of the free spirit, although he is also dubious about the notion of free will as a mere invention of philosophers. He does ally himself closely with the demand for union with nature—especially through Dionysian experience. Finally, he is unresponsive to the expressivist demand for unity with others—a demand that is highly valued by Hegel.

Nietzsche's interest in self-exploration outweighs his concern with self-objectification. The aim of self-exploration is well demonstrated in the subtitle of *Ecce Homo,* "How One Becomes Who One Is." Indeed, Nietzsche goes on to proclaim there that "to become what one is, one must not have the faintest notion of *what* one is" (EH, "Why I Am So Clever," #9). This exemplifies Taylor's point that with self-exploration it is assumed that one must explore oneself because one does not already know who one is. When Nietzsche praises the idea of giving "style to one's character" in the *Gay Science,* we find further confirmation of his commitment to self-exploration (GS, #290).[4]

What about Nietzsche's relation to self-objectification? Nietzsche is clearly not friendly to the idea of disengagement, viewing it as a posture that philosophers have seen as obligatory. He insists that underlying postures of disengagement are the inescapably personal needs of human beings. In the *Gay Science,* Nietzsche muses: "Perhaps you know some people near you who must look at themselves only from a distance in order to find themselves at all tolerable or attractive and invigorating. Self-knowledge is strictly inadvisable for them" (GS, #15). This idea can be linked to the opening passage of the *Genealogy of Morals,* in which Nietzsche argues that so-called men of knowledge do not have knowledge when it comes to themselves. As he avers: "We have never sought ourselves—how could it happen that we should ever *find* ourselves?" (GM, preface, #1). It would seem, then, that according to Nietzsche, the inclination to objectify oneself is opposed to the openness required in order to explore oneself.

Although Nietzsche is not swayed by self-objectification, he does not necessarily disavow the other component of modern inwardness, self-control. There are numerous passages, especially from his middle period, in which he praises self-mastery and moderation (HAH, I, preface and #464; HAH, II, #326). Book V of the *Gay Science* contains passages in which he praises self-determination and connects it to being a free spirit. In *Twilight of the Idols*, Nietzsche proposes that freedom is grounded in responsibility for oneself (TI, "Skirmishes of an Untimely Man," #38).

At a number of points in the *Will to Power*, he defends self-control in terms of control of affects. For example, in a passage from 1887–1888, he claims: "Blind indulgence of an affect, totally regardless of whether it be a generous and compassionate or a hostile affect, is the cause of the greatest evils. Greatness of character does not consist in not possessing these affects—on the contrary, one possesses them to the highest degree—but in having them under control" (WP, #928 (November 1887–March 1888)). Thus, Nietzsche's commitment to self-exploration in no way precludes the value of self-control. For him, self-control organizes and restrains affects; it does not attempt, however, to expunge them. Self-control affirms the expressivist emphasis on emotion. One can also detect here the influence of the ancient Greeks on Nietzsche's thinking, especially the Aristotelian notion of "megalopsyche."

Nonetheless, one must be careful not to misinterpret Nietzsche to be siding with Apollo against Dionysus. Along with the many passages that praise self-control, Nietzsche encourages us to let go, to forget, and to revel in the absence of regulating oneself. A revealing example is found in his conclusion to the aphorism titled "Self-Control" in the *Gay Science*: "For one must be able to lose oneself occasionally if one wants to learn something from things different from oneself" (GS, #305). In this passage, Nietzsche seems to be proposing a loose sense of agency in which valuing agency is not inconsistent with abandoning it. Nietzsche's advocacy of losing oneself occurs in the context of asserting a specific claim about exposing oneself to "things different from oneself." His qualification about "occasionally," too, is important to observe, because perhaps it can be used to save Nietzsche from drifting into contradiction.

We might read Nietzsche as claiming that, generally speaking, self-control is desirable, although exceptions exist when it is desirable to open ourselves to displace such control. The problem with interpreting "losing oneself" as a kind of reasonable, occasional exception, though, is that it still might fail to register a full appreciation of the Dionysian impulse. Nietzsche values overflowingness of character that refuses to be harnessed and that is modeled on sexual passion. So, however much Nietzsche does appreciate self-regulation, he finds self-abandonment appealing as well.

Although Taylor acknowledges the tension between self-exploration and self-objectification, he does not seriously consider the relation between self-exploration and self-control. He discusses self-control in connection with Plato and the Stoics; he has relatively little to say about the Aristotelian paradigm in which it is possible to shape and modulate affects. Taylor's description of expressivism offers important background for understanding the philosophical projects of Hegel and Nietzsche. In particular, we can compare the two philosophers: Hegel's concern about attaining unity with others is not matched by Nietzsche, and Nietzsche's interest in affects and drives was subordinate in Hegel because of his commitment to rationality. Moreover, we have ascertained that Hegel attempts to embrace both self-objectification and self-exploration, whereas Nietzsche regards them as in tension and values self-exploration over self-objectification. Hegel and Nietzsche both appreciate self-control, although Nietzsche does so more ambivalently. Framing the views of Hegel and Nietzsche in these ways is helpful, but it is still too general. In the next two sections, I take a closer look at their respective views of agency.

II Hegelian Recognition

Hegel's fundamental interest in modernity is apparent with the concept of recognition. Recognition has epistemological, sociopolitical, and psychological dimensions. It concerns both one's relation to others (mutual recognition) and to oneself. The ultimate significance of recognition, for Hegel, is its potential to address the promise and anxiety forged by modern culture, and, more specifically, to overcome the danger of empty subjectivity and self-division. Hegel postulates a seamless web in which self-recognition and recognition of others might be mutually reinforcing. The value of both self-recognition and recognition of others can be defined in terms of the satisfaction they bestow. Correspondingly, Hegel repeatedly demonstrates throughout the *Phenomenology of Spirit* that problems with recognition doom us to dissatisfaction.

That recognition involves self-recognition has not always been appreciated. In my reading, self-recognition coincides with self-knowledge. It contains two elements: that the self comes to know itself as socially constituted and as self-identical. Just before the master/slave section, Hegel spells out the concept of *Geist* as "We that is I and I that is We" (PhS, 110). Although this concept is not realized until later in the work, what happens in the self-consciousness chapter prompts a reformulation of the starting point of the work. Initially, consciousness explores the content of its own mind in a vacuum. There is something lacking in such solipsism, because it overlooks the existence of others and obscures their fundamental importance. The major discovery at the next juncture in consciousness' journey is the fact that "self-consciousness achieves its satisfaction (*Befriedigung*) only in another self-consciousness" (PhS, 110). This discovery is about understanding oneself as related to others, and it must be held distinct from the discovery that emerges later in the spirit chapter—that the self is socially constituted. At the stage of self-consciousness, consciousness comes to appreciate that there is a lack of satisfaction in ignoring and/or withdrawing from others.

The second aspect of self-knowledge is that the self comes to know itself as self-identical. This is conveyed by means of experience, a process wherein what has been concealed is revealed. Self-identity is attained and lost countless times in consciousness' journey. Self-identity is predicated on facing and overcoming self-division. Hegel uses phenomenological language in describing the struggle to attain self-identity: "being for-itself" and "being for-another." This terminology is intended as an original and precise way to capture the internal experience of being a subject.

The phrase "being for-itself" has a range of meanings. It designates the actualization of potentiality—that is, "being in-itself." Yet, being for-itself has connotations that go beyond this: the term suggests that consciousness is motivated by "desire" and by the pursuit of its own self-interest. One even might argue that being for-itself is the engine that propels consciousness in the direction of self-knowledge. Being for-itself can legitimately be conceived of as the source of a sense of agency.

Being for-itself is an affirmation of freedom achieved through self-determination. In the master/slave section of the *Phenomenology of Spirit*, Hegel describes being for-itself in terms of independence. At the same time, Hegel stresses that self-consciousness "does not see the other as an essential being, but in the other sees its own self" (PhS, 111). Even more pointedly, he informs us that "self-consciousness is, to begin with, simple being for-self, self-equal through the exclusion from itself of everything else" (PhS, 113). In other words, being for-itself in its initial form entails the denial of being for-another.

Being for-itself can be linked with narcissism. Narcissism is at the source of consciousness' oscillations in self-esteem; narcissism can also be discerned in consciousness' impulse to see itself as a self-enclosed unity and to reduce others to be part of itself. Narcissism explains the tendency to obscure the fact that we are also constituted as being for-another. From Hegel's standpoint, being for-itself is not necessarily antithetical to being for-another. In particular, there is no reason to assume that narcissism is, in and of itself, problematic. It becomes problematic only insofar as it pushes consciousness to disregard being for-another.

Hegel depicts the narcissistic side of human beings in equating the desire for recognition with the desire for prestige. Psychologically speaking, Hegel shows the need to be admired and honored by others to be prompted by an even more fundamental wish—to feel well, to enjoy a positive sense of self-esteem. This raises another aspect of being for-itself, which is consistent with what has been suggested about self-fathoming as well as about self-exploration: that people's need to feel good about themselves is a specifically modern need.

Being for-itself varies according to different historical and cultural contexts. In modern culture, being for-itself has a heightened importance, since it is no longer possible for us to look to customs and tradition. This creates a hardship because it must bear more weight, but also a new opportunity for fulfillment. As Hegel emphasizes, being for-itself does not coerce us into being self-enclosed atoms. In trying to conceptualize agency, though, we must not focus on being for-itself to the exclusion of being for-another.

Being for-another is Hegel's way of affirming that human agency is defined by "relatedness." The term *relatedness* expresses the desire to be connected to others. As an agent, one interacts with others, one depends on others, and one comes to see that others offer insight into oneself. The result is that one becomes acquainted with being for-another as a part of oneself. This realization is distinct from and should not be equated with the discovery of one's own sociality. Although being for-another can be understood as the basis of sociality, it is worth preserving the difference between the quality of this early interaction and later, self-conscious stages of development. Hegel is describing an elemental awareness that is implicit and must unfold.

There is a danger in being for-another negating being for-itself, just as there is of being for-itself negating being for-another. Hegel regards the latter, however, as the more likely danger: we are more likely to err in the direction of being selfish as opposed to being selfless. The struggle between being for-itself and being for-another is crucial because it reveals Hegel's appreciation of conflict as inherent in human agency. Hegel affirms the legitimacy and desirability of integrating being for-itself and being for-another, yet one should not underestimate the difficulty of this challenge.

From a Hegelian point of view, it is misguided and unhealthy to define oneself strictly in terms of narcissism or relatedness. Pursued to the exclusion of the other, either of these alternatives offers the illusion of satisfaction, but, in truth, dissatisfaction will result. By emphasizing that being for-another is a part of self-identity, Hegel claims that the two aspects of self-knowledge are not opposed. Self-knowledge is not bifurcated in comprising self-identity and the socially constituted self. Instead, the idea of the self as socially constituted means that the individual accepts that the universal dwells within him or her as an individual. The self as self-identical embraces being for-another and being for-oneself as potentially complementary. The former is a matter of one's relation to others, and the latter is a matter of one's relation to oneself. Put another way, being for-another has ramifications for both one's external relation to others and one's internal relation to oneself. Moreover, being for-another clarifies that the project of self-fathoming cannot be carried out in isolation from others.

For Hegel, agency is not merely an assertion of the rational truth that humans are related to others and social in nature. Self-deception and the ineluctability of struggle between being for-another and being for-itself are prominently featured. Genuine satisfaction hinges on the challenge of integrating being for-another and being for-itself. Hegel's depiction of agency oscillates between satisfaction and dissatisfaction, and emphasizes that there is no straightforward path to becoming an agent.

III Nietzschean Will to Power

Nietzsche offers a harsher evaluation of modern culture than Hegel, pointing out that over the course of the nineteenth century, despair supplants mere alienation as enormous changes take place, which result in a sense that things keep speeding up and spinning out of control. These changes include political events, like the revolutions of 1848, wars, nationhood for Germany (and the growth of nationalism in general), and the abolition of slavery; social changes like the expansion of the bourgeoisie and of mass culture; and scientific developments like the emergence of the theory of evolution and the development of industry and technology. These changes lead Nietzsche to conclude that the illusion of progress obscures that something has gone wrong with modern culture.

At times, he uses language similar to Hegel's, hoping that philosophy can play a role in altering "our unsatisfied (*unbefriedigten*) modern culture" (BT, #23). Nietzsche departs from Hegel, though, in ascribing pathology to modern culture and in being pessimistic about widespread social change. Modern culture, in Nietzsche's view, fosters mediocrity: "a useful, industrious, handy, multi-purpose, herd-animal" (BGE, #176). He forecasts a coming "catastrophe" in European culture (WP, #2) and offers the diagnosis that there is "a disorder in the modern soul which condemns it to a joyless unfruitfulness" (UM, (SE), #2). According to Nietzsche, modern culture perpetuates sickness: "Hence each helps the other; hence everyone is to a certain extent sick, and everyone is a nurse for the sick" (TI, "Skirmishes of an Untimely Man," #37).

The threat of nihilism requires a new view of agency, and this generates a project that, for Nietzsche, is elitist. Nietzsche is uncomfortable with the idea of a universal model of agency, although one can find passages to the contrary (for example, HAH, II, pt.1, #223). Following Hegel, Nietzsche regards conflict as a persistent feature of agency; however, he denies the possibility of any conventional notion of unified agency. Still, Nietzsche does defend a sense of agency wherein the self can achieve coherence and determination through "self-overcoming," although not transparency. Nietzsche's view of agency differs from Hegel's, most obviously in that it does not presume that integration produces social integration. He also departs from Hegel's commitment to founding agency on self-knowledge—especially with its claim of absoluteness.

Nietzsche's description of agency emphasizes that it has multiple components. Multiplicity is invoked as a way to capture what it is like to have a "soul," and Nietzsche understands being a "subject" as constituted through the attempt to pull together and organize disparate experiences of the soul. Two points are implied: (1) that being a subject depends on eclipsing the nature of a soul—that is, fabricating something in its place, and (2) that we ought to entertain an alternative conception, wherein the subject is understood as a matter of multiplicity. Nietzsche derides what he sees as a fantasy of "the subject"—because it simply assumes concordance and does not face that it must be created. As he tells us in the *Will to Power* (entry dated 1883–1888), "The 'subject' is not something given, it is something added and invented and projected behind what there is. Finally, is it necessary to posit an interpreter behind the interpretation? Even this is invention, hypothesis" (WP, #481). While this passage underscores the first point, it does not explicitly make the second point. The second point is clearly introduced in the following passage from the *Will to Power* (entry dated 1885): "The assumption of one single subject is perhaps unnecessary; perhaps it is just as permissible to assume a multiplicity of subjects, whose inter-action and struggle is the basis of our thought and our consciousness in general? A kind of aristocracy of 'cells' in which dominion resides? To be sure, an aristocracy of equals, used to ruling jointly and understanding how to command? *My hypotheses:* The subject as multiplicity" (WP, #490). In *Beyond Good and Evil,* Nietzsche amplifies this point, inviting us to question "soul atomism," which he links to Christianity, and to entertain new, alternative hypotheses: "such conceptions as 'mortal soul,' and 'soul as subjective multiplicity,' and 'soul as social structure of the drives and affects,' want henceforth to have citizens' rights in science" (BGE, #12). In *Human, All Too Human*, Nietzsche observes: "For the thinker it is disadvantageous to be tied to one person all the time" (HAH, II, pt. 2, #306).

Agency requires an ongoing challenge in Nietzsche's account. In an aphorism titled "We Incomprehensible Ones," he introduces a striking analogy: "Like trees we grow—this is hard to understand, as is all of life—not in one place only but everywhere, not in one direction but equally upward and outward and inward and downward; our energy is at work simultaneously in the trunk, branches, and roots; we are no longer free to do only one particular thing, to *be* only one particular thing" (GS, #371). For Nietzsche, the challenge of being an agent also means grappling with the past:

> To determine this degree, and therewith the boundary at which the past has to be forgotten if it is not to become the gravedigger of the present, one would have to know exactly how great the *plastic power* (*die plastische Kraft*) of a man, a people, a culture is: I mean by plastic power the capacity to develop out of oneself in one's own way, to transform and incorporate (*umzubilden und einzuverleiben*) into oneself what is past and foreign, to heal wounds, to replace what has been lost, to recreate broken moulds. . . . And this is a universal law: a living thing can be healthy, strong and fruitful only when bounded by a horizon; if it is incapable of drawing a horizon around itself, and at the same time too self-centred to enclose its own view within that of another, it will pine away slowly or hasten to its timely end. Cheerfulness, the good conscience, the joyful deed, confidence in the future—all of them depend, in the case of the individual as of a nation, on the existence of a line dividing the bright and discernible from the illuminable and dark; on one's being just as able to forget at the right time as to remember at the right time; on the possession of a powerful instinct for sensing when it is necessary to feel historically and when unhistorically. (UM, #1)

Nietzsche's investment in a dynamic view of agency is conveyed in the notion of a "plastic power" that involves the ability both to forget and to remember. In invoking "transformation" and "incorporation," Nietzsche is laying out a process of working through the past. The key point here concerns erecting "boundaries" that are neither too permeable nor too rigid. Nietzsche sees the creation of boundaries as enabling one to differentiate between inside and outside, and between self and other. While Nietzsche acknowledges a concern about being self-centered, it is much more characteristic for him to endorse the value of narcissism.

A healthy sense of agency, according to him, entails recognition of the desirability and legitimacy of self-interest. As he suggests in *Zarathustra*: "Indeed, this ego and the ego's contradiction and confusion still speak more honestly of its being—this creating, willing, valuing ego, which is the measure and value of things" (Z, I, "On the Afterworldly"). Let us also recall

Nietzsche's enthusiasm for *Selbstsucht*, a concept that closely resembles narcissism. In another passage from *Zarathustra*, he proclaims: "It happened for the first time—that his word pronounced selfishness (*Selbstsucht*) blessed, the wholesome, healthy selfishness that wells from a powerful soul—from a powerful soul to which belongs the high body, beautiful, triumphant, refreshing, around which everything becomes a mirror" (Z, III, "On the Three Evils," 2). This passage is revealing as an affirmation of healthy narcissism; it shows the mirroring effect of narcissism as well as its close connection to the body. The passage also serves to remind us of Nietzsche's belief that narcissism and the will to power mutually reinforce each other.

Indeed, the concept that underlies everything Nietzsche believes about agency is the will to power. The will to power, "the strongest, most life-affirming drive," is what allows us to thrive, not just to survive (GM, III, 18). It is an all-encompassing way to account for the multiple aspects of agency. The will to power derives from our bodies and instinctual endowment—it is a kind of synthesis of libido and aggression. It has connotations of both mastery and domination. Yet it is also linked to intellectual life: the will to power contributes to "spontaneous, aggressive, expansive, form-giving forces that give new interpretations and directions" (BGE, #12). Nietzsche specifically links the will to power to affects and affective interpretations (WP, #556).[5]

Nietzschean agency is more concerned with narcissism than relatedness. Nietzsche does not reject the category of relatedness per se; he offers, for example, many reflections on friendship. However, his account of relatedness is confusing and ultimately less satisfying than his examination of the cluster of issues around narcissism.[6] He provides a rich and multivaried way to think about narcissism and about irrationality in general.

In resorting to psychoanalytic language in discussing Nietzsche, we are taking much less of a leap than with Hegel. Nietzsche relishes his identity as a psychologist, and the affirmation of psychology is an important theme in his work. From one perspective, Nietzsche looks to psychology as a way to escape from the limits of the philosophical tradition. From another perspective, however, he is seeking to enlarge the domain of philosophy so that it becomes open to and inclusive of psychology.

Nietzsche anticipates Freud in a number of ways. He suggests that consciousness is a developmental modification that arises out of exigency; it is a mere tip of the iceberg, and as he puts it, our "weakest and most fallible organ" (GM, II, #16). Nietzsche suggests that the unconscious, the repository of the id and instincts, has been ignored as a factor in mental life. As he proclaims, "For the longest time, conscious thought was considered thought itself. Only now does truth dawn on us that by far the greatest part of our spirit's activity remains unconscious and unfelt" (GS, #333). Nietzsche also anticipates Freud in reminding us that the demands of our instincts need to be satisfied, as well as in worrying about the cost of deferring and/or forego-ing satisfaction. Nietzsche develops a notion of sublimation in which instincts are transmuted for the sake of a higher purpose, although sublima-tion is more important for Freud than for Nietzsche. In honoring our instincts, Nietzsche is less sanguine than Freud about accommodation.

IV Intersubjective, Decentered Agents

In this final section, I develop my reading of how Hegelian and Nietzschean agency dovetail in a psychoanalytic conception of agency and maintain that any contemporary model of agency ought to take psychoanalysis into account. I have argued that it is important to contextualize the concept of agency, and that the particular form in which it has been postulated in modernity is "self-fathoming." I have also claimed that Hegel and Nietzsche both advocate self-fathoming, and that self-fathoming entails a dynamic process of defining oneself, wherein conflict, struggle, and even failure are inevitable. Self-fathoming depends on self-understanding, but it culminates in self-realization and life satisfaction.

Hegel and Nietzsche are very different kinds of philosophers, but they both bring a psychological sensibility to the understanding of human agency. The concept of recognition allows Hegel to reinforce the twin dangers of defining oneself exclusively either in terms of being for-itself or being for-another. Hegelian agency, therefore, seeks to balance and synthesize narcissism and relatedness. Hegel's appreciation of how constitutive others are for our own sense of identity is a superb insight, which has become documented further in attachment theory and psychoanalysis (Winnicott 1965; Bowlby 1969; Mahler, Pine, and Bergman 1975; Stern 1985; Fonagy et al. 2002). Recognizing/being recognized are not optional phenomena; they represent a fundamental need that no human willingly abdicates. Trauma is that only thing that can lead a human being to be indifferent to its allure.

It is worth placing special emphasis on the birth of mutuality as a creative and transformative experience (all the more so because Hegel's awareness of mutuality is not matched by Nietzsche). Regardless of the value of Hegel's perspective on intersubjectivity, though, it remains unclear how meaningful it is to imagine mutual recognition being realized on an abstract, universal level, especially in our current global society. While recognition can be a guide in terms of everyday, interpersonal interactions, it needs to be supplemented by detailed analysis of the economic sphere.

Nietzsche's approach to agency focuses on motivation more exhaustively than Hegel's does. Nietzsche's interest in "depth psychology" leads him to heed how much of human behavior is governed by elemental and unconscious sources. His affirmation of irrationality is not intended to be hostile to reason; rather it is a call to grasp irrationality in its own right. Nietzsche anticipates psychoanalysis in arguing that facing up to irrationality, and giving up fantasies about its elimination, produces a more honest kind of self-assessment. Nietzsche accepts the limits of agency; at times, he seems to be infatuated by and to give license to more extreme forms of conduct, but he is inconsistent on this issue. The fact that Nietzsche countenances "letting go" should not obscure that he values self-control and a coherent sense of agency. Nietzschean agency worries about socialization as mere conformism, but it is less enlightening on its potential value or the dangers of living without it.

As a conclusion, I would like to enumerate five points about a psychoanalytic conception of agency, drawing from my genealogical account, which might serve as the basis for a contemporary model. The first point about a psychoanalytic conception of agency is the assertion that narcissism and relatedness are necessary features (regardless of how much cultures might differ in terms of the emphasis they place on one or the other or the ideal balance they would justify). A healthy sense of agency is implicit here, and, by contrast, a pathological sense as well. Blatt and Blass (1996) have cogently argued, for instance, that underlying all forms of psychopathology are problems either in the area of self-definition or in the area of relatedness to others. Freudian, Kleinian, and Lacanian analysts would be inclined to take a harder line about the inevitability of conflict between narcissism and relatedness. Winnicott, Self-Psychologists, and Relational theorists affirm the interrelation of narcissism and relatedness, emphasizing how coregulation produces self-regulation in infants. Winnicott (1965) suggests that "good-enough mothering" requires toleration of the child's need for omnipotence, which then results in a modulated form of narcissism that is less dismissive of others.

My second point follows directly from the first point. A psychoanalytic conception of agency demands that the question of how one becomes an agent—a point of weakness in philosophical accounts—be taken seriously. Developmentally, the sense of agency emerges from the affective relationship between infant and primary caregiver.[7] More specifically, the sense of agency comes into being through "affect mirroring," by virtue of which infants not only begin to understand what they feel by seeing it reflected by the caregiver, but see that they have the potential to control or modulate those feelings (Fonagy et al. 2002). The capacity for affect regulation is crucial for a child to be able to mentalize—that is, to learn to read and interpret the mental states of others as well as his or her own. Mentalization, which occurs at four to five years of age, enables children to move beyond the assumption that what is in their mind must be in the minds of others ("psychic equivalence") and to appreciate more complex assessments of reality (Fonagy and Target 1996). This faculty helps us hold onto different interpretations of reality, without prematurely settling on one or the other. Mentalization clearly depends on cognition, but it also enables us, as adults, to reflect on our own affect states ("mentalized affectivity"), making it possible to understand affect states in terms of our own history and representational world as well as in terms of our culture (and the interaction between where we come from and where we live).

This brings us to the third point: that it is impossible for agents to possess transparent and complete self-knowledge. That affective experience can be understood retrospectively does not mean that we are necessarily fully aware of the meaning of our affects as they occur. Misunderstanding affect, thinking we feel one thing rather than another, and being confused about what we feel are central to a psychoanalytic way of conceiving of affects (Jurist 2005, 2006, 2008). It belongs to the nature of agency, therefore, to experience both moments of aporia and self-deception. This serves as a useful reminder of the limits inherent in human agency.

The fourth point highlights a feature of the mind, "dissociation," that helps to explicate the limits of agency. Dissociation has come to occupy an increasingly important role in psychoanalytic theory. In line with Nietzsche's insight about multiple self-states, dissociation helps us to see that the mind is defined by having separate mental states. Dissociation can be understood as one of the main consequences of trauma. Bromberg (1989) offers a perspective that is more complex: he countenances dissociation as a normal and even healthy quality of the mind, a way, for instance, to tolerate affect states that otherwise would be too painful.

The cultural significance of dissociation is worth pausing over. Hegel characterizes modern culture in terms of alienation; Nietzsche dramatizes this by invoking despair and sickness. Dissociation can be seen as the contemporary, postmodern equivalent, indicating that we experience an even more disturbing kind of disconnection (not just between ourselves and others, but within ourselves as well). Moreover, dissociation is evocative of a traumatized consciousness, one that has trouble being able to feel at all.

The fifth point concerns the vexing issue of the relation between agency and society or, perhaps better put, between individual and social agency. All psychoanalytic views would concur that society ought to make room for narcissism, that narcissism can be construed as healthy and can be differentiated from mere selfishness. All psychoanalytic views would agree, too, that aggression is exacerbated when narcissism is thwarted. Kohut (1971) is a well-known proponent of this view, and it has been adopted by relational theorists who wish to challenge Freud's supposition that aggression is an elemental part of human motivation.

The issue of whether aggression is fundamental or epiphenomenal is crucial in terms of how social agency is imagined and constructed. Some thinkers—like Hegel, Marx, Habermas, and Honneth—hope that socialization can flourish through relatedness. Other thinkers—like Nietzsche, Lacan, Foucault, and Judith Butler—view relatedness and socialization ambivalently, in that they see socialization as violent, coercive, and oppressive. Freud and Adorno have sympathies for the former camp but fall into the latter camp. The latter perspective does a better job of holding onto tensions between individual and social agency. The former perspective is preferable in establishing a vantage point from which to limit and condemn the exploitation of others.

Psychoanalysis offers a promising contemporary view of agency because it derives from both Hegelian intersubjectivity and Nietzschean decenteredness. It upholds the ideal of keeping both in mind without minimizing the difficulty of doing so. It directs us to look at the development, limits, and complications of agency. Philosophical accounts of agency cannot afford to be indifferent to a psychoanalytic point of view, just as psychological accounts of agency can benefit from philosophical analysis.

Notes

1. The literature on personal identity is too vast to summarize here. Although Locke's view on personal identity sets the agenda for a large portion of this literature, recent works challenge this domain of inquiry. As Schechtman (1996, ix) observes, "The contemporary philosophical discussion of identity omits a great deal that seems central to the topic of personal identity." She goes on to argue that "the reidentification question" will never satisfy the demands of "the characterization question," the latter of which appeals to "an individual's inner life and her attitude toward her actions and experiences" (p. 95). The issues raised by the characterization question, according to Schechtman, rely upon a "narrative self-constitution" view.

2. Some philosophers want to emphasize that we ought to think of persons and agents as closely related. For example, in "Personal Identity and the Unity of Agency," Korsgaard (1989) uses Kant's notion of agency, which is a practical standpoint that is based on viewing ourselves as free and responsible, against Parfit.

3. Taylor's first extended discussion of expressivism was in *Hegel* (1975), which proposes that this background is critical for understanding Hegel's philosophical proj-

ect. In *Sources of the Self: The Making of the Modern Identity* (1989), Taylor develops his narrative to a greater extent through the nineteenth and twentieth century. In the article "Inwardness and the Culture of Modernity," Taylor (1992) does not contend with the theme of expressivism.

4. Nehamas's (1985, 196) work has made an important contribution in specifying how self-exploration is played out in Nietzsche: the author invents himself as a character in his work.

5. Generally Nietzsche stresses the value of affects: "*In summa: domination* of the passions, *not* their weakening or extirpation!—The greater the dominating power of a will, the more freedom may the passions be allowed. The "great man" is great owing to the free play and scope of his desires and to the yet greater power that knows how to press these magnificent monsters into service" (WP, #933, entry dated spring-fall 1887). Contrasting the "good man" who lives moderately and combines the "harmless and the useful," Nietzsche's point is that the great man has access to his affects, is adept at their expression, and refuses to stifle them. In referring to affects as "magnificent monsters," however, Nietzsche does acknowledge that affects are powerful and potentially dangerous. In another passage from the *Will to Power* (entry dated March–June 1888), Nietzsche observes that if one is weak, one will fear the senses, desires and passions because one feels unable to restrain them. He moves on to suggest, on the other hand, that if one is strong, then the excess associated with passions is not a threat. He hypothesizes that passions have acquired a bad name precisely because they overwhelm those who are weak. Nietzsche again acknowledges that passions can be akin to sickness, but he tells us here that they should not be avoided.

6. In chapter 12 of *Beyond Hegel and Nietzsche,* I focus on what Nietzsche has to say about our relation to others, particularly friendship. He values others, but worries about being negatively affected by them and defends solitary life.

7. Benjamin (1987) and Honneth (1996) are critical theorists who have looked to psychoanalytic developmental theory, particularly Winnicott, in their accounts of agency. I am sympathetic to their accounts and will add to them by utilizing recent developmental research.

References

Benjamin, J. 1987. *The bonds of love: Psychoanalysis, feminism, and the problem of domination*. New York: Pantheon Books.

Blatt, S. J., and Blass, R. 1996. Relatedness and self-definition: A dialectical model of personality development. In G. G. Noam and K. W. Fischer, eds., *Development and vulnerabilities in close relationships*, 309–338. Hillsdale, N.J.: Erlbaum.

Bowlby, J. 1969. *Attachment and loss, Vol. 1: Attachment*. London: Hogarth Press and the Institute of Psycho-Analysis.

Bromberg, P. 1989. *Standing in the spaces: Essays on clinical process, trauma, and dissociation*. New York: Analytic Press.

Fonagy, P., Gergely, G., Jurist, E. L., and Target, M. 2002. *Affect regulation, mentalization, and the development of the self.* New York: Other Press.

Fonagy, P., and Target, M. 1996. Playing with reality: I. Theory of mind and the normal development of psychic reality. *International Journal of Psycho-Analysis* 77:217–233.

Hegel, G. W. F. 1971. *Hegel's philosophy of mind (Part III of the encyclopedia* [abbreviated PM]. Trans. W. Wallace. Oxford: Clarendon Press.

Hegel, G. W. F. 1977. *Hegel's phenomenology of spirit* [abbreviated PhS]. Trans. A. V. Miller. Oxford: Clarendon Press.

Honneth, A. 1996. *The struggle for recognition: The moral grammar of social conflicts*. Cambridge, Mass.: MIT Press.

Jurist, E. 2000. *Beyond Hegel and Nietzsche: Philosophy, culture, and agency*. Cambridge, Mass.: MIT Press.

Jurist, E. 2005. Mentalized affectivity. *Psychoanalytic Psychology* 22:426–444.

Jurist, E. 2006. Art and emotion in psychoanalysis. *International Journal of Psycho-Analysis* 87:1315–1334.

Jurist, E. 2008. Minds and yours: New direction for mentalization theory. In E. L. Jurist, A. Slade, and S. Berger, eds., *Mind to mind: Infant research, neuroscience, and psychology*. New York: Other Press.

Kohut, H. 1971. *The analysis of the self.* New York: International Universities Press.

Korsgaard, C. 1989. Personal identity and the unity of agency: A Kantian response to Parfit. *Philosophy and Public Affairs* 28:101–132.

Mahler, M., Pine, F., and Bergman, A. 1975. *The psychological birth of the human infant*. New York: Basic Books.

Nehamas, A. 1985. *Nietzsche: Life as literature*. Cambridge: Harvard University Press.

Nietzsche, F. 1954. *The Portable Nietzsche*. Ed. and trans. W. Kaufmann. New York: Viking Press.
Twilight of the idols [abbreviated TI].
Also spoke Zarathustra [abbreviated Z].

Nietzsche, F. 1968a. *Basic writings of Nietzsche*. Ed. and trans. W. Kaufmann. New York: Random House.
Beyond good and evil [abbreviated BGE].
The birth of tragedy [abbreviated BT].
Ecce homo [abbreviated EH].
On the genealogy of morals [abbreviated GM].

Nietzsche, F. 1968b. *The will to power* [abbreviated WP]. Trans. W. Kaufmann and R. J. Hollingdale. New York: Viking.

Nietzsche, F. 1974. *The gay science* [abbreviated GS]. Trans. W. Kaufmann. New York: Vintage.

Nietzsche, F. 1982. *Daybreak*. Trans. R. J. Hollingdale. Cambridge: Cambridge University Press.

Nietzsche, F. 1983. *Untimely meditations* [abbreviated UM]. Trans. R. J. Hollingdale. Cambridge: Cambridge University Press.

Nietzsche, F. 1986. *Human, all too human* [abbreviated HAH]. Trans. R. J. Hollingdale. Cambridge: Cambridge University Press.

Schechtman, M. 1996. *The constitution of selves*. Ithaca, N.Y.: Cornell University Press.

Speight, J. 2001. *Hegel, literature and the problem of agency*. Cambridge: Cambridge University Press.

Stern, D. 1985. *The interpersonal world of the infant*. New York: Basic Books.

Taylor, C. 1975. *Hegel*. New York: Cambridge University Press.

Taylor, C. 1985. *Philosophical papers*. 2 vols. Cambridge: Cambridge University Press.

Taylor, C. 1989. *Sources of the self: The making of the modern identity*. Cambridge, Mass.: Harvard University Press.

Taylor, C. 1992. Inwardness and the culture of modernity. In A. Honneth, T. McCarthy, C. Offe, and A. Wellmer, eds., *Philosophical interventions in the unfinished project of Enlightenment*. Cambridge, Mass.: MIT Press.

Taylor, C. 1995. *Philosophical arguments*. Cambridge, Mass.: Harvard University Press.

Winnicott, D. W. 1965. *The maturational processes and the facilitating environment*. Madison, Conn.: International Universities Press.

3 Understanding Persons as Relational Agents: The Philosophy of John Macmurray and Its Implications for Psychology

Jeff Sugarman

Charles Taylor (2002) has remarked that the most pressing challenge of this century for politics and the social sciences is "understanding the other." However, in recent times, this task has become complicated by two factors. First, we have begun to recognize the far-reaching implications of a legacy of belief that Europeans and other Westerners are the epitome of cultural maturity to which all other cultures should aspire and against which their assumed lesser merits can be measured. But granting legitimacy to the beliefs and practices of alien cultures and societies appears to undermine Western epistemological traditions and systems of warranting that have been understood as central to the social-scientific enterprise, leaving many to contemplate relativism and its associated difficulties.

Second, even if we overcome such hubris, many critics argue that this project is further impaired by the dominant scientification and technicization of cultural discourses that restrict our horizon of reflection and pose a threat to the integrity of our interpretations of forms of life—both our own and those of others. With the entrenchment of science and instrumentalism in our modes of inquiry, ordinary capacities for practical judgment and rational reflection are seen as anathema to methodological veracity and met with distrust, if not outright derision. Relatedly, many psychological phenomena, though compelling in everyday human functioning and experience—freedom of choice and action, for example—are taken to be too ephemeral and insufficiently objective to fall within the purview of legitimate scientific inquiry. But any examination of the human condition that excludes psychological phenomena on such grounds seems weak science at best. As will be discussed, sooner or later the questions it poses and answers it provides will be revealed as highly restricted both in theory and application, if not entirely distorted.

In this chapter, I present the view that the Other should be regarded as person, not object. Moreover, I claim that persons are distinguished by a human agency whose nature takes shape through its immersion and participation in communal relations with others. The upshot is that as the source of human understanding (both understanding others and our own self-understanding), agentic personhood demands a central role in any adequate conception of human psychology. In articulating this view of persons as relational agents, I will be following and elaborating the work of the twentieth-century Scottish philosopher, John Macmurray. Macmurray's speculative philosophy has remained relatively inconspicuous, having been eclipsed by the analysis of logic and language that dominated British philosophy of his era. Macmurray was concerned with distinguishing "the form of the personal" and articulating those respects in which persons differ uniquely from other animate and inanimate entities. This task seemed to him a matter of urgency. For without any clear conception of personhood, he feared the psychological sciences susceptible to developing deficient and possibly damaging accounts of human nature, while politics was likely to be misguided and potentially destructive.

Macmurray asserted the metaphysical and epistemological primacy of action over reflection, and located the seeking and acquisition of knowledge in the active and differentiating agentic engagement of persons with the world. While Macmurray claimed that thought is derivative of action, he also held that the human individual not only is an intentional agent who chooses and constructs experience through action, but also a person who exists, from birth, in dynamic interaction with other persons, and whose particular kind of self-conscious agency arises as a consequence of embeddedness in human relations. Personal existence, in Macmurray's view, is a relational becoming, ongoing agentic activity in which we are constituted mutually by and with each other as persons. We discover and realize our personhood in a pervasive relational dynamic of self-revelation by which we become present to ourselves though the actions of others. In Macmurray's summation, persons not only are agents, but moreover, they exist as agents in relation: "We need one another to be ourselves. This complete and unlimited dependence of each of us upon the others is the central and crucial fact of personal existence . . . the basic fact of our human condition" (1961, p. 211).

Macmurray's philosophy of the form of the personal bears close kinship with the works of others who have sought to comprehend personal existence in terms of relational or dialogical agency. Readers will note particular similarity between Macmurray's ideas and those of Martin Buber and Gabriel Marcel, both of whom were contemporaries and acquaintances of Macmurray (Costello 2002), as well as affinity with other Continental philosophers, including Ferdinand Ebuer, Eberhard Grisebach, Karl Jaspers, Friedrich Heinrich Jacobi, Eugene

Rosenstock-Huessy, Franz Rosenzweig, and Max Scheler (see Friedman 2002). Commonalities can be detected as well with other traditions of thought that developed independently, but that also trace the development of personal agency to our immersion and participation in interpersonal relationships. Examples include the symbolic interactionism of James Mark Baldwin, Charles Horton Cooley, and George Herbert Mead (see Harter 1999), in addition to cultural-historical activity theory, as advanced by Vygotsky, Leontiv, and their collaborators (see Stensenko and Arievitch 2004).

Building on his philosophy of the form of the personal, Macmurray wrote extensively about the kinds of human association and collectivities best suited to personal possibility and fulfillment. He advocated the ideal of community which, in his view, consists in a harmonious interrelation of agents that springs not just from mutual need and interdependence, but also from the kind of affiliation found in friendship. In light of Macmurray's ideas, understanding the Other is not simply an epistemological endeavor. It is profoundly ontological, moral, ethical and, most importantly, personal. In this chapter, Macmurray's work is examined as a rich and largely unexplored source to be mined for ways in which psychologists and psychotherapists might more adequately conceptualize persons as relational agents and the nature of academic and professional psychological pursuits. I begin by sketching Macmurray's philosophy of the form of the personal. Subsequently, I turn to the relevance and possible implications of his work for understanding others and for understanding how academic and professional psychology is positioned with respect to these endeavors.

The Form of the Personal: Relational Agency

Macmurray interprets metaphysics as the attempt to configure human experience into a set of categories by which it can be comprehended. However, he finds traditional approaches that have attempted to grasp human life in mechanistic or organic categories inadequate. According to Macmurray, neither analogy does justice to what is uniquely entailed in personhood. The predicament of philosophy, he thus submits, is to discern the form of the personal and identify ways in which it is metaphysically sui generis and irreducible. In Macmurray's estimation, meeting this challenge demands no less than wholesale rejection and remaking of two deep-seated metaphysical presumptions. He observes that modern philosophy has been, first, excessively theoretical and, second, egocentric. It is overly theoretical in that it seeks proof of existence in thought, and proceeds as though the self were a pure subject capable of withdrawing completely from action and participation in the life of the world. It is egocentric in presenting a view of the subject isolated in contemplation, separated from others and unable to verify its existence.

Macmurray addresses these presuppositions in two volumes comprising his 1953–1954 Gifford Lectures collectively titled *The Form of the Personal*. In the first volume, *The Self as Agent* (1957), Macmurray contests the theoretical disposition of metaphysics by asserting the primacy of action over reflection. He alleges that the influence of Cartesian philosophy has been to obscure the logical priority of action. Since Descartes, much philosophy has been premised on the idea that mental experience is self-evident, and we can grasp our nature as thinking beings directly in reflection. But building metaphysics on the foundation of a reflective self, Macmurray claims, overamplifies the importance of thought and, in so doing, creates a host of intractable dualisms that separate the self from its embodied dealings in the everyday world of practical reality. The outcome is philosophies incapable of dealing adequately with extramental reality and that only can accept the existence of action and other minds on faith.

The solution Macmurray proposes is to reverse the relation between reflective subjectivity and agency by giving precedence to action. He argues that it is action, not thought, that is self-evident to a human agent acting in the world. If we examine the phenomenology of immediate experience, knowledge of ourselves as active agents interacting dynamically with each other and with the world is at least as well founded as knowledge of ourselves as thinking subjects for whom the world is an object. Macmurray insists that human life is, first and foremost, action. Thinking, as one possible mode of activity, always serves the ends of action, and its verification only is available by its practical reference. Thought is contained within the active self as one moment in its being and is an abstraction from the practical reality of an engaged agency.

Thus, agency encompasses thinking, and involves intention and choice, not as antecedent mental events that preface and cause what we do, but rather, as necessary features of action. Moreover, intentionality is unique to human agents, and marks a crucial difference between material or organic events and human acts. Unlike material or organic events, which have nonvolitional causes, human acts are intentional. Acts express intentionality, which requires human agents as their source. The distinctively human capacity to act according to our intentions and choices makes our actions self-initiated in a way that material or organic events are not.

Our ability to act with intention is not a matter of logical deduction, but one of freedom. Freedom, Macmurray defends, is a practical reality expressed in action, by forming intentions and attempting to achieve them. Further, if our actions are truly agentic, and we are capable of affecting the things on which we act, as well as ourselves in acting on them, our actions cannot be predetermined by mechanistic or organic events. In Macmurray's metaphysics, the world in which we act is not fixed and universal but rather mutable, particular, and contingent. Such a world is required for human freedom and the agency by which it is expressed.

Macmurray's emphatic appeal to regard agency as a vital feature of persons antedates and accords with a number of contemporary proposals for its indispensability in psychological accounts (e.g., Bandura 2001; Greenwood 1991; Harré and Gillett 1994; Howard 1994; Jenkins 1997; Martin, Sugarman, and Thompson 2003; Rychlak 1999; Slife 1994; Williams 1992). For example, Martin, Sugarman, and Thompson (2003) have argued that agency is an irreducible and defining aspect of what it is to be a person, and have articulated a developmental theory of situated, deliberative agency that emerges from the embeddedness of biological individuals in preexisting historical and sociocultural lifeworlds. In this conception, human agency is the deliberative, reflective activity of a human being in framing, choosing, and executing his or her actions in a way that is not fully determined by factors and conditions other than his or her own understanding and reasoning. In this definition, agency need not be unaffected by factors and conditions other than an agent's own authentic, reflective understanding and reasoning. It only must not be determined fully by such other factors, a state of affairs referred to as *underdetermination*. In claiming that agency is underdetermined by "other factors," this does not mean that agency is necessarily undetermined, only that it must itself figure in its own determination. Once a psychologically capable person has emerged developmentally, his or her interpretations will be active in the further constitution of his or her personhood.

Martin, Sugarman, and Thompson's account of agency does not deny the necessary requirements of physical, biological, and sociocultural factors in the constitution of agentic persons. However, it recognizes a crucial distinction between requirement and identity—that is, while agentic persons can never stand outside the determining influence of relevant physical, biological, and socicocultural factors and conditions, their agentic self-understanding is underdetermined by such factors and conditions, and they are capable of entering into the choosing, framing, and execution of actions in ways that transcend their biological and sociocultural constitution. By championing a psychological agency in this way, Martin, Sugarman, and Thompson have attempted to resist the hard determinism that has been, and continues to be, a hallmark of scientific psychology for many psychologists.

In the second volume of the Gifford lectures, *Persons in Relation* (1961), Macmurray disputes the presupposition of philosophical egocentricity. According to him, the self as agent remains an abstraction unless properly contextualized as a relational being. Against the notion of the isolated self, Macmurray develops the claim that personal existence only can be realized in dynamic relation with others. All of our capacities for knowing and understanding arise from our immersion and participation in a world of personal relations. Macmurray refuses the view that psychological development is driven principally by biological impulses or evolutionary forces. Persons do not begin as infantile organisms that develop by surviving and adapting to their environments. Quite conversely, it is our total inability to survive and adapt on our own that creates a relation of dependence on others that steers the course of psychological development. Macmurray asserts that every aspect of the form and direction of psychological development is initiated and guided by others who equip us not simply to survive as organisms, but to take our place as members of a personal community.

Macmurray theorizes that our capacities for knowing and understanding are sown in infancy, and psychological development begins by distinguishing the presence and absence of the primary caregiver. Knowledge is acquired by making discriminations. However, as infants, we are unable to act intentionally, and the caregiver who acts on our behalf is undifferentiated in the unity of infantile experience. The infant's first discrimination is that of the caregiver whose intermittent tactile presence in response to the infant's cries registers a very basic recognition of the caregiver's repetitive pattern of withdrawal and return. This seeds the development of memory and expectation. As the infant's awareness expands, the presence of the caregiver becomes an expectation stirred by memory. In waiting, the past is imagined in order to recover the sense of security experienced previously in being touched and held.

Development flows from the caregiver's rhythm of withdrawal and return, as this pattern becomes incorporated inextricably into the infant's existence. The initial prereflective understanding of the presence and absence of the caregiver leads not only to early awareness of succession, expectancy, refusal, and reconciliation, but also, eventually gives rise to reflective activity and differentiation of fantasy from reality, true from false, right from wrong, and good from bad. Macmurray details how in attempting to comprehend and cope with the dependency of motives and needs on a nurturant, but also resistant, personal world, the child is compelled to make these intellectual and moral distinctions and steered toward the development of an intentional reflective agency.

As development proceeds, what gradually appears is an integrated assemblage of skills gained through conscious learning, many of which eventually become habitual and automatic. Practical activity is mainly prereflective and occurs for the most part automatically. However, when our actions are impeded or interrupted, reflective activity arises, and this occasions the conscious acquisition of new skills. Most important among the skills we acquire is speech, which enhances not only our powers of expression, but also our capacity for understanding. The most salient aspect of speech, according to Macmurray, is that it permits us to enter into reciprocal communication that facilitates the sharing of experience and furthers the acquisition of skills. Thus, in his developmental analysis, the world and other persons both support and resist our actions and act on us, and in so doing, create a relational context of possibility and constraint in which an intentional reflective agency can develop psychologically.

Not only do our psychological capacities find their initial form through the care others provide that both supports and limits our actions, but also, it is from within this tension that self-consciousness emerges. Macmurray dismisses the notion of an agent able to manufacture self-awareness in contemplative isolation. We first become aware of the existence of others; self-awareness follows. The differentiation of things from persons follows from the discrimination of persons, ensuing much later, and only when the child's capacities have been augmented significantly by speech and abstract thought. We begin our psychological development with the realization of a personified world—an Other who cares for us—not a world of impersonal objects. Self-awareness emerges from resisting, opposing, and contrasting ourselves with our caregivers who attempt to impose their intentions on us. If not for their opposition to our actions, it is difficult to see how we ever would come to recognize ourselves in existence or apprehend our agentic purposes.

So vital is the personal interrelatedness of human life that without it, Macmurray remarks, any knowledge whatsoever would not be possible, including knowledge of our own existence. Our first knowledge is that of the Other, and this awareness is the presupposition for all successive development. It is with this insight that Macmurray can be placed in the company of Buber, Marcel, and other Continental philosophers (see Friedman 2002). These thinkers took issue with the epistemological assumption that knowledge of other persons is derived from the relation of a knowing subject to an external world. They argued for a fundamental reversal of this epistemology. The "I-Thou" relation precedes "I-It" relations, to use Buber's terms. It is only because we are already in a personal "I-Thou" relation that we are able to acquire knowledge of an external world or awareness of ourselves.

Macmurray maintains that self-consciousness is created in the ongoing and ever-present dynamic exchange by which we make ourselves present to each other. Self-consciousness emerges and develops as a kind of mutual self-revelation that transpires only within the context of relationship. By revealing and contrasting ourselves in relation, we convey our appreciation of the Other's unique significance to us and, in so doing, participate in their self-constitution. The caregiver interacts with the child, not simply as a being requiring the fulfillment of needs, but as a being of value: a person. The child becomes present to herself through the actions of the caregiver, who communicates the nature and significance of the child's presence to the child. At the same, the child responds to the caregiver with love, and in the child's communicative expressions, the caregiver is informed of her significance and value as caregiver.

Thus, it is not simply that our personhood is constituted in relation with others. It is constituted in the mutuality of self-revelation. Personhood is mutual in its very being and we remain forever embedded in the mutuality of the "I and You" relation of which we are part, but from which we strive to distinguish ourselves. As Macmurray (1961, 91) describes,

> The "You and I" relation . . . constitutes the personal, and both the "You" and the "I" are constituted, as individual persons by the mutuality of their relation. Consequently, the development of the individual person is the development of his relation to the Other. Personal individuality is not an original given fact. It is achieved through the progressive differentiation of the original unity of the "You and I."

The mutuality of self-revelation permeates individual development throughout the many and varied relations we encounter over the course of our lives. We come to know and experience ourselves through revelation by the Other and in contrast with them.

It is of interest to note that some contemporary developmental psychologists have advanced the view that it is through our active engagements with others, not in thought, that we normally come to comprehend one another and ourselves as intentional beings (Hobson 2002; Reddy 1996; Reddy and Morris 2004). According to this perspective, relational engagement is the process by which minds to be known are created. For example, Reddy and Morris claim that "the problem of other minds" (i.e., the gap between third-person perceptions and first-person experience) that currently occupies much of infancy and child research, can be addressed by greater attention to the features of relational engagement. As Reddy and Morris explain, "In engagement they [infants] are not confronted with objects whose movements they need to match with (or interpret through) something else in order to understand what they mean. . . . The infant is not observing others as objects from a third-person perspective, but rather is experiencing them as intentional beings in relation with their own intentionality, as second persons" (p. 659).

Reddy and Morris, drawing explicitly from Macmurray, argue that infants relate to their caregivers in the second person, as a Thou, rather than as an object—a He or a She. Reddy and Morris further observe that a second-person or Thou relation is marked in early development by a certain emotionality that distinguishes it from third-person relations, and that this emotionality persists throughout our development as a constitutive feature of our relations. Similarly, Benjamin (1995), in her reinterpretation of object relations theory, differentiates relations between subjects from those between the subject and the subject's object. For Benjamin, we possess an intrapsychic need for recognition, and grasping our subjectivity fully in the course of our development requires that others genuinely recognize us as subjects, not simply as objects. It is to this key distinction in conceptions of human beings as persons or as objects, articulated by Macmurray as that between personal and functional relations, that I next turn.

Forms of Human Relations

Among Macmurray's unique contributions is his analysis of kinds of human association, and advocacy of those he takes to be best suited to a personal existence in which our agentic being and becoming are dependent on mutual relations with others. Pivotal to Macmurray's (2004) account is a distinction between functional and personal relations that he first draws in a 1941 essay, *Persons and Functions*, later elaborated in the Gifford Lectures as the contrast between personal and impersonal relations. Functional relations are defined by their instrumental worth in achieving a common purpose. These are the sorts of transactions ubiquitous in daily life in which we attempt to get something done—purchase groceries, obtain an estimate for an automotive repair, undergo an optometric examination, and so forth. Our relations to those with whom we are dealing are defined by functional purposes and the social roles that circumscribe the manner of the encounter. Typically, functional relations terminate at the conclusion of the transaction when the purposes of those involved have been achieved. At the root of functional relations is an impersonal attitude. In an impersonal relation, we treat the Other less as a person than as an object to be known. In such cases, Macmurray remarks, we attempt to negate or withdraw from the personal relation, and our attitude toward the other is self-centered or egocentric.

Personal relations, by contrast, have no purpose beyond expression of the relation itself. Personal relations exist for their own sake, and are expressive of personhood in the fullest sense of its aspects of agency and mutual relation. In genuine personal relations we do not subordinate our agency to social functions, but rather, reciprocally express our mutual significance and value as persons. In Macmurray's view, not only does personhood emerge in our relations as mutuality for its own sake, but also, the mutual interdependence of equals found in friendship is the exemplary form of a personal relation. The relation expressed in friendship is heterocentric rather than egocentric—that is, each person acts principally for the benefit of the other, out of such motives as love, loyalty, and generosity, rather than out of self-interest. Friendship is not founded on common purposes, but rather, stems from a genuine mutual concern and the enjoyment that friends take in being together. To consider what purpose a friendship serves is to put it into question and cast doubt on its authenticity.

Macmurray does not believe that functional life can be separated from personal life, but he recoils at the notion that our primary purposes are to serve social roles. He maintains that while both functional and personal relations are indispensable to human life, they are of differential importance. Specifically, Macmurray emphasizes the priority of the personal over the functional. Further, he articulates their interconnection: "The functional life is *for* the personal life; the personal life is *through* the functional life" (2004/1941, 149). By this, Macmurray means that the entire complex of our social, political, and economic affairs poses no value in and of itself, but only insofar as it serves the ends of personal life and human fulfillment. However, at the same time, personal life is cultivated through functional activities. Personal life is agentic action and expressed in our daily encounters as we provide for one another's needs and find value and significance in doing so. The goods of personal life are made manifest in our concrete engagements with others.

The distinction between functional and personal involvements bears implications for the kinds of collectivities facilitative of personal life and human fulfillment. In Macmurray's interpretation, individual fulfillment only can be realized by persons in relation, and the degree of fulfillment each of us is capable of securing is relative to that attained by others. Personal fulfillment depends on the mutual communication of the significance individuals hold for one another. In highlighting the ways different forms of collective life are framed by particular kinds of association, Macmurray uses the terms *community* and *society* to designate collectivities built on personal versus functional relations, respectively.

According to him, societies rest on the functional devices of politics, law, and other means of maintaining social orders. The impersonal structure of contemporary liberal democracies, for instance, typically sets moral obligations to the lowest common denominator by the imposition of laws governing the extent to which individuals can realize their intentions without infringing on those of others. This is because the chief purpose of liberal political orders is to protect the pursuits of individuals whose prime motive is to maximize their own self-interests. The attempt to regulate human interaction by externally imposed rules, in turn, promotes impersonal relations and an individualistically oriented, egocentric society.

Macmurray contends that the impersonal character of many societies is determined by a root motive of fear—that is, fear for self, fear of the Other, and fear of the threat the Other poses to the worldly possessions and social status with which one falsely identifies his or her personhood. In societies where fear prevails, freedom to express one's personhood is restricted. There is reluctance to embrace others openly and forgo our own interests for theirs if we fear that doing so comes at a cost to our own identities and self-fulfillment. When a primary motive of self-interest is presumed by all, trust is eroded, along with the kinds of caring relations that promote and underpin personal life.

By contrast, communities, as conceived by Macmurray, are not established through functional structures. Rather, they are founded on personal relations and the intention to create felicitous conditions for each member's development and fulfillment. Communities are built on the understanding that it is only through the flourishing of others who receive our care and concern that our own fulfillment may be secured. Central to Macmurray's vision of community are two constitutive and interconnecting principles: freedom and equality. Personal relations depend on the intention to preserve our freedom as agents. To deny another's freedom is to deny her agency and thus her personhood. Moreover, in the absence of freedom, there is fear of the Other, and the urge to overcome it by seeking power and control over its object. The principle of equality is necessary to ensure freedom, for if we fail to regard others as our equals, freedom is undermined.

Macmurray affirms the mutuality of freedom and equality. My freedom of action depends on yours, and likewise, we only find friendship by treating each other as equals—not equivalent in capacities or competence, but equal in our status as agentic persons and our need to create a relationship between us. From Macmurray's standpoint, community constitutes a form of life through the enactment of freedom and equality by its members. Community is defined neither by geography nor by regarding others at a distance with some vague, warm and fuzzy sentimentality. If community is to exist, it must be instantiated in action.

In sum, according to Macmurray, we can only be and become ourselves to the extent that we are included as members of a community of others and when individual and collective significance is actively elaborated and shared among its members. The goal of personal development is not eventually to dissolve our dependence on others. Rather, it is to achieve mutual interdependence among equals. Macmurray argues that human development and fulfillment is the common good, and describes the ideal collectivity as a personal community in which friendship, and the equality and freedom it permits, is offered unreservedly to each member. As Macmurray (1957, 15) encapsulates his agentic and relational philosophy of the personal, "All meaningful knowledge is for the sake of action, and all meaningful action is for the sake of friendship."

Understanding Persons

Macmurray's conception of the form of the personal provides a compelling account of features in which personhood resides—an account that I would suggest any psychology vested in understanding and bettering the condition of others ought to consider. Macmurray draws attention to the importance of understanding humans as persons, persons as agents, and the form and development of agentic personal existence as intrinsically relational. Further, his distinction between functional/impersonal and personal relations, and between communal and social collectivities, speaks directly to the means and ends of psychological inquiry and practice. In what follows, I wish to elaborate possible implications of Macmurray's work with an eye toward their value in understanding and bettering the lives of persons and, more specifically, the ways psychologists and psychotherapists might start to consider more critically their role toward these ends.

In the attempt to model psychology after approaches to the natural sciences, there has been a strong tendency to treat psychological phenomena as objects reducible to their biophysical or sociocultural constituents whose functioning can be formulated in causal explanations (Martin, Sugarman, and Thompson 2003). Contemporary psychology is replete with ongoing programs of research that attempt to reduce human agency, self, thinking, learning, and other kinds of psychological phenomena to biology, behavior, neurophysiology, computation, or other machine mechanisms, and even to disembodied systems of language and social practice. The outcome not only is to identify psychological phenomena as objects to be reduced, but also to construe human personhood in these terms. While psychologists rarely have undertaken explicit defenses of their ontological, epistemological, and methodological assumptions and commitments to natural-scientific approaches, there is, by contrast, an impressive accumulation of criticism both from within and outside the discipline by those who have examined these assumptions and found them wanting.[1] The belief that humans are objects to be studied like phenomena investigated by natural science, rather than persons to be encountered, makes all sorts of assumptions that are weakly warranted, if not incoherent and untenable. Nowhere perhaps is this more evident than in psychological conceptions of agency.

The treatment of human agency by disciplinary psychology is riddled with incoherence (Martin, Sugarman, and Thompson 2003). On the one hand, agentic freedom of choice and action is inimical to psychology as a highly deterministic, reductive science that aims to discover causal conditions for human action and experience. Because scientific determinism is irreconcilable with the freedom of choice and action entailed by agency, disciplinary psychologists have tended to disavow agency and reduce its effects to biophysical and/or sociocultural determinants. On the other hand, professional psychology, by and large, takes human agency for granted, and presumes that clients are capable of making choices and actively initiating change in ways that can transform their lives. Moreover, it is difficult to see how persons, including psychologists, could conduct their lives without some conception of agency. In the absence of agentic freedom of choice and action, we cannot be said to be responsible for our deeds, merit the respect or contempt of others, deserve the fruits of our labors, or invent, discover, or be capable of entering into relations such as friendship and love that demand agentic moral and ethical commitment.

Clearly psychologists cannot have it both ways. We cannot presuppose that human action and experience are determined by biophysical or sociocultural causes and, at the same time, regard our own and others' everyday choices, actions, and experiences as significant and influential in our lives. Macmurray's account situates personhood and the constitutive feature of agency at the center of all psychological theory, inquiry, and practice. In light of Macmurray's work, to deny agency is to disclaim our personhood. To dismiss human agency is to reduce our actions to mere events and to conceive of humans as deterministic objects rather than persons who, as a consequence of their agency, are presumed to bear certain rights, have interests and recognize what is and is not in their interest, possess capacities for rational choice and originating genuine purposes, forge their own unique autobiographies, or decide who can be said to be justly deserving of praise or blame.

In short, any understanding of ourselves as fully human requires the idea of agentic freedom, and to treat another person as a person necessitates recognition of his or her agency. One might well wonder what value professional psychology possesses if both psychotherapists' and their clients' actions and experiences are fully predetermined by fixed causal sequences that preclude human agency.

The incoherence in psychologists' conceptions of agency also is evident in the separation of thought from action that has pervaded psychological theorizing. The history of psychological theorizing has persistently been divided by this schism as theorists have endlessly debated formal and functional models, and mental/cognitive and behavioral orientations. By asserting the priority of action, Macmurray's philosophy indicates a remedy for many of the theoretical ills spread by dualism. As Dokecki (1990) suggests, in overcoming the traditional dualism of thinking and acting, Macmurray also provides an avenue to resolving the dualism of theory and practice that has divided, and continues to divide, academic and professional psychology. Theory does not supersede or preside over practice, nor need we be encumbered by difficulties entailed in conceptualizing how an abstract thinker is motivated to act. In view of Macmurray's construal, theory, like thought, is furnished by agency. Theory flows from an engaged and situated agentic existence in the everyday world of practical activity. All thinking is related to purposes that arise within the basic condition of human life as the embodied agentic activity of persons. This grounding of the thinker (psychologist or psychotherapist) firmly in the world as a consequence of an engaged and situated agency also helps to stem the postmodern fragmentation that results when selves are conceptually disembodied from their agentic worldly being (Martin, Sugarman, and Thompson 2003).

For example, some influential postmodern psychological theories (e.g., Gergen 1997) have attempted the total deconstruction of agentic psychological capacities. On this account, ontological posits of mind, self, agency, and other psychological phenomena can be made to yield to conceptual analyses of rhetorical devices and narrative conventions. In turn, such devices and conventions are believed to be further reducible to processes of social interaction. Encapsulating this view, Gergen (1997, 740) asserts that "we can envision the elimination of psychological states and conditions as explanations for action, and the reconstitution of psychological predicates within the sphere of social process." Those such as Gergen may be warranted in drawing attention to the ethnocentrically assumed foundationalism and excessive individualism of much psychology, as well as advocating for far greater emphasis on relational activity as a constitutive feature of what it is to be human. However, by radically eliminating agentic human interpretive activity and the ontology of psychological phenomena, Gergen also does away with the possibility of societal and cultural innovation and change. If persons are fully determined by sociocultural conventions and practices, societies and cultures would remain static, and clearly they do not (Martin and Sugarman 1999). Analogously to the manner in which scientific theories are underdetermined by evidence, human understandings and interpretations, and the actions they support, are underdetermined by sociocultural conventions and practices.

Macmurray's portrayal of personhood not only reveals its agentic character, but also the manner in which the development and expression of an agentic personhood is profoundly relational. We cannot understand persons by examining their discrete aspects as isolated individuals. Rather, persons only can be comprehended by the way they are immersed in, and constituted by, their relations with others. Personhood is not simply existence. It is inescapably coexistence. We only become present to ourselves and develop psychologically in mutual relation with others. In addition, not only does self-awareness emerge in mutual relation, but also, our understanding of relationships between things and between people is circumscribed by our own relationships to them as conceived in early development. Throughout the course of our lives, changes in the nature of our relations can affect our understanding of ourselves, and conversely, new self-understandings can alter our comprehension of relationships. In either case, however, our understandings of others and ourselves are always the expression of an active agentic relatedness in which we elaborate our mutual significance as persons.

Macmurray's distinctions between functional/impersonal and personal relations, and between communal and social collectivities, are germane to discussion of psychological inquiry and practice as a technical undertaking versus personal engagement. The notion that disciplinary psychology principally is concerned with the understanding of persons seems increasingly lost amid the contemporary zeal for technical precision and instrumental skill. A vast and exponentially expanding literature attests to the fact that our discipline has become dominated by what appears to be largely the painstaking pursuit of trifling detail and a penchant for arcane technical quarrels beyond the comprehension and interest of most of us seeking to understand persons and what they are about. It would seem that as our psychological interests and aims grow more technical and instrumental, our inquiries become less a matter of genuine human encounter and understanding than of technical correctness.

A technical and instrumental disposition tends to ignore the integral relationship between means and ends, between what psychology is about and how we go about doing it. Elevating functional over personal dimensions of psychologists' disciplinary and professional endeavors in our efforts to understand and address the human condition occludes our wider purposes and influence on the communities and societies in which we are embedded. Psychological inquiry and practice do not stand apart from the everyday world of human activity. They are part of it, and contribute to the ways we understand ourselves as persons (Danziger 1997). Increasingly, ordinary people comprehend themselves and describe their lives in distilled psychological vocabulary (Woolfolk 1998). Psychologists' efforts to understand and theorize about various aspects of human life are an expression of our personhood, and are always ultimately concerned with being and becoming more human. Even the narrowest of social-scientific inquiries are, at root, in the service of this aspiration.

Psychology participates in the mutuality of self-revelation. All told, psychology, like all of our other disciplinary and practical pursuits, is an aspect of human life through which personal relations are established and maintained, and that attempts in some fashion to contribute to human understanding and fulfillment. The implication is that psychologists need continually to be aware of the ends of personal life and the ways our inquiries and interventions always are inevitably in their service. When psychological theories and practices cause us to reduce all of our personal encounters to functional exchanges, we denude ourselves of the personal significance of agentic being on which all our functional activities and engagements rest.

However, as Macmurray points out, we cannot dispense with the functional and its necessary role in sustaining personal life. In fact, Macmurray accepts that just as impersonal relations are necessary to maintaining the economic and political structures of a functioning society, so an impersonal scientific comprehension of persons may be both feasible and justifiable if it ultimately is placed in aid of the personal. To illustrate, Macmurray describes a situation in which a psychology instructor and student who also maintain a friendship meet and converse in the manner of a personal relationship. As the conversation proceeds, however, the instructor notices something abnormal about the student's behavior. Trying to determine the nature and cause of the abnormality, the instructor begins to analyze the student from the perspective of a psychologist. The psychologist's attitude toward the student shifts from the personal to the impersonal, but with the understanding and intention of applying his or her knowledge in the effort to understand and help the student as a person.

Macmurray is not naive in his prioritizing of personal over functional relations and advocacy of communities in favor of societies. He does not suppose that impersonal relations ever can be supplanted entirely by personal ones. The functional and personal are inextricably connected and always are present in every human interaction. When we intend a personal relationship with another person, an aspect of our intention to regard the Other functionally as an object is always present. This attitude never is displaced completely even with those with whom we are most intimate. However, an important part of what is entailed in being a person is the freedom and particularity of one's own agency, features of agentic existence that never are entirely within another's grasp. The Other, as agent, always possesses attributes that resist us and are unyielding to our will. Even though there may be much understanding between us, we never quite fully comprehend one another and, as a result, there always remains the possibility for new or elaborated awareness and appreciation.

Psychological inquiry and practice must attend to the functional activities of which human forms of life are comprised. However, if we truly believe in the value of communities and promoting the merits they possess for psychological well-being, then we must look to the ways communities are constituted by personal relations and to how such relations might be fostered and enhanced in daily life. In light of Macmurray's ideas, it is clear that the furtherance of communal life is not abetted by the proliferation of laws, rules, or procedures, or, for that matter, the sort of facile do-it-yourself prescriptions for individual happiness and successful relationships now commonly advertised by our profession. The proliferation of social and political rules and procedures, as well as of recipes for better living, not only is a meager substitute for sound practical judgment and rational reflection, it also insinuates that a society's members no longer possess those virtues and dispositions that characterize responsible personal agency and genuine human community.

Macmurray's notion of community is profoundly emancipatory and inclusive, and provides warrants for why functional approaches to relationship can never substitute adequately for genuine personal encounters. However, the idea that we might transform our societies into communities, especially given the enormity and complexity of societies comprising modern nation-states, is wishful thinking in the extreme. There are far too many persons in modern societies whom we do not know, but on whom we depend indirectly to function effectively in order for us to go on with our lives. There also are deep differences that divide people even when they act in good faith. There seems no end in sight to many political, ethical, and religious disagreements. In addition, to put it bluntly, some people just are not equipped or disposed toward open and reasonable discussion.

Nonetheless, what Macmurray's work seems to suggest is that it is important to be able to comprehend the importance and function of impersonal relations, to be able to distinguish them from personal relations, and appreciate the ways these two vital forms of human relations are connected in the nexus of human agentic and relational existence. Further, it is important to recognize that the kinds of personal relations that bind communities together cannot be legislated or instrumentally engineered. Macmurray attributes the failings of contemporary societies to the mistake of disregarding the personal in favor of more mechanistic and organic forms of knowing, understanding, and instrumental action.

This, however, does not preclude the possibility of social reform. With awareness of conditions by which communities are constituted, we are equipped to hold our social institutions and practices up to scrutiny, and critique and reform them in ways that might better serve the goods of community and personal existence. The development of a capacity for reflective, intentional agency makes it possible for us to achieve some measure of critical distance from our practices and traditions, and, in so doing, critique and revise our practices, ends, and inevitably ourselves. Individuals' interpretations can create possibilities for present and future understanding and action that are not entirely constrained by past and present sociocultural circumstances.

Psychologists are likely to agree on the importance of friendship and its merits for individual and collective well-being. But they also probably would agree that friendships with clients are entirely another matter. Further, we understand our relationships with clients differently from those with students, even though we occasionally might help clients become students and vice versa. However, the cultivation of friendships with students, like those with clients, is something of which we are wary and that raises questions of mutual freedom and equality. In addition, although it becomes more and more difficult for academic psychologists to solicit subjects for our research projects, we would hardly call these folks who assist us by participating voluntarily, our friends. Both academic and professional psychology have been cast as functional and impersonal pursuits. It would seem we psychologists are not out to make friends despite the newly adopted goal of positive psychology to become the science of happiness (Seligman and Csikszentmihalyi 2000).

While friendship may not be an appropriate goal given the functional designs of our discipline and profession, there is perhaps an aspect of the personal to be found in the sense of feeling obligation and commitment to others, even if it is limited to the mutual aspiration to be and become more human through greater understanding of our individual and collective condition as agentic and relationally constituted persons. The notion that the foundation of psychotherapy consists in mutual confirmation of our condition as persons or "healing through meeting" has been elaborated by Friedman (1985, 2003). Friedman, drawing from Buber, suggests that at the heart of the genuinely therapeutic encounter is "confirmation," being made present as a person. According to Friedman, confirmation observes the ontology of our mutual interrelatedness as expressed in dialogue. The confirming relation is one in which "I am called into being by you and you by me. . . . Our very sense of ourselves comes only in our meeting with others as they confirm us in the life of dialogue" (Friedman 2003, 54–55).

Our psychological development as persons consists largely in expanding the reach of our agency by attempting to know the nature and value of our encounters in the world. What becomes intelligible as knowledge issues from action. Conversely, action is informed by knowledge, and as knowledge increases, there is a corresponding increase in the possibilities for reflective intentional agentic action. Personal life involves the mutual interrogation and exploration of individual and collective possibilities in various settings of dialogical interaction with others. This includes discovering, realizing, questioning, and reformulating the significance of our own unique agentic personhood. Among his striking insights, Macmurray's notion of the mutuality of self revelation suggests that it is through others that we are introduced to new possibilities of being and understanding. In other words, understanding others is less to be looked on as a problem to be overcome than as an opportunity to be embraced. His work implies that we might comprehend our own personhood more deeply, not by looking inward, but by looking outward. From Macmurray's perspective, openness to Otherness is, at the same time, openness to possibilities in oneself. Macmurray reveals how we might comprehend more of our own personhood by sincerely attempting to look at ourselves from the perspective of the Other who is unfamiliar and familiar, stranger and companion, but always, person.

Note

1. The pages of journals such as *The Journal of Humanistic Psychology, The Journal of Theoretical and Philosophical Psychology, New Ideas in Psychology*, and *Theory and Psychology* are replete with examples of such critical work. There have also been a spate of texts critical of the assumptions pervasive in mainstream psychology. Some notable examples are Koch 1999, Robinson 1985, Taylor 1964, and more recently, Richardson, Slife, and Reber 2005.

References

Bandura, A. 2001. Social-cognitive theory: An agentic perspective. *Annual Review of Psychology* 52:1–26.

Benjamin, J. 1995. *Like subjects, love objects: Essays on recognition and sexual difference.* Hew Haven, Conn.: Yale University Press.

Costello, J. E. 2002. *John Macmurray: A biography*. Edinburgh: Floris Books.

Danziger, K. 1997. The historical formation of selves. In J. D. Ashmore and L. Jussim, eds., *Self and social identity: Fundamental issues,*137–159. New York: Oxford University Press.

Dokecki, P. R. 1990. On knowing the person as agent in caring relations. *Person-Centered Review* 5:155–169.

Friedman, M. 1985. *The healing dialogue in psychotherapy*. New York: Jason Aronson.

Friedman, M. 2002. *Martin Buber: The life of dialogue*. London: Routledge.

Friedman, M. 2003. Martin Buber and dialogical psychotherapy. In R. Frie, ed., *Understanding experience*, 52–76. London: Routledge.

Gergen, K. J. 1997. The place of the psyche in a constructed world. *Theory and Psychology* 7:723–746.

Greenwood, J. D. 1991. *Relations and representations: An introduction to the philosophy of social psychological science*. New York: Routledge.

Harré, R., and Gillett, G. 1994. *The discursive mind*. Thousand Oaks, Calif.: Sage.

Harter, S. 1999. Symbolic interactionism revisited: Potential liabilities for the self constructed in the crucible of interpersonal relationships. *Merrill-Palmer Quarterly* 45:677–703.

Hobson, R. P. 2002. *The cradle of thought*. London: Macmillan.

Howard, G., ed. 1994. Freewill and psychology. Special issue, *Journal of Theoretical and Philosophical Psychology* 14:1–101.

Jenkins, A. H. 1997. Free will and psychotherapy: The enhancement of agency. *Journal of Theoretical and Philosophical Psychology* 17:1–12.

Koch, S. 1999. *Psychology in human context: Essays in dissidence and reconstruction*. Ed. D. Finkelman and F. Kessel. Chicago: University of Chicago Press.

Macmurray, J. 1957. *The self as agent*. London: Faber and Faber. (Reprint, Atlantic Highlands, N.J.: Humanities Press, 1991.)

Macmurray, J. 1961. *Persons in relation*. London: Faber and Faber. (Reprint, Amherst, N.Y.: Humanity Books, 1999.)

Macmurray, J. 2004. Persons and functions. In E. McIntosh, ed., *John Macmurray: Selected philosophical writings*,141–155. Exeter, UK: Imprint Academic. (Original work published 1941.)

Martin, J., and Sugarman, J. 1999. *The psychology of human possibility and constraint*. Albany: SUNY Press.

Martin, J., Sugarman, J., and Thompson, J. 2003. *Psychology and the question of agency*. Albany: SUNY Press.

Reddy, V. 1996. Omitting the second person in social understanding. *Behavioral and Brain Sciences* 19:140–141.

Reddy, V., and Morris, P. 2004. Participants don't need theories: Knowing minds in engagement. *Theory and Psychology* 14:647–665.

Richardson, F. C., Slife, B. D., and Reber, J. S., eds. 2005. *Critical thinking about psychology: Hidden assumptions and plausible alternatives*. Washington, D.C.: American Psychological Association.

Robinson, D. N. 1985. *Philosophy of psychology*. New York: Columbia University Press.

Rychlak, J. F. 1999. Social constructionism, postmodernism, and the computer model: Searching for human agency in the right places. *Journal of Mind and Behavior* 20:379–390.

Seligman, M., and Csikszentmihalyi, M. 2000. Positive psychology: An introduction. *American Psychologist* 55:5–14.

Slife, B. D. 1994. Free will and time: That "stuck" feeling. *Journal of Theoretical and Philosophical Psychology* 14:1–12.

Stetsenko, A., and Arievitch, I. M. 2004. The self in cultural-historical activity theory: Reclaiming the unity of social and individual dimensions of human development. *Theory and Psychology* 14:475–503.

Taylor, C. 1964. *The explanation of behavior*. London: Routledge.

Taylor, C. 2002. Understanding the other: A Gadamerian view of conceptual schemes. In J. Malpas, U. Arnswald, and J. Kertscher, eds., *Gadamer's century: Essays in honor of Hans-Georg Gadamer*, 279–298. Cambridge, Mass.: MIT Press.

Williams, R. N. 1992. The human context of agency. *American Psychologist* 47:752–760.

Woolfolk, R. L. 1998. *The cure of souls: Science, values, and psychotherapy*. San Francisco: Jossey-Bass.

II Clinical and Developmental Contexts

4 Perspectival Selves and Agents: Agency within Sociality

Jack Martin

Psychologists and disciplinary psychology have put themselves in an awkward position with respect to human agency. Agency, as used herein, refers to the capacity of human beings to self-determine their decisions and actions in ways not entirely dictated by biophysical and/or sociocultural constituents and factors outside of their control. The awkwardness arises from the fact that much scientific psychology attempts to offer a strongly deterministic account of human action and experience that eliminates or reduces human agency to its biophysical and sociocultural origins, leaving less room for self-determination. On the other hand, professional psychology, which often claims to rest on scientific psychology (as per the much vaunted scientist-practitioner rhetoric of the American Psychological Association), assumes a rather robust form of agency. This is an agency, at least when bolstered by the ministrations of expert psychological practitioners, strong enough to enable individuals to ameliorate whatever difficulties are troubling them. So, the agentic self-determination assumed by most professional psychologists flies in the face of the biophysical and sociocultural determinism assumed in much psychological research.

One way disciplinary psychology and psychologists have responded to the foregoing awkwardness and difficulty is to insist that human agency is both determined and determining. In this general view, agency is determined by relevant biophysical and sociocultural factors and constituents, yet somehow manifests as a particular kind of self-determination. This is a kind of self-determination that cannot be reduced back to its biophysical and sociocultural determinants, and that exerts demonstrable influence on the subsequent decisions and actions of the agent, allowing the agent to influence significantly both her circumstances and herself: "People are both producers and products of social systems. . . . It is because self-influence operates deterministically on action that some measure of freedom is possible" (Bandura 1997, 6–7). Moreover, such self-determination is held by many to be a developmental achievement: "The emergence of processes of intentional self-development marks a dialectic shift in the relation between action and development. To the extent that development gradually forms intentionality and the self, intentional action comes to form development" (Brandtstädter and Lerner 1999, xi–xii). In short, humans develop as agents during ontogenesis. Agency is determined by the activity of biophysically evolved human infants/children within sociocultural contexts, but manifests in the emergence of forms of self-determination that can exert influence on these contexts and determinants.

In philosophy, the term *compatibilism* is used to describe the general view that agency is both determined and yet is capable of exerting its own determining influences. Typically, compatibilists are determinists who subscribe to some notion of self-determination, such that as far as persons are concerned, deterministic accounts of choice and action must include the self-determination of choosers and actors. (*Incompatibilists*, on the other hand, are either libertarians or hard determinists. Libertarians believe that because free will or self-determination exists, determinism is false. Hard determinists believe either that because determinism is true, free will or self-determination does not exist, or that incompatibilist free will is unintelligible whether or not determinism is true (see Kane 1998).)

Despite the suggestion that a compatibilist approach to the question of agency might serve to safeguard the interests of disciplinary psychology as both a social scientific and professional practice, the theoretical details of exactly how such a compatibilism might develop and operate have been mostly absent. In 2003, with the collaboration of my colleagues Jeff Sugarman and Janice Thompson, I published a book titled *Psychology and the Question of Agency*, the purpose of which was to provide conceptualizations, arguments, and a compatibilist, developmental theory to explain how selfhood and agency emerge within sociality. This work employed several ideas developed by Vygotsky (1978, 1986) and hermeneutic scholars like Heidegger (1962), Gadamer (1995), and Taylor (1985, 1995).

Since then, I have attempted to build on the sociocultural and interpretive account of agency provided in Martin, Sugarman, and Thompson 2003 in ways that clarify a central claim in that work. The claim in question is to have provided a coherent account of agency as determined by a combination of biophysical and sociocultural processes, which does not preclude the idea of agency as at least partially self-determining of decisions and actions in ways that are not reducible to these other determinants. The central matter involved in my more recent theoretical extension (Martin 2003, 2005a, 2005b, 2006)) concerns the necessity of theorizing a kind of emergence capable of explaining how self-determining agency might arise from complex interactions of biophysical and sociocultural processes associated with, and occasioned by, human activity in the world. To do this, I have borrowed from the social psychology and theory of self development advanced many years ago by George Herbert Mead (1934, 1938, 2002) and from a variety of contemporary developmental psychologists whose theoretical and empirical work provides important support for my own emergentist perspective. My interpretation of Mead's ideas concerning self and agency emphasizes the perspectival realism that he developed toward the end of his life—a theoretical framework that, to date, has been insufficiently emphasized by many psychologists who have examined and commented on Mead's social, developmental psychology.

In this chapter, I interpret Mead's work to strengthen the conceptualization and explanation of the emergence of selfhood and agency during ontogenesis, thus building on recent theoretical extensions (Martin 2003, 2005a, 2005b, 2006) to Martin, Sugarman, and Thompson (2003). When agency is understood as self-determination, its developmental emergence goes hand in hand with the developmental emergence of selfhood. I also illustrate the relevance of my theorizing about agency to psychology and psychotherapy by reworking a case example presented by Peter Hobson (2003). Finally, I discuss the uniquely human capabilities of self-interpretation and self-reactivity as enabling of a kind of agency that is determined, determining, and constantly emergent across the life course of a human being.

The Ontogenetic Emergence of the Agentic Self within Social Interactions and Practices

At a macroscopic level of interpretation, to say that selves are socially constituted to any significant extent is to claim that human ontogenetic development can best be understood as a process in which human beings, through their activities and interactions in the sociocultural and biophysical world, take up the artifacts and practices of their culture. This appropriation can be understood as taking and reacting to the perspectives of others and the broader society, and eventually makes possible forms of collective and individual activity capable of transforming the very cultural artifacts and practices that are available for appropriation. Socioculturally spawned agentic selves are best thought of as "culture carriers" whose actions in the world serve both to perpetuate and to transform cultural traditions, practices, and ways of thinking, acting, and living (Giddens 1984). At the same time, these agentic selves owe their very existence and ongoing constitution to the dynamically evolving, sociocultural practices and perspectives in which they are always embedded. These practices and perspectives both constrain and enable the constantly emergent worldly activity of agentic selves throughout the course of individual lives (Bickhard 1992; Harré 1984; Lave and Wenger 1991; Martin, Sugarman, and Thompson 2003).

In ontogenesis, human infants are born as members of a biologically evolved species of *Homo sapiens sapiens* into existing societies and cultures with historically established traditions, practices, and worldviews. A first-person perspective emerges gradually from the preconceptual worldly activity of a newborn that is biophysically evolved to orient to others and to their ministrations. Immediately following birth, human infants do not differentiate between themselves and other persons and things, let alone between possible points of view (their own and others') (Baldwin 1906). However, this fact should not be taken to mean that human infants begin as asocial beings. Human infants are social from the very beginning, showing an interest in the faces and behavior of other people (Stern 1985), and engaging in rhythmic interactions and gestural sequences with their caregivers (Trevarthan 1979), all within minutes of birth. Neonatal mimicking and protoconversation (very initial and primitive forms of orienting and reacting to others) are uniquely human (when compared to the newly born of all other animals), and are also evident very early on. Such behavior, called primary intersubjectivity by Trevarthan (1993), is both preconscious and preconceptual. The neonate does not differentiate between herself and others. Further, because the inner and outer also are not initially differentiated by the infant, she does not interpret mental states, intentionality, and emotions as lying behind the behavioral expressions of others. Such differentiation is a developmental attainment.

Although many contemporary developmental psychologists, including some whose work is mentioned here, have been associated with the so-called analogical argument, there is little reason to suppose that human infants can understand themselves prior to differentiating others and their actions in the world. The analogical argument, which assumes that infants derive their knowledge of other minds and selves from knowledge of their own mind and self, runs into several important and informative difficulties. First, the establishment of any similarity between one's experience and that of another assumes the ability to take an external, third-person perspective on one's own experience, and fails to explain how this is possible in the absence of any understanding of others and their perspectives. Second, it is doubtful that young infants can model another's experience on the basis of experiences of their own that they very well may not be experiencing at the moment. Third, what possible criteria might the analogically reasoning infant use to establish identity across his own and another's experience if such an identification is based only on his own experience? Finally, the only logical conclusion that follows from the argument from analogy is that "there is one of my experiences," hardly an adequate basis for knowing others and their perspectives (see Müller and Carpendale 2004). None of this is to say that once developed as selves and persons, human beings do not reason analogically from their own experiences to those of others. It is just that as a means of describing how infants initially attain knowledge of others and self during very early stages of development, the argument by analogy fails. However, when the analogical argument is set aside, and attention is directed first at activity with others within the context of development, such difficulties begin to evaporate.

Differentiation of self and others and inner and outer begins in interpersonal bodily engagement. Triadic interaction between the infant, another person, and the world is the basis for such differentiation and for other forms of knowledge (Chapman 1991; Mead 1934). Within the first few months of life, infants actively explore their surroundings, observing and touching themselves, others, and things, and being observed and touched by others. Such prelinguistic, practical activity sows the initial seeds of a primitive, preconceptual sense of first-person perspective (Archer 2000; Merleau-Ponty 1962). Further development of differentiation and perspective taking unfolds over the first year to year and a half of life in increasingly sophisticated ways (Müller and Carpendale 2004). Convincing evidence of gaze following, as a very early precursor to what eventually becomes joint attention, is available for infants as young as three months of age. At this age, infants are able to move their eyes in the direction of an adult's head turn toward a target object (D'Entremont 2000). By four months of age, infants' attention to a target can be cued by an adult's eye movements alone (Farroni et al. 2000).

However, even at six months, the gaze following of infants is far from established firmly. For example, at this age, they still experience problems turning toward objects that are either further away or moving (D'Entremont 2000). Nor can they be trained to turn their heads to examine interesting events that occur outside of their visual field when the occurrence of such events is made contingent on the head turn of another person (Corkum and Moore 1995). However, at eight months, such training is possible. And by twelve months, infants spontaneously (without training) follow the head turn of another person, and are able to locate the target of an adult's gaze even when it is the second object along their scan path (Butterworth and Jarrett 1991; Corkum and Moore 1998). By this time, infants have become capable of using the other person's head turn as an indicator, and are able to establish spatial relations between another person and a target object even in the absence of movement cues (Moore, Angelopoulos, and Bennett 1997). However, their ability to follow another's gaze in the absence of a target is fragile, indicating that they do not fully differentiate another's perspective.

Nonetheless, toward the end of the first year of life, there also are other indicators of the infant's manifestation of triadic interaction. For example, at about this age, infants start to point to objects in order to direct adults' attention to them. At this age, a rich interpretation of children's capabilities might be taken to indicate that infants now can understand that other people have intentions and attention that can be directed to parts of the world and things in it (e.g., Tomasello 1999). Rich interpretations of this kind sometimes are made even earlier. For example, Tomasello (1993) maintains that at approximately nine months of age, human infants begin to behave with apparent growing awareness of others as psychological beings, looking where others look, observing how others approach objects and what they do with them, and directing communicative gestures to others, but not to inanimate objects. In minimal ways, they begin to act toward themselves as others do, and to attribute intentionality to others and themselves in early, preconceptual ways (Tomasello 1999). On the other hand, a more conservative interpretation (e.g., Müller and Carpendale 2004) indicates that there is still some way to go in the development of capacities for triadic interaction and full differentiation of self, others, and perspectives.

A Meadian interpretation of the foregoing research in contemporary developmental psychology (Martin 2006) would incline toward the view that it is the developing child's increasing participation in more advanced forms of "gesture → reaction → consequence" sequences with others that enables all forms of perspective taking and associated capabilities. For Mead, it is the child's active and repeated occupation and experience of different roles and perspectives in conventional practices and sequences of interactivity (such as rolling a ball back and forth, attempting early versions of "peekaboo," and so on) that permit the child gradually to differentiate different phases of intersubjective activity and the interactors themselves, including himself.

By eighteen months of age, infants are capable of following another's gaze when the other's attention is directed outside of their own visual range and target objects are absent to them (Corkum and Moore 1995). In general, by this age, infants are able to differentiate objects, others, and the object-related actions of others from themselves and their own actions. Even on conservative interpretations, others are now understood, at least implicitly, as autonomous centers of activity. By this age, there is little question that infants now can use gaze following and pointing as means of engaging in joint attentional activity with others about the world, others, and themselves.

From this point onward, human infants engage in learning that is not just interpersonal, but that is increasingly cultural. Of particular importance in this regard is the Meadian process of taking the perspective of others as a necessary condition for self-consciousness, conceptual self-understanding, and more reflective forms of first-person perspective and experiencing. For Mead (1934, 225), "Self-consciousness involves the individual's becoming an object to himself by taking the attitudes of other individuals toward himself within an organized setting of social relationships." Developed abilities to achieve joint attention and to understand other people's referential intent are basic to this kind of perspective taking. Such developmental milestones only can be acquired in the context of ongoing interactions with others in social contexts. They open up more fully cultural forms of human ontogenetic development in which young children participate with others in joint attentional activities and begin to comprehend and reproduce the intentional actions of others with respect to various material and symbolic artifacts (Tomasello 1999).

As I have already explained, a first-person perspective first appears in a prelinguistic, preconceptual sense. With the emergent, socially enabled capabilities of joint attentional focus, intentional referencing, and perspective taking, language acquisition commences and extends the cultural line of development more efficiently and completely. Mastery of this one special cultural artifact transforms the capabilities and actions of the child. With language, children are able to engage intersubjectively with others and to adopt the communicative conventions of their cultures. Because linguistic symbols are both subjective and perspectival, when children learn to use words and linguistic forms in the manner of adults, they understand that the same objects and events are construed variously in relation to different points of view and communicative purposes. Through language and its use, children learn the criteria for words people in their society use to talk about human activity. They come to understand talk of the psychological world in terms of patterns of activity that constitute criteria and referential contexts for the use of psychological language. With such criteria in place, they can reflect on the psychological world, learn even more about others' experiences and perspectives, and thus expand their own bases for actively participating in their sociocultural contexts. The ability to talk about the psychological world provides a resource with which to understand and reflect on others and oneself.

Full differentiation of self and other now is attained, and sophisticated, abstracted perspective taking and coordination become possible. Sociocultural learning no longer is limited to immediate social interactions with others. The emergence of enhanced forms of self-consciousness and agentic understanding and capability owes much to the intersubjective, perspectival nature of language, and to the communicative exchanges and constructions it makes possible. And, once again, all of this issues from participation with others within human societies and cultures. Knowledge of the world, others, and oneself develops through constantly coordinating other peoples' perspectives with one's own, and acting on the bases of the perspectival amalgamations and insights that emerge.

Over time, the socioculturally enabled acquisition of enhanced linguistic capability and social awareness facilitates more complex forms of self-consciousness and conceptual understanding of oneself in sociocultural context. Psychological personhood (including selfhood, agency, and identity) emerges both materially and relationally. Caregivers and others interact with developing children in ways that provide relational practices, forms, and means of personhood and identity extant within particular societies and cultures. Psychological development proceeds as these appropriated sociocultural, linguistic, and relational practices are employed as bases for private language, and eventually for thought and reflection (Mead 1934; Vygotsky 1986). This ongoing sociocultural, relational constitution of the psychological tools and understandings required for selfhood is accompanied by enabling and more substantive processes of biophysical maturation, adaptation, and learning (Edelman 1987).

Over time, the young individual's activity in the world is transformed from one of prereflection to one in which reflective, intentional agency emerges and fosters an increasingly conceptual self-understanding and personal identity linked to one's particular existence and personal history of activity. Such psychological continuity imbues an individual life with meaning and significance. Open to the lifeworld, the psychological person starting from a basic, preconceptual, embodied first-person perspective develops self-consciousness, conceptual self-understanding, deliberative agency, and a personal identity defined by commitments and concerns associated with her particular existence and activity in the world (Martin, Sugarman, and Thompson 2003).

It is the activity of human beings in the biophysical and sociocultural world that creates the dynamic sites at and through which full selfhood emerges. Personal development in ontogenesis is not to be found in biologically developing and maturing human beings alone, nor is it located in their sociocultural settings and relations. Rather, it lies in the linkage of biophysical beings with their sociocultural settings, routines, and conventions through activity associated with a first-person perspective. Understood in this way, the ontogenetic development of the self moves from a basic, preconceptual form of first-person perspective, made possible by a primary intersubjectivity associated with a primitive social orientation, to a more self-conscious activity in the world. Associated with this more self-conscious activity is a more reflective first-person perspective, together with more conceptual forms of self-understanding. A basic sociality and interactivity are thus prior to our first-person perspectives, which gradually become caught up in more conceptual forms of self-consciousness and self-understanding.

As ontogenetic development advances into adolescence and beyond, our selfhood becomes increasingly perspectival as we engage in discursive interactions in school and other settings that are mediated by an ever more complex and diverse array of intersubjective and perspectival linguistic symbols, conceptions, and imaginative constructions. Through our participation in educational and other life contexts that provide us with more varied, complex, and multiperspectival tools of thought and action, we are immersed in ever-widening horizons of sociocultural experience. Problems, perspectives, and ways of life that might be quite distant from what has been personally experienced bring with them a deeper and broader sense of our own situations and life experiences, even as they pull us toward alternative possibilities for our future existence. In all of this, particular perspectival selves acquire a wider view of the world and their place within it. This is a historical, cultural, and contemporary world populated by ideas, debates, problems, issues, and challenges that command attention, and that encourage and enable the cultivation of increasingly complex forms of understanding, acting, and being.

Elaborating a Neo-Meadian Approach to the Question of Agency

Our activity in the world (which, with our entry into symbolic means of communication, is always a social world, even in those instances in which we may only be conversing with ourselves) is constantly unfolding, and within it, so too are our minds and selves. Because activity in the world always may be framed from a variety of social, interpersonal, and personal perspectives, and from overlapping temporal perspectives that locate the present in both the past and the future, our selfhood has both sociocultural/interpersonal and temporal/psychological aspects that permit a kind of agency that is both determined and determining, exactly in the manner argued by Mead (1934, 1938, 2002). Not only is this the kind of agency that contemporary psychological theory and practice seem to require, it is a kind of agency consistent with most philosophical thought, both past and present, that favors an account of agency as compatible with both determinism and meaningful self-determination. By taking the perspectives of others and our broader, historically established cultures, and reacting to them (especially in novel and problematic situations), we transform both ourselves and our societies. Our agency is constituted by our activity as uniquely culture-capable beings in interaction with others within our social, cultural world. In Mead's terms, because we simultaneously occupy both the past and the future in a fleeting present, and because we inevitably stand within a multiplicity of perspectives, our worldly activity is inevitably both determined and transformative.

It is important to stress that Mead's emergent self is not a simple product of social, symbolic interactivity with others. The worldly conduct of such a self is not mechanistically determined by the actions and words of others, or the structures and practices of the broader society. Within the social process, the emergent, self-conscious person actively decides on courses of action in response to the perspectives of others. In Mead's view, the taking of perspectives always is accompanied by an individual's reactions to those perspectives. For Mead (1934), the "Me" is the socially organized set of perspectives of others that one takes. (Mead understands perspectives as orientations to situations and things that are related to possible conduct.) The "I," on the other hand, is the response that an individual makes to these perspectives. I am a "Me" in that I make use of (actually or imaginatively) the words and actions of others within sequences of social interactions, but my "I" is an emergent, creative response to the symbolized action sequences and structures of my "Me." Whereas the "Me" is knowable and highly predictable, the "I" is not an object of experience. Its trace may be detected in memory, but only as it appears ex post facto. I only can access my "I" by remembering the responses it makes to my "Me." In temporal terms, the "I" is a response to the "Me" that occurs in an immediate, momentary, and already passing present, with the aim of restructuring the "Me" in the future. When the "I" has acted, "we can catch it in our memory and place it in terms of that which we have done," even though, within the newly emergent present, it already has passed into the restructured "Me" (Mead 1934, 203). The "I" and the "Me" coexist in a dynamic, temporal relation within which the "I" responds unpredictably and freely to the "Me" that arises through taking the perspectives of others and the broader society. For Mead, the self and its activity are conditioned, but not determined entirely, by the social processes within which they emerge. Human agency is conditional but free.

For the self to become an object to itself, it is not enough to see oneself as others do. Rather, it is necessary to act toward oneself with the words and actions of others (actually and/or imaginatively), and to reflect on the self that appears in memory as a consequence of engagement in such action sequences. This is a self that has an objective reality such that it can be acted on as an ontological object. In consequence, Mead's self appears as an "I" in action in the present, which can be grasped in a remembered "Me" because one is able to take the perspectives of others with whom one is interactively engaged in the social process. This remembered self has an objective existence that invites reflection and reconstitution in novel and problematic situations. Indeed, the agency of the "I" is especially apparent in situations in which the self must be reconstituted according to complex interactions between the perspectives of others, past and existing perspectives of the self, and situational demands that do not yield readily to any combination of these perspectives. It is in such contexts that the responses of the agentic self, the "I," are most carefully recorded in recollections of problem-solving activity that involves the sharing and critical consideration of self and other perspectives in the context of broader social practices and perspectives. In this sense, the Meadian self may be understood as a first-person perspective on one's interactional history and action possibilities that is enabled by interactively taking the second-person perspectives of others in the context of third-person perspectives common to the broader sociocultural context in which one is embedded at birth and in which one lives out one's life. (Note that Mead himself did not use the terms first-, second-, or third-person perspective; see Habermas 1992 for a somewhat related, but nonetheless different, interpretation.)

For Mead, the immediate moment of action brings together a concern of the present with both recollections of relevant past activity and anticipations of a future in which the concern or problem to which the action of the present is directed is resolved or somehow made manageable. Such concerns typically are emergent in the field of activity within the ongoing dynamic interplay of social, interpersonal, and personal perspectives described above. They arise in the immediate context of novel, unpredictable occurrences that constitute a change in past action sequences and perspectives. If such emergent change were not common, our minds and selves would be determined entirely by our past interactions in our biophysical and sociocultural world, and our worldly conduct would not be punctuated and experienced in temporal terms. It is precisely because of the emergence of change that our temporal experience and agency also arise. Psychological time requires markers, and change supplies them.

To understand this rather abstract set of claims, it is helpful to think of the "I" as not only reacting to a "Me" that is determined by past activity and the perspectives acquired through such activity, but also to an immediate present in which circumstances and conduct are not unfolding exactly in accordance with past activity and existing perspectives. For example, a new mother finds herself confronted with previously unexperienced childcare situations in which she reacts to herself through emergent first-person, parental perspectives that reflect, in part, what she previously had experienced only as second-person perspectives in interaction with her own and other mothers, all configured within a broader set of societal third-person perspectives concerning parenting. In such situations, the "I" cannot cease all activity, but acts on the basis of a complex of perception, remembrance, and anticipation that cannot be predicted at the exact moment of acting, even though all of the remembrances and anticipations involved may be determined on the basis of past activity and existing perspectives. At such moments, Mead claims that the self is simultaneously in two temporal/psychological perspectives at once. On the one hand, the "Me" to which the "I" is reacting is determined within a knowable past. On the other hand, the "I" of the moment must act in circumstances that are not entirely predictable from the past, and that are in part explicable in terms of an imagined future state in which the concern or problem of the moment somehow has been ameliorated. In these instances, the "I" occupies two distinct temporal perspectives, one in which the "Me" as object is determined (e.g., seeing oneself in the role of mother through previously experienced second- and third-person perspectives), and another in which the "I" as agent is not so determined (e.g., the emergently unfolding, newly experienced first-person "mother" perspective of the immediate moment). Of course, once the action in question takes place, it, together with whatever perspective or perspectival transformation it might occasion, is part of a "new" knowable past, which can be used to anticipate a newly emergent concern of the moment and a "new" future (e.g., one in which the new mother gradually enters into her own first-person maternal perspective). And so it goes.

A Psychotherapeutic Illustration

When considered in light of the foregoing perspectival account of self and agency, psychotherapy may be understood as a kind of social interaction in which the psychotherapist helps clients to enlarge and adjust their self and other perspectives. The goal of such perspectival construction and fine-tuning is to allow clients to act together with others in their life circumstances in ways that might resolve problems and difficulties that currently seem intractable. In most such situations, the client is stuck in perspectives that somehow limit her agentive efforts. In speaking to and acting toward the therapist, the client reveals the perspectives that constitute her self and her situational understanding and conduct. In listening and reacting to the responses of the therapist, the client is caught up in newly emergent alternative perspectives that can be applied to herself and her circumstances. As a consequence, her paralysis in the face of the problems she confronts begins to dissipate, and she regains some degree of agentive possibility through a shift in those perspectives within which she now is able to be and to act. In short, she experiences herself in new ways that open up new avenues of possible action. With these perspectival acquisitions, participations, and shifts, she is able to undertake a symbolic reconstruction of her past self and experience, and to assimilate and utilize these reconstructed perspectives in her ongoing present experiences and actions as she looks toward a future in which her problems might be alleviated or ameliorated. Psychotherapy, then, is a process of intersubjective engagement in which perspectives that constitute the client's self and situational understanding and conduct are reconstructed in ways that recover agentive possibilities as a consequence of new symbolizations of past, present, and future (see Cronk 1974; Martin 1994).

Consider the following case description by Hobson (2003, 23–24) that recounts the first ten minutes of an initial interview between Hobson as psychotherapist and a male client:

> The man arrived and we shook hands as I introduced myself and explained that the meeting would last for ninety minutes. The patient said that was fine, and paused expectantly. He said he wondered what I wanted him to talk about, and then seemed to realize that, instead of my asking questions, he might need to take the lead in saying what he thought was relevant and important. What he did was engage with me as though I had been both solicitous and encouraging towards him. It was as if I was already a confidant. He talked with some animation and feeling about how he had seen a range of other doctors, but nothing had really helped. As his account unfolded, it appeared that not only were the treatments ineffective, but also the doctors he had seen were in various ways inadequate or unprofessional. He seemed to be conveying to me how I might succeed in helping him, where everyone else had failed.
>
> Yet it did not feel to me that this man had any confidence in what I might achieve on his behalf. For example, he had been speaking nonstop for ten minutes, and at no time did he seem interested in my view of his story. I felt that I might as well have been a fly on the wall, and I was very pessimistic that he would pay any attention to me if I tried to offer a comment. In the end I decided to interrupt what appeared to be an increasingly elaborate and entangled account to say, "I wonder if I might stop you for a moment there. You are speaking to me as if I had been very helpful to you at the

beginning, and as if you have confidence in me and what I might offer in this interview. Yet I wonder what is really going on."

At this the patient looked dumbfounded, then exclaimed, "You mean you want me to be honest?" I said yes, I wanted him to be honest. What subsequently emerged was that, far from having confidence in me, this patient was already convinced that I, too, was unprofessional and inept and the last thing he expected was that I would be able to do anything worthwhile.

Then it was possible to address how what had been happening in the interview was actually quite typical of this man. When he came into a dependent relationship with someone else, he would convince the other person and even himself that all would be well, but underneath there was suspicion and mistrust. In relation to me as a psychotherapist, he was repeating a familiar storyline, one in which he began as compliant and ended up disillusioned and frustrated by those who should have been taking care of him. Yet, because I did not join him in living out the customary succession of events, we were able to think about the recurring patterns in his attitudes and behaviour. We could examine in detail what was shaping the current interview and could pinpoint what he was feeling and doing right then and there in relation to myself. Together we could identify what was actually going on. We could do so because it was possible to track how the patient felt and then deal with his feelings, moment by moment. And we could see that what was going on had far-reaching importance for the patient's complaints and for his emotional life.

It is relatively easy to interpret Hobson's (2003) description of the interactions between himself and this particular client in terms of the foregoing conceptualization of psychotherapy as an intersubjective restructuring of the client's perspectives that restores agentive possibilities for client conduct in relation to his problems and concerns. By refusing to take a conventional part in the client's enactment of his typical pattern of interpersonal relating, the therapist disrupts the client's existing perspectives on himself in relationships. Then, by asking the client what was actually going on, the therapist encourages the client to explore perspectives and possibilities different from those that had proven so ineffectual in his past and current relationships with others. Although this is a very brief, initial foray into what is likely to be a much more extensive and elaborated psychotherapeutic intervention, both the actuality and possibility of psychotherapeutically induced perspectival change have been engaged and demonstrated in the first ten minutes of this initial interview. Of course, a great deal probably remains to be done to develop and entrench alternative perspectives in the client's social conduct outside of psychotherapy. Nonetheless, the process of perspectival change resulting in the emergence of new self-understanding and agentive possibilities has been initiated, and the ground prepared for revamping the client's interpersonal conduct with others in ways reflective of such change and emergence.

Self-Interpreting, Self-Reactive Agents

Human agency is constantly emergent through our ongoing interpretation of, and reactivity to, possibilities and constraints available in our historically shaped sociocultural practices and interactions with others. The theory of agency presented here makes use of several ideas that have been developed more fully by a number of developmental psychologists (e.g., Tomasello 1999; Vygotsky 1978, 1986), ontological hermeneuts (e.g., Gadamer 1995; Heidegger 1962; Taylor 1995), and pragmatists (especially Mead 1934, 1938, 2002). The goal has been to describe the emergence of an agentive form of human being-in-the-world that differs from other forms of existence. Ian Hacking (1995, 1999, 2002) captures this difference nicely in his distinction between interactive, human and noninteractive, natural kinds. Unlike natural, noninteractive kinds, human kinds can be understood only within a discursive context in which they interact with the classifications and descriptions applied to them. For example, it does not matter to a rock or a cat if it is described as valuable or mean-spirited. However, human persons who have experienced the kind of ontogenetic development described here find significance in such descriptions and react to them. It matters to us if we are categorized by others as lazy, talented, ambitious, and so forth. Moreover, our reactions to such descriptions and classifications are part of what constitutes us as the kinds of persons we are. An individual labeled as learning disabled may give up dreams of going to college, or may seek professional assistance to overcome his disability. A heavy drinker who is labeled an alcoholic may despair, seek assistance, or decide to maintain his current habit. Moreover, such choices (whether consciously deliberate or not) inevitably affect how human persons understand themselves and the kinds of persons they are. Both our descriptions and the kinds of persons we are constantly emerge as we interpret and react to ourselves on the basis of the perspectives and descriptions we apply to ourselves.

The ongoing self-interpretation and self-reactivity of human beings are much discussed not only by pragmatists like Mead, but also by hermeneuts like Heidegger (1962), Gadamer (1995), and Taylor (1985). It is precisely because we are self-interpreting and self-reactive that we are capable of developing as self-conscious agents in interaction with others. Philosophical and psychological theories and positions that deny the possibility that human agents can be both determined and determining tend to overlook this critical feature of being human. We are constantly emergent as human agents because we are caught up in ongoing processes of self-interpretation and self-reactivity. What this implies is that whatever biophysical and sociocultural phenomena

enter into our determination at point A do not fully determine our choices and actions at point C, because our self-determination (self-interpretation and self-reactivity) intervenes at point B in ways that cannot be reduced to those determining biophysical and sociocultural phenomena at point A, but that are required for any reasonable account of our choices and actions at point C. Thus, the classic form of logical transitivity (of the form: if A determines B, and B determines C, then A must determine C) insisted on by hard determinists simply does not hold for human agents in interaction with others as it may for natural, noninteractive kinds. The developmental scenario presented in this chapter provides considerable detail with respect to the ontogenetic emergence of selfhood and agency, understood as human kinds, and supports the kind of compatibilism that sanctions talk of human agents as both determined and determining. (Note that some theoretical psychologists, like Joseph Rychlak (1988, 1997), use the term *soft determinism* to describe something similar to the kind of compatibilist position advanced here.)

Conclusion

The sociocultural, relational, and perspectival approach to agency discussed here bears some striking similarities to several other recently forged approaches to selfhood and agency that also emphasize the relational ontology of human persons (e.g., Slife 2004), the critical importance of cultural-historical activity (e.g., Stetsenko and Arievitch 2004), the ongoing dialectic between societies and selves (e.g., Falmagne 2004), and the agentic characteristics of human kinds (e.g., Brinkmann 2005). However, all of these approaches, like Martin, Sugarman, and Thompson 2003, fail to provide a specific articulation of the ways self and agency are constituted, internalized, and emergent through interactivity within sociocultural practices. It is here that the current neo-Meadian extension to Martin, Sugarman, and Thompson 2003 goes significantly beyond what is available in these other theories.

The neo-Meadian account provided here understands selfhood and agency as emergent within conventional practices of sociality through a process of perspective taking that moves from a preconceptual, prereflective immersion in different phases of routine sequences of interpersonal, social interaction to a more self-reflective consideration and evaluation of alternative possibilities that may be conducted prior to further direct social, interpersonal engagement. The ability to coordinate and evaluate perspectives and possibilities within ongoing activity is what enables the agentive self to act in consideration of past experience in relevant social practices without ignoring the inevitably novel aspects of currently unfolding circumstances. In this way,

the "I" of the present reacts to the "Me" of the past in the context of an ongoing social process with a view to continuing the constantly emergent social-self dialectic. Agency understood as the continuous reactivity of a perspectival self that always is embedded within dynamically evolving social, interactive circumstances is not the detached self-reflection and choice championed by much traditional Anglo-American philosophy and contemporary cognitive, information processing psychology. Nor is it reducible to biophysical properties of our brains and bodies or only an aspect of a depersonalized sociocultural process. Agency is a property of the perspectival functioning of human persons immersed in sociocultural practices. If perspectives are orientations to situations with respect to acting within them, agency is a reactivity to first-, second-, and third-person perspectives that are experientially associated with situated practices of interactivity. It is a reactivity that is both enabled and constrained by situational activity and perspectives.

References

Archer, M. 2000. *Being human: The problem of agency*. Cambridge: Cambridge University Press.

Baldwin, J. M. 1906. *Thought and things*. Vol. 1. New York: Arno Press.

Bandura, A. 1997. *Self-efficacy: The exercise of control*. New York: Freeman.

Bickhard, M. H. 1992. How does the environment affect the person? In L. T. Winegar and J. Valsiner, eds., *Children's development within social contexts, Vol. 1: Metatheory and theory*, 63–92. Hillsdale, N.J.: Erlbaum.

Bickhard, M. H. 1999. Interaction and representation. *Theory and Psychology* 9: 435–458.

Brandtstädter, J., and Lerner, R. M. 1999. Introduction: Development, action, and intentionality. In J. Brandtstädter and R. M. Lerner, eds., *Action and self-development: Theory and research through the life span*, ix–xx. Thousand Oaks, Calif.: Sage.

Brinkmann, S. 2005. Human kinds and looping effects in psychology: Foucauldian and hermeneutic perspectives. *Theory and Psychology* 15:769–792.

Butterworth, G., and Jarrett, N. 1991. What minds have in common is space: Spatial mechanisms serving joint visual attention in infancy. *British Journal of Developmental Psychology* 9:55–72.

Chapman, M. 1991. The epistemic triangle: Operative and communicative components of cognitive development. In M. Chandler and M. Chapman, eds., *Criteria for competence: Controversies in the conceptualization and assessment of children's abilities*, 209–228. Hillsdale, N.J.: Erlbaum.

Corkum, V., and Moore, V. 1995. Development of joint visual attention in infants. In C. Moore and P. Dunham, eds., *Joint attention: Its origins and role in development*, 61–83. Hilldale, N.J.: Erlbaum.

Corkum, V., and Moore, V. 1998. The origins of joint visual attention in infants. *Developmental Psychology* 34:28–38.

Cronk, G. 1974. A symbolic interactionist account of the process of psychotherapy: An application of Mead's central concepts. *Darshana International: An International Quarterly* 11:17–25.

D'Entremont, B. 2000. A perceptual-attentional explanation of gaze-following in 3- and 6-month-olds. *Developmental Science* 3:302–311.

Edelman, G. M. 1987. *Neural Darwinism*. New York: Basic Books.

Falmagne, R. J. 2004. On the constitution of "self" and "mind": The dialectic of the system and the person. *Theory and Psychology* 14:822–845.

Farroni, T., Johnson, M. H., Brockbank, M., and Simion, F. 2000. Infant's use of gaze direction to cue attention: The importance of perceived motion. *Visual Cognition* 7:705–718.

Frankfurt, H. G. 1971. Freedom of the will and the concept of a person. *Journal of Philosophy* 68:5–20.

Gadamer, H.-G. 1995. *Truth and method*. Trans. J. Weinsheimer and D. G. Marshall. 2nd ed. New York: Continuum. (Original work published 1960.)

Giddens, A. 1984. *The constitution of society: Outline of the theory of structuration*. Cambridge: Polity.

Habermas, J. 1992. Individuation through socialization: On George Herbert Mead's theory of subjectivity. In J. Habermas, ed., *Postmetaphysical thinking: Philosophical essays*, trans. W. M. Hohengarten, 149–204. Cambridge, Mass.: MIT Press.

Hacking, I. 1995. The looping effect of human kinds. In D. Sperber, D. Premack, and A. J. Premack, eds., *Causal cognition: A multi-disciplinary approach*, 351–383. Oxford: Clarendon Press.

Hacking, I. 1999. *The social construction of what?* Cambridge, Mass.: Harvard University Press.

Hacking, I. 2002. *Historical ontology*. Cambridge, Mass.: Harvard University Press.

Harré, R. 1984. *Personal being: A theory for individual psychology*. Cambridge, Mass.: Harvard University Press.

Heidegger, M. 1962. *Being and time*. Trans. J. Macquarrie and E. Robinson. New York: Harper and Row. (Original work published 1927.)

Hobson, P. 2003. *The cradle of thought: Exploring the origins of thinking.* New York: Oxford University Press.

Kane, R. 1998. *The significance of free will.* New York: Oxford University Press.

Lave, J., and Wenger, E. 1991. *Situated learning: Legitimate peripheral participation.* New York: Cambridge University Press.

Martin, J. 1994. *The construction and understanding of psychotherapeutic change: Conversations, memories, and theories.* New York: Teachers College Press.

Martin, J. 2003. Emergent persons. *New Ideas in Psychology* 21:85–99.

Martin, J. 2005a. Perspectival selves in interaction with others: Re-reading G. H. Mead's social psychology. *Journal for the Theory of Social Behaviour* 35:231–253.

Martin, J. 2005b. Real perspectival selves. *Theory and Psychology* 15:207–224.

Martin, J. 2006. Re-interpreting internalization and agency through G. H. Mead's perspectival realism. *Human Development* 49:65–86. Martin, J., Sugarman, J., and Thompson, J. 2003. *Psychology and the question of agency.* Albany: SUNY Press.

Mead, G. H. 1934. *Mind, self, and society from the standpoint of a social behaviorist.* Chicago: University of Chicago Press.

Mead, G. H. 1938. *The philosophy of the act.* Ed. C. W. Morris. Chicago: University of Chicago Press.

Mead, G. H. 2002. *The philosophy of the present.* Amherst, N.Y.: Prometheus. (Original work published 1932.)

Merleau-Ponty, M. 1962. *Phenomenology of perception.* Trans. C. Smith. London: Routledge and Kegan Paul.

Moore, C., Angelopoulos, M., and Bennett, P. 1997. The role of movement in the development of joint visual attention. *Infant Behavior and Development* 20:83–92.

Müller, U., and Carpendale, J. I. M. 2004. From joint activity to joint attention: A relational approach to social development in infancy. In J. I. M. Carpendale and U. Müller, eds., *Social interaction and the development of knowledge,* 215–238. Mahwah, N.J.: Erlbaum.

Rychlak, J. F. 1988. *The psychology of rigorous humanism,* 2nd ed. New York: New York University Press.

Rychlak, J. F. 1997. *In defense of human consciousness.* Washington, D.C.: American Psychological Association.

Slife, B. 2004. Taking practice seriously: Toward a relational ontology. *Journal of Theoretical and Philosophical Psychology* 24:157–178.

Stern, D. N. 1985. *The interpersonal world of the infant: A view from psychoanalysis and developmental psychology*. New York: Basic Books.

Stetsenko, A., and Arievitch, I. M. 2004. The self in cultural-historical activity theory: Reclaiming the unity of social and individual dimensions of human development. *Theory and Psychology* 14:475–504.

Taylor, C. 1985. Self-interpreting animals. In *Philosophical papers: Vol.1. Human agency and language*, 45–76. Cambridge: Cambridge University Press.

Taylor, C. 1995. *Philosophical arguments*. Cambridge, Mass.: Harvard University Press.

Taylor, C. 2002. Understanding the other: A Gadamerian view of conceptual schemes. In J. Malpas, U. Arnswald, and J. Kertscher, eds., *Gadamer's century: Essays in honor of Hans-Georg Gadamer*, 279–298. Cambridge, Mass.: MIT Press.

Tomasello, M. 1993. On the interpersonal origins of self-concept. In U. Neisser, ed., *The perceived self: Ecological and interpersonal sources of self-knowledge*, 174–184. New York: Cambridge University Press.

Tomasello, M. 1999. *The cultural origins of cognition*. Cambridge, Mass.: Harvard University Press.

Trevarthan, C. 1979. Communication and cooperation in early infancy: A description of primary intersubjectivity. In M. Bullowa, ed., *Before speech: The beginning of human communication*, 321–347. New York: Cambridge University Press.

Trevarthan, C. 1993. The self born in intersubjectivity: The psychology of an infant communicating. In U. Neisser, ed., *The perceived self: Ecological and interpersonal sources of self-knowledge*, 121–173. New York: Cambridge University Press.

Vygotsky, L. S. 1978. *Mind in society: The development of higher psychological processes*. Ed. M. Cole, V. John-Steiner, S. Scribner, and E. Souberman. Cambridge, Mass.: Harvard University Press.

Vygotsky, L. S. 1986. *Thought and language*. Trans. A. Kozulin. Cambridge, Mass.: MIT Press. (Original work published 1934.)

5 Agency and Its Clinical Phenomenology

Jill Gentile

The status of personal agency in clinical psychology and psychoanalysis is directly related to the definition of the human subject. While the human subject is no longer seen as an isolated or individually defined entity, the proposition that human experience takes shape in interactional contexts creates its own conundrum: it has been read, by some, as spelling the demise of the human subject and, by others, as giving birth to it.

This chapter takes as its premise that the persistence of this conundrum reflects, at least in part, a tendency to situate the so-called relational construction of experience on an overly narrow dyadic or two-person edifice. The problem is that an understanding of relationality as a relation *between two* subjects bypasses the influence of what is now commonly referred to as a Third. The concept of "thirdness" has many incarnations and meanings, but generally refers to an ethical framework of meaning creation that transcends the two-person dyad. For purposes of this chapter, I refer to the foundational *Third* (and to *thirdness*) as the interpretive space between two subjects in which meaning is created and personal agency is experienced.

I focus primarily on the idea of a semiotic code as a foundational Third. I argue that transformations of personal agency and meaning creation emerge in tandem with transformations of semiotic empowerment—our capacity to use signs to communicate our desires and intentions, and to interpret the communications of others. From this point of view, a phenomenological trajectory of meaning creation (guided by personal agency) and a trajectory of semiotic empowerment are inseparably linked and may be seen as different sides of the same coin. In turn, psychoanalysis can be seen as an enterprise dedicated to the evolving phenomenological expression of meaning creation that has its blueprint in what can be seen as a foundational Third (and that is rooted at once in biology and culture).

I recognize that, in light of the lessons of postmodernism and its rejection of foundational aspects to the organization of experience, this may be a controversial argument. Beyond that, it is a paradoxical argument insofar as it suggests that the very shift toward an understanding of psychoanalysis as a hermeneutic, relational enterprise is what may allow us to discover an organization of experience that is both distinctly personal and that is grounded in a Third. If we contemplate or even accept this presumption, we may have a basis not only for rejecting the so-called death of the subject and of personal agency but for actually reaffirming its triumph. The birth of the human subject as personal agent is, in part, born of surrender to something that lies beyond both the individual and the dyad. This surrender gives rise to a trajectory of psychological agency and human experience that is both deeply personal and idiosyncratic even as it is anchored in something shared and transcendent (see Gentile 1998).

Although these themes go well beyond the confines of this chapter, they set the stage for what I will discuss. First, I define a conception of personal agency grounded in psychoanalytic considerations. I then explore the idea that experience evolves as a function of a semiotic code that, following Muller (1996), I refer to as a foundational Third. In turn, I examine how the experience of agency emerges in tandem with a semiotic space of "thirdness." By contrast, I explore the correspondence between a semiotic state of "twoness" and experiential states of impasse in which personal agency is imprisoned. Clinically, I suggest that the therapeutic challenge is to "follow" this agency and to help our patients discover themselves as personal agents in both the destruction and creation of personal meaning.

What Is Agency?

I understand agency as the fundamental capacity to create personal meaning, to initiate and "own" the communication of desire and intent, and to make the "spontaneous gesture" (Winnicott 1965). Following Sander (1983), I locate the origins of human agency in the "open-space" periods of the infant-caretaker system that are characterized by relative disengagement and that provide the infant with an opportunity for the "initiation of experience" (p. 323). This "open-space" quality is also invoked by Winnicott in his understanding of the genesis of the spontaneous gesture, made possible by the nonintrusive but facilitating presence of the "environmental mother." In this sense, agency is fundamentally derived from within (including within our sensual and bodily experience), as several recent conceptions of agency in the psychoanalytic literature also suggest (e.g., Benjamin 1995; Gentile 2001; Klugman 1997; Rustin 1997). Put differently and in counterpoint to postmodernist claims that privilege the relational construction of meaning creation, agency is not *constructed* within relationship; rather, it is the basis from which authentic relatedness evolves.[1] Indeed, our status as distinctive personal agents impels us to "contribute in" (Winnicott 1963) to relational, cultural, and political life.

In that sense, it is through relatedness that our potential for agency becomes transformed into an experienced sense of agency. Both Benjamin (1995, 1998) and Slavin (1998) have emphasized that, although agency emerges from within, its transformation into a sense of agency requires an experience of impact within a relational context. As Benjamin (1995, 33) notes, agency "requires the other's confirming response, which tells us that we have created meaning, had an impact, revealed an intention." While Benjamin refers to "recognition," Sander (1983) describes "moments of meeting" to capture this interplay between the personal and the relational, between agency and the intersubjective.

Agency requires intersubjectivity to be experienced as a sense of agency, and yet intersubjectivity cannot arise in a vacuum. It requires the presence of two potential agents who, paradoxically, cannot come into being in the absence of an intersubjective milieu. In that sense, as many within psychoanalysis have argued and as abundant philosophical precedent contends (see Frie and Reis 2005 for an overview), agency and intersubjectivity are mutually constituted. But, recalling my thesis that personal agency and intersubjectivity are constituted not only between themselves but in a context of thirdness, let me now examine this interplay.

Agency, Intersubjectivity, and Thirdness

If agency involves the initiation of personal meaning and if the evolution of a sense of agency involves coming to experience an impact on the Other, then the transformation of agency into an experienced sense of agency involves the idea that someone or something "out there" is made meaning of, is acted on, is interpreted. In that sense, agency implicates what Winnicott referred to as the world beyond omnipotence—both the material world (the realm of the "thing in itself") and the world of subjects that we do not create and that exist independently of us, and that we can know and become known to through our acts of meaning making.

Winnicott's (1951) conception of transitionality captured this realm of meaning creation that consists both of subjective omnipotence and of that which defies our omnipotence, be it the unyielding realm of matter or a mother's independent subjectivity. He refers to this terrain as the realm of "me/not-me." However, this relationship between agency and the "me/not-me" world has been undertheorized in conceptions of agency. Once we connect the idea that a potential for agency is inborn and that it requires both an intersubjective outlet and an outlet in transitional space, we have a vision of subjects who come into being as embodied and symbolic agents not only between subjects but between subjective and material (including bodily) life.

In turn, we may understand Winnicott as grounding his intersubjective relationship between mother and infant in a relationship of thirdness in which the realm of matter stands as the third to the dyad. The relationship between transitionality and intersubjectivity may itself be seen as a dialectical relationship between dyadic and triadic processes in which intersubjectivity is constituted between two subjects as well as in relation to the Third (see Gentile 2007). How does this conception of agency and intersubjectivity as constituted between each other and in relationship to transitionality relate to the idea of a foundational Third?

The Semiotic Code and Its Relationship to Agency and Thirdness

The accumulation of recent infant research provides strong support for the idea that infants are born oriented toward the world beyond themselves, and toward the possibility of discovering, knowing, and using others to discover themselves as agents of their own bodily and psychological experience. Further, the infant empirical literature tells us about (what we may infer to be) an infant's first experiences of agency. Whereas we commonly conceive of psychological agency as requiring the effective use of gesture and language, recent research (see, for example, Muller 1996; Stern 1985; Fonagy et al. 2002) demonstrates that the infant is born and initiated quite quickly into a semiotic code and comes to know and master that code through interactional encounters with a caregiver.

Let me briefly elaborate by turning to Muller's (1996) discussion of the influential work on semiosis by Charles Saunders Peirce (1839–1914). For Peirce (1940, 282), semiosis means "an action, or influence which is, or involves, a cooperation of three subjects, such as a sign, its object, and its interpretant, this tri-relative influence not being in any way resolvable into actions between pairs." While Peirce (1891, 296) described a conception of "firstness" and "secondness," it was his conception of "thirdness" that he saw as a prerequisite for thinking because implicit in it "is the concept of mediation, whereby a first and second are brought into relation."

Muller describes this process of semiosis as "incessant," (p. 45) providing as an example the "mother's smiling gaze [which] functions for the infant as a sign . . . whose dynamic interpretant is the infant's smiling gaze in response . . .

[which] in turn, functions as a sign to the mother" (pp. 44–45). Elsewhere, Muller notes, "This ongoing process of signing is almost instantaneous, largely unconscious, and seems to lie at the heart of the 'talking cure' and of all dialogue" (p. 35). We may intuit glimpses of the origins of what will become Winnicott's realm of transitionality here: the smile is not simply a "thing in itself." By virtue of the semiotic code, it has status for both infant and mother from the start, suggesting the early origins of a realm between subjectivity and "thingness."

Muller argues that the semiotic code should be understood as a foundational Third because it frames and grounds the dyad in its communicative gestures. In a very similar sense, and as I have elaborated elsewhere (Gentile 2007), Winnicott's transitionality rooted the dyad in the sphere of material reality—in something beyond them and the realm of omnipotent fantasy. In that sense, neither infant nor mother is strictly a *personal* communicator, insofar as each communicates in part not only from her idiosyncratic humanity but also from what is encoded as an inborn capacity to develop in relationship to a communicating Other. This is the realm of the Third.

In health, the mother or caregiver maintains an engagement with the Third, grounding her communication with her infant in lawful cultural patterns that function to create limits to the dyad's idiosyncratic, unbounded freedom. The mother's engagement with the Third helps her to create a space for thirdness and thus, a space for personal agency for herself, her infant, and their relationship.

The infant empirical literature, as interpreted by Muller, suggests an initial period in which the infant's facial responses so strongly mirror the mother's emotional presentation that they reflect what Muller (1996, 23) calls an obligatory or "coerced empathy." However, this highly contingent responsiveness quickly gives way to something that begins to suggest that the infant "seems to be making 'choices' "(Wolf 1987, 239), suggesting an "apparent release from 'stimulus boundedness'" (1987, 124, cited from Muller 1996, 24) or from coerced empathy. We may infer that this represents a key marker in the infant's emergent experience of agency, because he can now exercise a rudimentary personal choice and "ownership" of his independent bodily gesture.

Further, the literature suggests that healthy communication proceeds in the context of what may be described, invoking Winnicott, as "good-enough matching" or "mirroring" by the mother of the infant's emergent cues. For example, studies of vocal rhythm matching and facial mirroring provide strong support for what Beebe and her colleagues (Beebe et al. 2003, 834) describe as a "balance model" in which "interactive coupling is present but not obligatory, and self-regulation is preserved but not excessive." In this view, *balance* is central to healthy communication. In such a case, the mother matches closely but not perfectly the infant's gesture, creating correspondence and difference at the same time. And importantly for the transformation of agency into an experienced sense of agency, it opens a space for the interpretation of meaning and for taking ownership of one's distinct experience and impact.

For example, in describing the development of the child's capacity for mentalization, Fonagy and Target (1998, 94) reported that "mothers who soothe their distressed eight-month-old babies most effectively following an injection rapidly reflect the child's emotion, but this mirroring is 'contaminated' by displays of affect that are incompatible with the child's current feeling (humor, skepticism, irony, and the like), . . . [ensuring] that the infant recognizes their [mother's] emotion as analogous but not equivalent to their [own] experience". Again importing from Winnicott, this "good-enough mirroring" may be understood as introducing a rudimentary symbolic space into the parent-child relationship, allowing the infant to begin to experience his own impact and not merely experience himself as a reactor to the Other's impositions of meaning. In preserving a simultaneity of separateness and connectedness, these early interactions plant the seeds for the infant's evolving experience of a linkage between mind and body, psyche and soma (Winnicott 1949), as well as for linkages between me and not-me, between me and you.

This interplay between me (and not-me), you, and a deeper code that frames our meaning-creation process grants a space for thirdness in which a personal, interpretive agent can emerge. In that process, we grant meaning to an otherwise impersonal reality—including a body, a teddy bear, and the body and face of the "environmental mother" (Winnicott 1965) who is not yet conceived by the infant as a personal subject with her own independent subjectivity. While we gain degrees of freedom in our subjective process of meaning creation here, we nonetheless also must contend with constraints, insofar as our body, the mother's physical presence, and the teddy bear all have properties as "things in themselves" and are not simply projections of our omnipotent fantasy.

This presumption leads naturally to an important consideration: What happens to personal agency when the semiotic code is bypassed and this process is derailed?

The Collapse of Symbolic Space and the Derailment of Personal Agency

If the mother's capacity to mirror her infant's cue, in healthy interaction, grants a space for the infant to experience his gesture as both meaningful and his own while also granting the opportunity to discover something new that is not strictly in his original communication, we can see that the road is paved for the rich possibilities of play and mutual discovery of oneself and an Other. However, in the case in which the mother either bypasses the infant's cue and imposes her own meaning or is slavishly attuned and too accurately mirrors the infant (while erasing her own agenda), we can see that the stage is set for both the constitution of personal agency and of intersubjectivity to go awry.

In such situations, the dyad loses the opportunity for creating symbolic potential and its space of thirdness collapses. The infant remains in a state of "stimulus entrapment" (Meares 1997) and nascent opportunities for a budding experience of agency are lost.

Not infrequently, in the clinical situation, we encounter someone who has come to experience futility about the project of personal meaning making and has retreated from the pressure of what Muller (1996) describes as the "suffocating baggage" of imposed meanings (in which another's agenda has eclipsed the individual's own meaning-making signs). Such a person may retreat to a sensory-dominated realm (see Ogden 1986, 1989) in which meaning creation (to the extent that it evolves at all) takes place in a private, internal landscape. It may be a very long process before the patient is ready to take a chance on creating meaning in a shared space between the patient and analyst, disrupting possibilities for both an experienced sense of agency and intersubjectivity.

Perhaps more often, we encounter a patient who experiences reality and subjectivity (his own and others') as matters of fact rather than matters of interpretation, as is the case in the "paranoid-schizoid" mode of organizing experience (Ogden 1986, 1994) or in complementary roles and power relations (Benjamin 1998, 2004). From a semiotic perspective, such relationships are organized by their structure of "twoness" insofar as they lack a third term.

Recalling our earlier discussion of semiosis, according to Peirce, (1891, 1940), the relation between symbol, symbolized, and an interpretant is fundamental to relationships of thirdness or among three. However, in states of "twoness," meaning is reduced to action/reaction, to a relationship between pairs. Psychological agency requires a space for interpretation—that is, a space of thirdness—and interpretation requires an interpreting personal agent. But clinically, we know that it may be a long journey from the organization of meaning in trapped dyadic states to an organization of meaning founded and enriched by the space of thirdness and its interpretive possibilities.

Therefore, returning for now to the semiotic structure of twoness, the question arises, where does personal agency reside in such states? As

I proposed elsewhere (Gentile 2001), in the absence of thirdness, agency itself remains confined and meaning creation remains trapped and bottled up. This gives rise to repetitive dynamics that lead the patient to experience an impact only on his mind and his body (via symptoms) or through fantasized or "brute-force" retaliation against the Other. Impact, in these states, is achieved through unmediated action/reaction, not through mediation and symbolic expression.

Just as we can understand psychopathology as a reflection of the collapse of semiotic structure (and of symbolic space) and the foreclosed phenomenology of agency, we can also guide clinical intervention to facilitate their evolution. For example, if states of "twoness" reflect an imprisoned agency, and if the transformation of personal agency emerges in tandem with increased semiotic empowerment, the question becomes: How do we open up a space for interpretation and for the patient's self-possession and experience of herself as an author of meaning? First, we must unleash the sequestered meaning and agency in trapped states of twoness. But how does this take place?

States of Twoness and the Phenomenology of Trapped Agency

In a previous investigation, I examined the meanings embedded in trapped states and proposed a "content/container" relationship between the phenomenology characterizing such "perversions of agency" and its accompanying structure of twoness (Gentile 2001). In this section, I will discuss this phenomenology, including clinical illustration of the patient's dawning recognition of his own contribution to this state of impasse, within which lie the seeds of a future sense of agency.

Time and again, we discover in the clinical situation that meaning has become organized around a split between loyalty and spite. The patient is simultaneously dedicated to being both loyal to an identity and loyal to an original attachment relationship (in which that identity was forged). On the other side of the split, the patient is engaged in an act of spiteful protest, often a morally indignant stance against that original attachment figure—usually one who was ruthless or transgressive and/or one who stood by and whose silence abetted acts of destruction against the patient's original acts of agency. Both sides of the split serve to seal the fate of the patient, who now remains locked in a subversive power struggle. This power struggle simultaneously sustains the integrity of the patient's very identity (and moral protest), even as it contradicts that very integrity insofar as it is rooted in spite and vengeance (and so, morally impoverished) and thereby ensures a life of self-defeat and relationships consigned to the status of power relations.

The clinical task at hand involves helping the patient to take some ownership of his own acts of meaning creation, which means simultaneously taking ownership of his own acts of meaning destruction. Not uncommonly, a patient in this predicament may be hard pressed to experience himself as a creator/destroyer of meaning, insofar as his identity (and its loyal and spiteful perverse agenda) is so often attached to an identity of being "done to" (Benjamin 2004), to a protest against an original perpetrator, to the erasure of personal agency. The accompanying clinical phenomenology reveals that spite and its meaning-destroying properties, in this developmental location, have achieved the status of virtue. One patient, for example, said, "I'm forever spiting myself but, to me, its being true to myself," and another, "I'll always root for the losing team but at least no one can say I'm not consistent and loyal."

In this exchange, the patient experiences, at best, a bittersweet triumph insofar as it comes at his own expense and precludes transformative relational experience. The patient, here, psychically robs the original aggressor of his power (agency) by becoming the author of his own demise. For example, they may refuse to experience excitement in order to preempt someone else's sadistic pleasure in the patient's fantasized (and feared) defeat. Or they may remain wedded to their self-defeat in order to preempt the Other from taking ownership over their successes (for example, when a parent lives vicariously through a child's academic or athletic success).

The clinical task must remain dedicated to the fostering of an experience of agency and to "follow the agency," as it were, wherever we find it. My experience has been that there is often a transformative moment—characterized by a sense of delighted discovery—in which the patient may recognize himself as an agent (however perversely) for the first time as having actively collaborated in building a relationship based on opposition and defeat, in which his signals conveyed meaning, at least to himself.

For example, one patient who had felt imprisoned in his subjective life, in his childhood role, and now in the corporate culture in which he found himself, often referred to his "life behind bars." Session after session, and day after day at work, this man wore a pinstripe shirt, as if personally condemned to a life behind bars but with no acknowledgment of actively perpetuating his own self-imprisonment. He experienced it as his uniform, or as we came to see it, as his prison (death) sentence—as if he had no choice. Only very gradually did the patient acknowledge to himself, let alone to me, that it was he who picked out his clothing each day and he who dressed himself. Gradually, he came to recognize that, in a cynical way, he was making a ridiculing statement toward the corporate culture in which he found himself (and its dehumanizing toll). Albeit at his own expense, this dawning responsibility for his own communication granted the patient a budding sense of agency. He took both pride and some sadistic pleasure in discovering that he had created such a clever means to ridicule the Other.

Only with the patient's gradual recognition that his victory was an omnipotent one, with no impact beyond his own enslavement, on the corporate culture in which he found himself (after all, he was also very loyal, wearing a very conformist attire) that he experienced both a fury and a determined desire for something more meaningful in life. This experience was compounded by his emergent recognition that, in sustaining this perverse agenda, he had perpetuated his dreary existence as an alienated, imprisoned, and ultimately unknown "employee," thus robbing himself of his own freedom to dress or to be recognized in a personally distinctive way.

Such splits between loyalty to a victimized, martyred identity and an identity founded in spiteful, indignant protest are commonplace in states of perverse agency and always reflect a failure of intersubjectivity insofar as the patient does not experience himself as an interpreting, meaning-granting subject in relationship to other subjects.

My patient's perverse power dynamic not only exacted the price of self-defeat, but the seeds of a budding sense of agency and pride could be found in it. Yet, at this semiotic and phenomenological juncture, the patient remains trapped in a realm of subjective omnipotence characterized by loyal but vengeful dynamics, not in engagement with the rest of the meaning-making world. The strategy of burying oneself can actually yield devastating consequences in real life, especially when compounded by cumulative losses in the face of the march of real time and missed opportunities for the ameliorative impact of new experience and a life well lived. Therefore, even as the patient may gain a glimpse of his potential as a creator of meaning, he must also come to acknowledge that this very potential is embedded in a vicious path of destructiveness. It is in gaining a sense of ownership over both one's participation in a destructive agenda and in the possibilities of a creative agenda that the patient begins to experience mounting frustration and desire, fueling a determination to make changes and choices, ushering in the further evolution of a phenomenological trajectory of agency.

Resistance, Therapeutic Action, and Agency

We may understand, in these contexts, the emergence of what we commonly refer to as resistance in therapy as a transitional state in the establishment of agency. Here, we see evidence that something is happening in the treatment and that it is the patient who is the catalyst for therapeutic action, originally camouflaged as therapeutic inaction (Gentile 2001). The patient's split agenda is coming into the treatment. The patient is resisting participation in a role-based relationship defined by the analyst's action, even as he simultaneously evades direct expression of his conflicting or controversial agenda (and so, sustains loyalty to his role as "patient"). In that sense, resistance is a significant but insufficient step in the pathway toward claiming a sense of agency: it both pries open and obscures a space for interpretation. Here the patient seeks and refuses change at the same time, remaining locked in a repetitive dyadic process but making incremental gains in personal agency at the same time.

Implicit in this conversation is the idea that therapeutic action must, ultimately, be action that is guided by the patient's agency. However useful the analyst's or therapist's action may be (through empathy, interpretation, creating a holding environment, self-disclosure, and so on), the patient must become the initiator of meaning creation in order to own his own treatment and in order to transform his very identity from patient to experiencing subject.

In that sense, transformative therapeutic action lies in the patient's acts of agency, which often begin to occur as acts of refusal. For example, the patient may signal refusal to participate in the treatment on terms set by the analyst, or may communicate boredom or contempt for the analyst's communications. Troubling as such acts may be to the analyst, they represent a sign that the patient is now willing to expose previously concealed conflicting agendas and now feels entitled to question the etiquette of the analytic setup by challenging the role-based relationship that has been constructed thus far in the treatment. The patient first must act to "destroy" what most likely had previously been useful to him but has now become boring, useless, or predictable conventions within the treatment. Here, the patient's expanding sense of entitlement to initiate change by challenging the treatment and the analyst signify the patient's increased status as a desiring subject with a newfound sense of agency and goal directedness.

In the next section, I turn to signs that the patient is beginning to own this new status as meaning maker and to use this capacity increasingly to create new experience. As he does so, he moves beyond the confines of a world in which reality, fantasy, and identity are all organized in an unquestioned "is what it is" interpretation-defying manner. With each incremental gain in semiotic capacity, the tides of personal experience begin to turn, increasingly now dominated by an experienced sense of agency.

Phenomenological Markers of Transformations of Agency

The Patient as Interpreter

In therapy, we often work with people who make assumptions about themselves and about their worlds as matters of fact rather than interpretation. These patients may live intractably in such a world, and considerable psychotherapeutic work may need to be done before the patient is able to contemplate that he has adopted the interpretations of others as matters of fact (often, of course, because they are imposed on the patient as if they are indeed matters of fact and not interpretations to be considered). Prying open the space for meaning creation can require an enormous strain on the part of the analyst and the patient, who are both fighting uphill in the face of the patient's defenses and relational history. But remarkable change can take place once a patient allows himself to question the very identity and worldview that until now have been taken for granted.

One patient who chronically tried to please others, came into treatment perplexed by what she regarded as her turn toward mediocrity and indifference. She had a history of anorexia and an obsessional perfectionism, but after years of careful self-scrutiny, had allowed her body to gain some weight and had assumed a more relaxed, if also self-sabotaging, stance toward her studies. Upset with herself for her "laxness," she desired to return to a size 0, a status she had achieved once before and in which she felt herself to be the envy of other women.

One day, my patient began a session indignant after glimpsing an article in a women's magazine in my waiting room. The magazine had conducted a survey in which readers rated two women on how sexy they were. As I remember it, one woman, very slim and fit, described herself as hard-working and self-critical. The other woman, quite a bit heavier, simply described herself as sexy. The readership overwhelmingly found the woman who had described herself as sexy to be sexy. My patient regarded this as fundamentally unjust.

Grudgingly, she recognized that indeed the spin people put on themselves has a real impact. She began to concede that her quest to diet and reduce her size not only reflected a very concrete solution to her desire to be sexy (as an object of envy) but also represented a collusion with those who had silenced her as a child, effectively robbing her of her true vitality and potential sexiness. Furious now that she had contributed to her own self-erasure, and that this had had a real impact, my patient did not sulk or stew but began instead to experiment with her own self-definition. Using her newfound anger, which she experienced as just as exhilarating as if she had suddenly discovered that she was "fluent in French," she now felt more entitled, empowered, and sexy. Determined to create a space for herself, free from her previous inclinations toward a knee-jerk accommodation, she became increasingly decisive, developing and implementing plans based on her own desires, which now she owned in a more direct and explicit way. With me and others she began to improvise a revised identity (Ringstrom 2001), based now on her own personal idiom (Bollas 1989) and freedom to create her own signs of self-expression.

There was, as in any treatment, considerable terrain yet to traverse. For example, at this juncture, my patient ascribed clinical usefulness to the magazine article in the waiting room but implicitly devalued my participation, which had aimed (over the course of months) to help her question what she took for granted about her identity and relationships. She was not yet ready to contemplate the therapy as a *personal* relational process—as one of mutual recognition. Nonetheless, the shifts in personal agency that accrued following this initial discovery of herself as capable of creating signs that had meaning for others and for herself were palpable, granting the patient not only newfound hope but fueling her real engagement with a previously postponed agenda for an intimate relationship and personally fulfilling career.

Beyond Role-Based Relating: Curiosity, Desire, and Thirdness

The patient may not realize that she has taken not only herself but the analytic relationship (including the analyst) for granted—as givens and not matters of interpretation (Gentile 2007). It is as if the infant never comes to contemplate that the blanket may be somehow more than a blanket, endowed with personal meaning and nuance (Winnicott 1971). Indeed, it can be stunning to the analyst to experience herself as so disregarded and unrecognized as a personal subject.

But it is the *patient's* realization that the analytic relationship (like the patient's own identity, subjectivity, and other relationships) has been taken as a matter of fact that is groundbreaking for the evolution of personal agency, a factor that contributes to the patient's own experience of being stunned to discover that the analyst is indeed in an affectively "real" relationship with him, even as it is a therapeutic one. Even patients who (in other aspects of their lives) value their capacity to deconstruct convention, often do not consciously consider their capacity to interpret this other person (the analyst), leaving the possibilities for the evolution of agency and intersubjectivity only dimly realized. As the analyst encourages this interpretive process (which obviously exposes the analyst to a greater level of vulnerability), the patient often comes to experience the analytic relationship itself as needing to be questioned, challenged, and transformed. By contrast, the failure of the analyst to encourage the questioning of the status-quo relationship—as well as the failure of the patient to do so—are among the most common sources of stalemate in therapies and in relationships at large. Let me briefly elaborate.

Patients come to reify their analysts, their parents, and their lovers or friends—inevitably with the complicity of the analyst, parent, lover, or friend. As personal agency evolves, patients are faced with relationships that bore them or that no longer work for them, but also with the predicament that the person feels they are fated to remain in such a limited relationship or that the relationship itself must be lost—as if there is no possibility for true relational transformation. Often enough, the patient accurately perceives the situation and must make an either/or choice. But the goal of the analytic relationship, at least ideally, is to remain in the relationship and transform it and oneself at the same time.

Aron (1996) emphasizes the huge importance of the analyst's curiosity about the patient's experience of who the analyst is personally, beyond the role that the analyst plays, by actively encouraging and welcoming the patient's emergent curiosity. I have come to see the patient's experience of boredom in the treatment as a telltale and welcome sign (however difficult) that the patient's sense of agency has some traction in the treatment. Inevitably, just beyond that boredom, lies the entrance of curiosity and desire for a more fully alive and genuinely "two-way" relationship in which both subjects in the relationship are present to be known, discovered, and interpreted.

One patient who grew bored and impatient with our process, became increasingly contemptuous of therapy. As she became more willing to be direct, she openly caricatured my words and the repetitive nature of my "interventions." Simultaneously, she refused to grant me status beyond the impersonal and circumscribed role that she allowed me to play and that I participated in playing. After several weeks in which I received and challenged her contempt and boredom, my patient was able to acknowledge some emergent (if grudging) curiosity about me as a person and, specifically, about me as a woman.

In that sense, the emergence of boredom signals that the patient is coming into being in an increasingly empowered and desiring way (Gentile 2001). Prior to the developmental capacity to be *interested*, the patient may have reacted to discoveries of the analyst's subjectivity as burdensome, as hypocritical, or as something to be ignored or annihilated. So, the emergence of curiosity is a significant accomplishment in the advancement of personal agency and relatedly, intersubjectivity. There is now emergent space for two human agents to be known, to experience desire.

Such gains in personal agency and intersubjective discovery vacillate with a strong retreat or backlash in the direction of preserving the relational and role-based status quo and to its reified, unquestioned assumptions of reality, fantasy, and identity. Whereas first patients may feel that they just somehow return to this state (often accompanied by a sense of despair, frustration, somatic turmoil, or mere indifference), gains in personal agency are notable ever so gradually. What changes through this cycle of engagement/ dissociation is an increased experience of choice as well as an expanded capacity to experience conscious motivations of both fear and desire.

For example, another patient acknowledged that, while much had changed in our work together, what remained unchanged was that he was unable to share his private fantasy life with me. Weeks later, he acknowledged that it was not that he was unable to share but that he *felt* he was unable to share, suggesting a hint of interpretive space. And some weeks after that, he conceded that he potentially could but did not want to share. Again, in this shift from a position of "I cannot" to "I will not," he was signaling to me important transformations in his sense of personal agency, transformations I believe are emblematic for all patients in their quest (and reluctance) to bear responsibility for what they do want, for their own desire.

Agency and the Third

Phenomenological markers, such as those described above, indicate that a long enduring power dynamic is giving way to an experienced sense of agency. They also signal that the patient has come to have some measure of faith or trust in the analyst—and particularly in the analyst's ability to position himself simultaneously as a member of the dyad and as a member of the Third (see Muller 1996). Put differently, the analyst's power derives not from a power dynamic but from his own sense of agency and foothold in something meaningful, ethical, and even nonnegotiable—something that transcends the entrapped dynamics of the dyad. This discovery allows the patient to develop greater trust that there will not be a "trading of places" (Gentile 2001) and that the analyst will not capitulate to an endless cycle of what Benjamin (2004) describes as a "doer–done to" dynamic.

These gains fuel the further evolution of agency. Just as importantly, as the patient comes to realize that he has actually enacted *real* damage—in relationships with others and/or in relationship to himself—the loyal/spiteful split on which his identity is founded receives a devastating blow. For example, one patient only came to recognize the real impact that his martyrdom had on his marital relationship when his wife announced her desire for a divorce. Another patient, after years of denial, came to acknowledge that chronic alcohol use had jeopardized her liver function. Genuine anger, regret, and sadness mount as the patient contemplates the futility and recklessness of his life's misguided agenda. Klein (1975) wrote of the relationship between the infant's destruction, guilt, and reparative gesture, while Winnicott (1968) elaborated on destruction as an inevitable conduit to and byproduct of the infant's discovery of the world "of externality." Similarly, in bearing responsibility for his own destructiveness to self and others, the patient may begin to bear responsibility as well for loving himself and real others, and for wanting "more" in life.

I think, above all, that it is the emergence of such desire that wreaks ultimate havoc on the old, fixed meanings sustaining identity and experience. One patient who had long held to a martyred stance in relationships (which, in the context of alcohol consumption, gave way to an abusive, defiant stance) came to acknowledge strong sexual desire within the analytic relationship. As this desire intensified, he was no longer able to tolerate his experience of me being "above him" as an idealized figure nor of him being "below me" in his martyred or abusive status. His desire fueled him to begin to discover me as a human being, with complicated feelings and a history of my own, and to more fully acknowledge the complexity of his own humanity, including his genuine power and creativity. He needed to level the playing field (as did I) in order to have a genuinely moral and mutually respectful relationship—in which we both could respect one another.

I believe this patient was on the verge of discovering a more fully intersubjective relationship in which we both come into being as subjects in and because of the interpretive space between us. This too signified that the patient's trajectory of semiotic empowerment (toward the realm of thirdness that Peirce described) and personal agency was becoming more fully realized.

Conclusion

The evolution of personal agency and its meaning-making trajectory, from the point of view of this chapter, ultimately implicates a paradox: to fully claim ourselves as personal agents, we must surrender to a Third (and its unconscious foundational moorings) and to the constraints this places on our subjective creations. We come alive in a space between limits and desire: we find *degrees* of freedom. In that sense, agency has its own teleology. To be realized, it must be anchored both in the world of subjects whom we do not control or possess and in laws of nature that we do not create.

Clinically, we commonly encounter patients in whom agency remains trapped and for whom the project of shared meaning creation has gone awry. Instead, what I have referred to as a "perversion of agency" predominates. Here, the patient is attached to a contradictory loyal and vengeful agenda toward original attachment figures. This gives rise to a perseverative, static process in which meaning is simultaneously generated and destroyed, thereby undermining the project of creating a personal and symbolic legacy in the world beyond oneself and beyond the confining dyad.

If a stymied trajectory of meaning creation is to become unlocked, the patient must begin to experience a sense of ownership of his destructiveness as well as of his stymied creative potential. In doing so, the patient gains a new experience of himself as a personal agent who owns both desire and responsibility. In this process, he discovers that he is capable of creating signs that can be interpreted and that can be transformative and, moreover, that he is capable of interpreting others. This opening of possibility for meaning creation fuels an experience of desire and curiosity, including a desire to discover the Other as a personal subject. And this desire, I believe, emboldens the patient to surrender to a world beyond his control and to take a chance on authentically "contributing-in" (Winnicott 1963) to meaningful relationships and to the possibilities for mutual recognition.

In our contemporary and often destructive era of globalization, facilitating this trajectory of agency and intersubjectivity bears tremendous relevance in the consulting room and beyond. In this trajectory, the birth of personal agency is inseparably linked (and cannot be realized apart from) our authentic expression and symbolic creations in the world beyond us, including the world of other subjects who possess their own needs and desires. Only through this process can the patient enter a realm of mutual dependence and survival—engaging, at last, in relationships that are imperfect and difficult, but real and loving.

Note

1. Although I use the term *authentic* here in its colloquial sense, the interested reader is referred to Thompson 2006 for a discussion of the concept of authenticity in psychoanalytic and philosophical thought.

References

Aron, L. 1996. *A meeting of minds: Mutuality in psychoanalysis*. Hillsdale, N.J.: Analytic Press.

Beebe, B., Rustin, J., Sorter, D., and Knoblauch, S. 2003. An expanded view of intersubjectivity in infancy and its application to psychoanalysis. *Psychoanalytic Dialogues* 13:805–841.

Benjamin, J. 1995. *Like subjects, love objects*. New Haven, Conn.: Yale University Press.

Benjamin, J. 1998. *Shadow of the other: Intersubjectivity and gender in psychoanalysis.* New York: Routledge.

Benjamin, J. 2004. Beyond doer and done to: An intersubjective view of thirdness. *Psychoanalytic Quarterly* 73:5–46.

Bollas, C. 1989. *Forces of destiny.* London: Free Associations.

Fonagy, P., Gergely, G., Jurist, E., and Target, M. 2002. *Affect regulation, mentalization, and the development of the self.* New York: Other Press.

Fonagy, P., and Target, M. 1998. Mentalization and the changing aims of child psychoanalysis. *Psychoanalytic Dialogues* 8:79–87.

Fredrickson, J. 2003. The eclipse of the person in psychoanalysis. In R. Frie, ed., *Understanding experience,* 204–224. New York: Routledge.

Frie, R., and Reis, B. 2005. Intersubjectivity: From theory through practice. In J. Mills, ed., *Relational and intersubjective perspectives in psychoanalysis,* 3–33. Northvale, N.J.: Jason Aronson.

Gentile, J. 1998. Listening for deep structure: Between the *a priori* and the intersubjective. *Contemporary Psychoanalysis* 34:67–89.

Gentile, J. 2001. Close but no cigar: The perversion of agency and the absence of thirdness. *Contemporary Psychoanalysis* 37:623–654.

Gentile, J. 2007. Wrestling with matter: Origins of intersubjectivity. *Psychoanalytic Quarterly* 76:547–582.

Klein, M. 1975. *Envy and gratitude and other works, 1946–1963.* New York: Delacorte.

Klugman, D. 1997, November. *Investment and divestment: Oneness, agentic relatedness, and self psychology's tripartite model of the person.* Paper presented at the 20th Annual International Conference on the Psychology of the Self, Chicago.

Meares, R. 1997. Stimulus entrapment: On a common basis of somatization. *Psychoanalytic Inquiry* 17:223–234.

Muller, J. 1996. *Beyond the psychoanalytic dyad: Developmental semiotics in Freud, Pierce, and Lacan.* New York: Routledge.

Ogden, T. 1986. *The matrix of the mind.* Northvale, N.J.: Jason Aronson.

Ogden, T. 1989. *The primitive edge of experience.* Northvale, N.J.: Jason Aronson.

Ogden, T. 1994. *Subjects of analysis.* Northvale, N.J.: Jason Aronson.

Peirce, C. S. 1940. Philosophical writings of Peirce. Ed. J. Buchler. New York: Dover.

Peirce, C. S. 1891. The architecture of theories. In N. Houser and C. Kloesel, eds., *The essential Peirce: Selected philosophical writings,* vol. 1, 285–297. Bloomington: Indiana University Press.

Ringstrom, R. 2001. Cultivating the improvisational in psychoanalytic treatment. *Psychoanalytic Dialogues* 11:727–754.

Rustin, J. 1997. Infancy, agency, and intersubjectivity: A view of therapeutic action. *Psychoanalytic Dialogues* 7:43–62.

Sander, L. 1983. Polarity, paradox, and the organizing process. In J. Call, E. Galenson and R. Tyson, eds., *Frontiers of Infant Psychology*, 315–327. New York: Basic Books.

Slavin, J. 1998. The innocence of sexuality. *Psychoanalytic Quarterly* 72:51–80.

Stern, D. 1985. *The interpersonal world of the infant.* New York: Basic Books.

Thompson, M. G. 200). Vicissitudes of authenticity in the psychoanalytic situation. *Contemporary Psychoanalysis* 42:139–176.

Winnicott, D. W. 1949. Mind and its relation to the psyche-soma. In *Through paediatrics to psychoanalysis: Collected papers*, 243–254. New York: Brunner/Mazel.

Winnicott, D. W. 1951. Transitional objects and transitional phenomena. In *Playing and reality*, 1–25. New York: Basic Books.

Winnicott, D. W. 1963. The capacity for concern. In *The maturational processes and the facilitating environment*, 73–82. New York: International Universities Press.

Winnicott, D. W. 1965. *The maturational processes and the facilitating environment.* New York: International Universities Press.

Winnicott, D. W. 1968. The use of an object and playing through identifications. In *Playing and reality*, 53–64. New York: Basic Books.

Winnicott, D. W. 1971. *Playing and reality*. New York: Basic Books.

Wolff, P. 1987. *The development of behavioral states and the expression of emotions in infancy: New proposals for investigation.* Chicago: University of Chicago Press.

6 Agency as Fluid Process: Clinical and Theoretical Considerations

Pascal Sauvayre

As we reflect on the course of our lives and our important life decisions, the question of agency often takes center stage. Could we have done things differently? Can we make up for past mistakes? Quite simply, are we truly the authors of our life's story? Within the clinical domain, questioning of this sort seems to yield complex and contradictory answers, including both yes and no. On the one hand, we may realize that all of our past actions and decisions that make us who we are have been chained to a context external to "us," and to that extent, we are determined by that context. On the other hand, this awareness may also lead to the realization that we can shape or endorse relevant parts of that context and thereby become the genuine authors of our lives: to this extent, we are free. This chapter addresses the incompatibility of the claims of freedom and determination for understanding personal agency within clinical contexts. I attempt to establish a perspective that moves beyond the traditional debate between freedom and determinism but all the while being careful not to lose the key points of each position that lead to the incompatibility. I also examine the lived experiences of freedom and determination through the use of a case illustration of a patient I refer to as "Patrick."

When Patrick came for therapy, he yearned for the exhilaration he had previously felt on making a series of bold life decisions encapsulated in "coming out" and in coming to America. He had felt he was breaking the chains of his past, but the excitement eventually waned and gave way to an oppressive feeling of being stuck, enchained. On reflection, the rush of excitement had been misguided and premature. He had overlooked numerous factors that, all told, revealed how the apparent liberation was firmly tethered to his past, and his perceived freedom was actually illusory. Paradoxically, at the very same time that he was accepting how profoundly his determining context had penetrated all facets of his life, he recovered neglected creativity linked to his childhood and developed what amounted to a new sense of his identity—one permeated by a deeper awareness of his own agency. The development of Patrick's self and of his agency go hand in hand, and as I will demonstrate, these concepts must rely on each other. Patrick's self, his ability to be himself, matured as he came to appreciate and own the limits of his self imposed by his determining context, but without disappearing in it. Patrick, as fully himself, was neither completely merged in his context, nor was he separate from it. This tension, or balance, is also the paradox of Patrick's agency—both determined as a part of the context, and free apart from it.

This paradox will be explored through the opposition between scientific determinism and the apparently conflicting goals of psychotherapy or psychoanalysis to enhance human freedom, despite their reliance on scientific principles such as determinism. This chapter proposes an account of agency as a movement between the self and the context that shapes it. By context I include all the traditional deterministic forces ranging from unconscious motives, to conscious beliefs and attitudes, to social forces, to biological determinants, to genetics, to biochemical events, and so forth.

If the self is subsumed by its determining context, then agency cannot exist. Most of our lives can be accounted for by determining factors to which we are tethered, and the attempt to "find" agency, free of contexts, is futile. Agency arises in the activity of the self in the flow of experience. The understanding of self and of agency are fully intertwined, and I would suggest the term *self-as-agent* to supplant both *self* and *agency*. Agency is best described as an activity that involves the construction and formulation of meaning through the struggle between self and Other. Specifically, Patrick's self emerged through the integrated rejection *and* identification of the Other.

To appreciate the self as agential, a different type of thinking, one that will be referred to as *dialectical*, to contrast it with *analytical*, is necessary in order to understand the self as entangled but not subsumed by its determining contexts. This kind of reflection lends itself better to the metaphor of time, in contrast to the spatial assumptions embedded in the attempt to locate agency. The notion of "flow" is more appropriate to the experience of freedom, in which the agent penetrates and is penetrated by the determining elements of one's life in an inextricable tangle—a dialectic. In elaborating this approach to agency, I will draw chiefly on the works of the French philosophers Henri Bergson and Maurice Merleau-Ponty. They applied dialectical thinking to the paradox of agency in order to overcome the limitations of the traditional freedom–versus–scientific determinism debate. I will also suggest that contemporary research into the inherent limitations of analytical thinking, and of formal systems of thought in mathematics and the sciences, suggests the presence of aspects of reality beyond the scope of scientific determinism that are best accounted for by notions such as "unpredictable flow."

The Case of Patrick

Patrick, a Frenchman in his early thirties, had been living in New York City for a couple of years when he sought out treatment for the first time. He was not quite sure why; all he knew was that he was stuck, frustrated, and anxious. This contrasted sharply to the way he felt only two years previously when he moved here from France in a state of agitated excitement. With a series of groundbreaking decisions that included "coming out," quitting the company that his father had worked for for his entire work life, and taking a job in New York, all against the strong objections and despair of his parents, he felt he had finally taken control of his life.

Up to that point Patrick had been following, or at least trying to, a path laid out in all the conventional ways. It included holding a secure job and career path like his father, and marrying a "nice" girl, a friend in fact, from a nearby town—a very cozy, predictable, and respectable life. He had finally come to the realization that no matter how much self-convincing took place, the person living that life was false, even to himself. So he believed that these courageous and radical steps would be the dawn of a new self, free from the burdens that an embittered father and a terrified mother had imposed on him and his brother. After so many years of subtle and corrosive oppression and repression, he felt as though *he* was choosing his destiny, choosing himself. As is the case for so many immigrants, the search for oneself beyond the oppressiveness of the old world is thought to be found in the freedom that resides in the new "land of freedom." America.

But just as a closer examination of America's claims to champion freedom reveals oppression and repression, so did Patrick's self-exploration put his initial feeling of freedom into serious question. As we explored further, it became clear that his decision to leave his job, his friends, his family, and his country was done in such a defiant and impulsive way that it actually reaffirmed his bond to them. In addition, it became clear that he had been acting out repressed wishes of his father to leave his home town and perhaps his wife as well, who in turn was determined to control any expression of independence. Was Patrick simply playing out his own version of the parental dynamics? Through his efforts to free himself from his destiny, had he actually been playing out his role in it? In light of these considerations, his current feeling of being enchained began to make sense.

Patrick was now consumed by his obligations toward the very same job that had represented his freedom, and by his obligations toward a failing relationship. America was losing its promise, its luster having been long gone. Although he possessed what for him were the accoutrements of freedom, a job in an artistic profession and a gay lifestyle in New York City, he knew himself to be repeating an all too familiar pattern. His own bitterness was frighteningly similar to his father's, and he found himself in a prison of his own making. In sum, his rebellion had wound up reinstating the oppressive status quo of his past.

As his acceptance and curiosity grew about the ways he was linked to his family, to his friends, and to me, a more separate sense of his own identity emerged. This simultaneous appreciation of the links to his context and his separateness from it is best thought of as an active balance, made up of multiple small and delicate movements comparable to a stable yoga pose that is achieved after much practice in order to master the ongoing imbalances. Fighting the chains had only tightened them, but this acceptance was not surrender either. Just as the recognition of his bonds to others paradoxically led to a more separate sense of himself, the recognition of his determining context allowed Patrick's "real self, (his) personal 'I' . . . inwardly free and spontaneous" (Guntrip 1969, 406) to emerge.

It was inspiring to witness Patrick rediscovering long-standing artistic affinities and passions that had been buried during adolescence in favor of more "mature" and "responsible" pursuits. Ironically, these were strongly linked to aspects of his relationship with his mother that were mutually enriching and free from the guilt-ridden power relations that had predominated. A new relationship developed with a man from a different racial, cultural, and socioeconomic background. It had all the trappings of an oppositional statement, but given the different way Patrick was approaching his family, he did not engage the same predictable reactions of worry and horror in them, finding instead a degree of openness and acceptance that had not previously been possible. His career seemed to open up with possibilities as well, even if that meant, among other alternatives, staying exactly where he was—only now as a matter of choice. He was neither obligated to stay, nor did he have to escape, and in the very questioning of these options, his life belonged to him.

Paradoxically, this experience of agency emerged from the recognition of the determining bonds that had previously oppressed him, and that, when unwittingly internalized, more effectively repressed his freedom. How the acceptance of these determinants releases the movement of agency is the central topic of this chapter. Let me first turn to the traditional philosophical version of this paradox.

The Dilemma of Free Will

The freedom-versus-determinism debate has a long and rich history in Western philosophy, and modern claims of freedom must face an all-encompassing scientific determinism. While mind and soul were thought to lie beyond the reach of science, the rise of psychology and related sciences has shown that not to be case. With the rule of science comes one of its fundamental assumptions, determinism, and therefore the abolition of prescientific notions of agency.

For instance, B. F. Skinner (1971), the founder of modern behaviorism and one of the most strident advocates of determinism, argues that if all human behavior can be understood in terms of scientific principles, then it can be predicted and controlled just like any other natural event. This lays the foundation for psychotherapy, or any other intervention, as long, of course, as we abolish such illusions as freedom and dignity. But if the object of psychotherapy, based on the scientific foundations of determinism, is to provide understanding and control for *desired* change, who, or what, is the agent of that change?

All psychotherapies, regardless of their underlying metapsychology, attempt to empower the person as agent. Terms such as *self-efficacy*, *self-determinism*, *self-realization*, *autonomy*, *choice*, and *agency* all reflect the same intent despite coming from different schools. Even Skinner (1971) says that the goal is to put "man" in the "role of controller, as the designer" of his environment (p. 53). It is precisely through science's "destruction of mystery" (p. 54) and of concepts such as freedom, that the empowerment of "intentional design" (p. 197) will be possible, both for the person and for the culture. Struggling with the apparent contradiction in identifying the person as the controller and designer of the environment without agency has been an important challenge for psychology.

This opposition between freedom and scientific determinism is also reflected in the schism between clinical theory and metapsychology as they are conceptualized in the psychoanalytic literature. How is it that metapsychologies firmly based on the tenets of science, and hence determinism, can lay the foundations for a clinical endeavor that intends to foster freedom of choice? On the one hand, Freud (1935, 95) is unequivocal: "Belief in psychic freedom and choice . . . is quite unscientific . . . and must give ground before the claims of determinism which governs mental life." The process of psychoanalysis indeed reveals how "overdetermined" (1953) our mental life is by unconscious motives, and how illusory our conscious freedom seems to be. But to what end do we then engage in psychoanalysis? Freud's answer was to "give the patient ego *freedom to choose one way or the other*" (1949, 72; original emphasis). But in turn, if we relinquish the claims of determinism according to Freud, we have "thrown over the whole scientific outlook on the world" (1949, 27) on which psychoanalytic therapy is based to begin with!

How to manage this contradiction? One way is to ignore it, and perhaps most clinicians do, or at least find some way to live with it as unsolvable.

For example, Gatch and and Temerlin (1965, 28–29) found that, regardless of whether clinicians subscribed to a philosophy that supported determinism or freedom, "all therapists spoke in a manner consistent with determinism when discussing the patient's past, but appeared to assume a choice-making capacity when speaking of the patient's behavior in the present or the future."

Another related approach among the clinically minded is to privilege lived experience to the exclusion of these "experience-far" philosophical considerations. The first problem here is that experience without reflection can be a deceptive guide, just as Patrick's experience of freedom was to begin with. Even before his rebellion, for that matter, he had initially "experienced" his choices as offered to him, not imposed on him, and therefore as genuine. Experience requires a reflective stance to gain perspective outside of the immanent experience, precisely the same stance that metapsychology takes vis-à-vis clinical theory. The second problem is that the privileging of experience over metapsychology cannot stand as a "solution" to the initial contradiction because it is itself a metapsychological position, so the contradiction between the clinical and the metapsychological positions has simply been displaced within radical phenomenology.

Metapsychological treatments of the contradiction most often maintain the claims of determinism and reinterpret the experience of freedom by assigning to the term *freedom* a particular feeling or way of experiencing the deterministic forces that shape our lives.

One argument is that our actions are embedded in a causal chain of physical, chemical, biochemical, physiological, and neurophysiological factors in which there is simply no room for "freedom," unless freedom is merely understood as a feeling on the same basis as all other feelings that are the effects of physiological events. This approach has historically been called *hard determinism* (James 1956). Internal events such as thoughts, emotions, beliefs, and so forth are simply the byproducts of impersonal biochemical events.

William James goes on to distinguish "soft" from "hard" determinism. "Soft" determinism recognizes the importance of the "warm" inner and social world in accounting for human action. This would include the commonsense notion that our decisions "cause" our actions. Soft determinism might even assign a significant role to the "will," as long as the will is also understood as just another epiphenomenon in which, if we go back "far" enough into the hard, cold world of biochemical processes, we will find the bedrock of computerlike determined neuronal connections. In fact, the will can be broken down into its essential components, motive-deliberation-choice-action, in such a way that it can hardly be said to be free (Sauvayre 1995). But then what we refer to as "freedom" is simply the feeling we have when we experience our actions as the result of determined processes that are *felt* to belong to our "self" (Dennett 1984). As I suggest later, this understanding of self drowns it into its determining context, and excises agency from the self. Dennett's soft determinism can be quite sophisticated in offering a more forgiving treatment of freedom, but the self-as-agent is still denied just as radically.

If freedom leads to the "breaking (of) . . . the causal chain of things . . . at any single point," Freud (1935, 32) concludes that one "has thrown over the whole scientific outlook of the world." If freedom threatens the very foundations of science, we can understand why it might be essential to deny it radically, whether one's approach is one of hard or soft determinism. While this radical rejection of freedom is often justified as a response to overblown visions of an individual's self-directed autonomy, it might also be worth wondering if part of the alleged incompatibility between freedom and the deterministic scientific outlook comes from an overly rigid vision of the causal chain.

I will briefly mention important scientific developments, linked to notions such as chaos, incompleteness, indeterminism, and unpredictability, that loosen the rigidity of the causal chain of traditional deterministic models as articulated by Freud and reduce its scope as well. In particular, Godel's incompleteness theorem in mathematics (Nagel and Newman 1958) and quantum indeterminacy in physics have been interpreted as debunking the linear and unidimensional notion of determinism that radically denies the possibility of freedom. For instance, in his study of the applicability of quantum mechanics to brain functioning, Satinover (2001, 7) suggests that "the human brain . . . has evolved a unique structure that harnesses subatomic 'choice,' concentrates it, and amplifies it upward, scale by scale, taking advantage . . . of the strange fact of 'chaos'" so that "the machinery of brain might prove the illusion, mind and will a more foundational reality." Also, studies of what are referred to as the *limitative theorems*, which include Godel's incompleteness theorem, has led DeLong (1970) to conclude that, due to the requirements inherent in any scientifically relevant operationalization (no matter how complex the operational definitions are), the process reveals an aspect of reality that it cannot apprehend, that escapes its scope. So "there is an incommensurability between reality and our ability to understand it completely, . . . no nonpoetic account of the totality of which we are part can be adequate" (p. 226). While the extent of these conclusions are hotly debated (Hofstadter 1979), they do address the claims of comprehensiveness and solidity of the causal chain that automatically make free will a categorical impossibility. Admittedly, these scientific developments are in no way "evidence" of freedom, yet they suggest that the existence of a phenomenon (freedom) that resists being put into the language of a formal system (determinism) cannot be questioned solely on the grounds that it would overthrow the scientific outlook as a whole.

As I try to show below, it is possible to use a language that does justice to the claims of freedom without contradicting the foundations of a deterministic science. If the language of a rigid determinism is maintained, whether hard or soft, all clinical efforts to enhance choice are correctly seen as fostering nothing more than an illusion, even if that illusion can be seen as "healthy" and "productive" (Knight 1946; Lefcourt 1973). If that is indeed the case, the therapeutic endeavor should then be viewed with extreme suspicion, since its aim is to foster an illusion. Where Knight and Lefcourt see something productive and healthy, others might correctly see oppressiveness and subtle coercion.

Is it possible to maintain the claims of agency without necessarily "throw[ing] over the whole scientific outlook of the world," as Freud believed? Yes, but only if we can move beyond the thinking that underlies that exclusionary perspective.

Analytical and Dialectical Thinking

The attempt to "locate" agency, and the self, among and within the objects that inhabit a world that can be "analyzed" is itself part of the problem. Having enough "room" for freedom assumes an objective world that can therefore only be inhabited by disparate objects. Nagel (1986) points out that the "agency dilemma" is tied to the classic philosophical subject-object split. As objects, "we" are no more free than billiard balls being knocked about the pool table, but as selves we are agents, authors of our lives—unless of course the self is made into just another billiard ball.

A world of disparate objects requires a certain kind of thinking, which Harris (1987) refers to as "formal." Formal thinking automatically engineers a world of objects that can be formally analyzed. In other words, each kind of reality is predicated on the kind of thinking used to apprehend it. Analytical thinking can only make sense of a world of analyzable objects, and whatever is not an analyzable object either does not exist or must be transformed into one. To apprehend things of a different nature, Harris suggests different kinds of thinking—one of which he calls "dialectical," consistent with the Hegelian dialectic.

In a dialectical world, things do not exist as objects, rather they "interexist" (Sauvayre and Auerbach 1990, 226). In such a world, we cannot talk of billiard balls slamming into each other, nor is it possible to see vectors being cleanly summed to provide a resultant force and direction. Things do not exist as discrete and separate entities, hence the notion of "interexistence." As we saw earlier, Patrick interexisted with others, most notably his family, in endlessly fascinating and complex ways. At first, he tried to get as far away as he could from his parents, only to find that the further he fled, the more they were present. As he began to appreciate all the ways he interexisted with them, the more he felt himself become independent from them. Finally, when he owned his independence, he could then come closer to them and rediscover points of genuine contact that energized his unique creativity. The person of Patrick, his self, is best understood as a movement to and from the context (i.e., parents and so on) within which Patrick lives, but that does not define him completely. The more he came to own himself as the product of his context, the more "he" became a relevant part of that determining context. The definition of Patrick's self, of Patrick, is in the back-and-forth movement. Perhaps a more accurate term would be *selfing*, so as to avoid the static connotations of *the self*.

Part of the problem in discussing the nature of this experience is the language we use. For example, the term *self* may suggest an entity to which there is a center, a center that would belong to a world of disparate objects, and those who call for the "death of the subject" rightfully point out important problems with this notion of the self. If the self is thought of as an entity, perhaps even with a "center" or "core," then any proper analysis will eventually crack this entity into its component parts if the analysis goes in the direction of the microlevel, and if the analysis goes in the direction of the macrolevel, then the self becomes just one billiard ball among others. Whether the context is micro or macro, the self essentially disappears. But we should not lose the notion of "being oneself" by throwing out that of "having a self." Postmodern approaches correctly throw away the notion of "*having* a center," but in my opinion they too often also lose the crucial notion of "*being* centered" as an organizing principle. "Being centered" is a movement, a delicate balance or oscillation to and from one's context. Analytical thought, in order to make "sense" of this, transforms "being oneself" into "having a self" and "being centered" into "having a center," and then loses, or destroys, the very experience that inspires these terms to begin with. A dialectical world does not deny or eradicate the world of objects but reconfigures it. And it is in this kind of worldview that dialectical thought permits that freedom moves about.

The dialectical perspective I am describing is represented in the philosophy of Maurice Merleau-Ponty (1908–1961) and of Henri Bergson (1859–1941), who took on the challenge of scientific determinism, analytical thinking, and freedom. Staking a ground between freedom and determinism, between subject and object, and between self and context, they are good examples of the existential-phenomenological tradition that, in my opinion, is best suited to explicating agency (Frie 2002).

Merleau-Ponty (1966) devoted a great deal of attention to the subject-object split, and like Nagel, he saw it as a problem for freedom. He explains that if the object is privileged over the subject, then any study of subjective activity (the self) makes the subject disappear. That is how the self disappears in a world of vectors. But by the same token objects disappear if there is no subject to perceive them as such. Hence, object and subject must mutually hold each other in existence; they interexist. To hold this gestalt of dialectical interdependence, one cannot rely on "objective thought and its stable-companion, analytical reflection" (p. 454), which has artificially separated subject and object.

This gestalt applies to the self and its determining factors. The self does not stand apart from the determining factors (the vectors), but neither is it simply a part of them. Or, the self is *both* apart from them *and* a part of them. As Merleau-Ponty points out, "All explanations of my conduct in terms of my past, my temperament and my environment are therefore true, provided they be regarded not as separable contributions, but as moments of my total being" (p. 455). My self and these determining factors are therefore best seen not as separate but as an "inextricable tangle" (p. 454): a dialectic.

Maintaining this dialectical gestalt is essential, and it should be noted that Merleau-Ponty is careful not to privilege the subject at the cost of the object in the other direction. He takes to task those he feels have done just that, like Sartre. In a sense we can see what that might look like in a concrete example by going back to Patrick when he first left France. Patrick's bold moves came back to haunt him not because of their content, but because they were done at the cost of denying the significance of his determining context, as if the boldness of his decision and the strength of his will could simply wipe away his determinants. The subject, the free self, the agent, can only assert himself or herself in the context of the determining factors that give freedom the traction it needs to move through life. As Merleau-Ponty says, "What then is freedom? To be born is both to be born of the world and to be born into the world. . . . There is, therefore, never determinism and never absolute choice. I am never a thing and never bare consciousness" (p. 453).

It was precisely when Patrick began to recognize and accept his interdependency with his context that his freedom began to emerge. Only after he could see and feel himself to be the product of his parents, among other determining factors, could he begin to appreciate his interexistence with his parents and others. Only at this point could he be separate from them as well and be the emerging author of his life. As Merleau-Ponty puts it, "We choose our world and the world chooses us" (p. 454). Holding this gestalt can also help us make sense of the dilemma Gatch and Temerlin (1965) wrestled with, namely, that clinicians across the board look on the patient's past from a deterministic perspective but use the assumption of freedom when looking at the patient's present and future. Holding these contradictory claims simultaneously in a unified gestalt is an expression of dialectical thinking, even if it remains latent or unarticulated.

Henri Bergson (1959) similarly devoted much attention to the limitations of analytical thinking. He focused specifically on the notion of time and the confusion it brought to the issue of freedom, arguing that analytical thinking splits time into a sequence so that moments in time, and therefore moments in human action, can be lined up one after the other. Analytical or scientific time is linear and lends itself to the very spatial metaphor that is at the heart of the distortions of freedom: "The problem [of free will] is born out of the fact that we wish . . . to interpret simultaneity as a sequence, and transform the idea of freedom into a language in which it cannot be translated" (p. 166). The question then becomes, what language can do justice to the notion of freedom?

According to Bergson, studies on the presence, or absence, of freedom and of free will, have often analyzed human action as part of a causal chain of events that can be spatially laid out on a time line. For instance, "external" forces cause a specific arrangement of motives and thoughts, which in turn cause a decision, and finally an action. This would be a highly simplified version of Freud's "causal chain." Once this sequence is laid out, is it possible to locate freedom? If it were, the chain would have to be loosened enough for a degree of unpredictability to be inserted. But as is correctly argued, *from this perspective*, a chain is only as strong as its weakest link, and the introduction of a loose link would be equivalent to breaking the chain. In turn, since there is no such thing as an unbroken causal chain, what is thought of as a loose or fuzzy link is so simply because of the limited state of our understanding. Once our understanding catches up, we will accurately perceive the tight chain-link pattern; then unpredictability, and freedom, will disappear. But equating freedom to an unpredictable event that must break the causal chain to demonstrate its presence is predicated on retrofitting human action to a framework of analyzable entities. In this case, Bergson explains that time is broken down into equal segments (0, 1, 2, 3, . . .), hermetically sealed to each other and leaving no empty spaces—a phenomenon he refers to as "scientific time."

But human actions do not occur exclusively in an analyzable world progressing along scientific time. They also take place in what he refers to as "experienced time," which behaves very differently. Experienced time is a fluid process. It is not divisible the way scientific time is, not just in terms of precise measurements, but also in terms of gross divisions such as past, present, and future. As Bergson points out, "simultaneity" is a feature of experienced time that cannot be translated into a linear sequence. Past, present, and future collapse into the present. This is a common phenomenon easily observable in psychoanalysis or psychotherapy, where the past and the future of a patient change according to the changes in the narrative they are constructing, or according to the state of mind they are in.

Bergson approaches the question of freedom by suggesting that time must be rethought so that scientific time gives way to experienced time. In a world where events occur in experienced time, simultaneity, rather than being the absence of time, actually provides the foundation—the space—for truly human events, and therefore freedom, to unfold. In contrast, scientific time "squeezes" freedom out of existence. When scientific time lines up determining factors beginning in the past in a linear sequence that leads to a (determined) choice in the present, the error is the assumption that the determining factors exist separately from the agent. Freedom is distorted "as soon as we seek to account for a state of consciousness in impersonal terms, external to each other . . . because at the heart of the whole . . . they penetrated into each other and melted into each other" (p. 123).

It is important to note the similarity between Bergson's concept of "melting into each other" and Merleau-Ponty's image of an "inextricable tangle," both of which refer to the interexistence of what would otherwise be understood as disparate objects in formal thought. To help grasp the interexistence of subject and object, of mind and body, and of the self and the world, Merleau-Ponty uses the phrase "inextricable tangle," which evokes the image of things in space tied into a ball of string. What Bergson adds here is the element of time. If the world consists of objects tangled in space, then events involving these objects unfold in entangled time, simultaneity, whereas events occurring in a world of discrete entities happen in linear time.

In the world of discrete entities, the self must be an entity, a billiard ball, that fits into the causal chain of events, and whose attributes (size, shape, personality, and so on) can be adequately analyzed or broken down. In this world, if we view the self from the perspective of the pool table, its movements are nothing but the result of the combination of external forces exerted by other billiard balls, the shape, texture, and evenness of the pool table, and the internal attributes of the billiard ball. All of these constitute the determining factors, and these do not allow for any meaningful autonomy for the self, and failing that, the self loses its meaning and is rightfully viewed as an arbitrary construction imposed on a random arrangement of attributes.

The dialectical world leads to an alternative perspective on the self. The self is neither acted on by the world nor does it act on the world, or rather, as we saw with Merleau-Ponty, it both acts on the world and is acted on by the world. But if the self is a product of a world of discrete entities and determining factors, how can it stand outside of it in any autonomous way? As mentioned above, part of the problem is language. The term *self* seems to automatically evoke the notion of a discrete entity. But in a dialectical world, there are no discrete entities, only the movements of entangled ones, so it is best to think of the self as movement—a movement that cannot be analyzed as taking place *from* point A *to* point B in space and time, but a movement that *includes both* A *and* B in space and time. From this perspective, Merleau-Ponty's gestalt flows naturally. Because the self is entangled in the world of determining factors, its movements are both of the world and upon the world.

That gestalt is present for Bergson (1959) as well. The determining "motives, to the extent that they have reached sufficient depth, represent the soul in its entirety. . . . And the external manifestation of this internal state will be precisely what is called a free act since only the 'I' will be its author, since it will express the 'I' in its entirety" (p. 124), which Bergson calls the "fundamental 'I'" (p. 129). Again, it is important to note almost identical phrases between Merleau-Ponty's "total being" and Bergson's "'I' in its entirety" or "fundamental 'I.'" These phrases refer precisely to the entangled inclusion of the self and *all* of its determining context in the movement of the agent. To the extent that this movement incorporates all the relevant aspects of the determining context (i.e., Patrick's bond to his parents, and the like), the self is autonomous and determined.

This notion of self is crucial for the possibility of freedom, just as the fragmentation of the self makes it disappear both in theory and in experience. In other words, if one's theory allows only for a perspective on the self that can be broken down (i.e., analyzed) into discrete components, all of which can be traced to determining components, then freedom has no "room." The self is found interwoven in all of its components, or rather, to avoid the tendency to objectify the self, it should be said that the self *is* the interweav*ing* of all of its relevant components, and a "free decision" is a reflection of that totality. Bergson states that "it is from the soul in its entirety, in fact, that the free decision emanates; and the act will be all the more free, the more the dynamic sequence to which it attaches itself will tend to identify itself with the fundamental 'I'. . . . We are free when our actions emanate from our whole personality, when they express it, when they possess with it this undefinable resemblance that is sometimes found between the artist and his work of art" (p. 129).

Bergson's notion of the "I in its entirety" and Merleau-Ponty's notion of the "total being" are sharpened not just by their absence in the theoretical world of discrete objects, but also by their potential absence in the concrete world of experience. As described above, agency is an active movement that balances and includes all relevant determining elements. If one or more of these elements is denied, a state of imbalance ensues that results in being controlled by those factors that have been denied, and agency is an illusion. We can understand Patrick's various states of unfreedom, both when he lived in France and when he left France, as manifestations of having excluded parts of his determining context. For example, and at the cost of oversimplification, Patrick was ruled by his denial of his homosexuality when he lived in France, and he was ruled by the denial of his bond to his parents after he left France.

Bergson believes that we indeed spend most of our lives in a state of unfreedom, with our self attaching itself to one determining force or the other and borrowing, or leeching off of, an external set of meanings or life "choices": "Here is formed, at the heart of the fundamental 'I,' a parasitical 'I' which will continuously intrude on the other (and therefore on freedom). Many live their lives in this fashion, and die without having known true freedom" (p. 129). I would suggest that this is a useful way to understand concepts such as "false self" and "inauthenticity," and that this is why the apparently simple advice to "just be yourself" is actually a lifelong project.

In sum, both Bergson and Merleau-Ponty use a dialectical understanding of the world to account for freedom. Otherwise it cannot be found in the analytical versions of reality, where there is no "room" for the self as agent. The two notions of self and agency go hand in hand. The concept, and the experience, of one's self as dialectically intertwined with its determining factors are necessary to appreciate freedom in all its fullness. Freedom is precisely that movement between self and context. How might this movement be described more concretely?

Conclusion

Agency as Flow: Patrick Revisited

The development of my argument has grounded the notion of freedom in a dialectical world where the agent interexists with her context and its determining elements. This perspective is based on a specific notion of the self as a part of its context as well as apart from it. The self would not exist without the context that shapes it. But not only is the self not subsumed by its context, the self also shapes the context that shapes the self.

To expand on Bergson's and Merleau-Ponty's notions of the total being, or of the I-in-its-entirety, as belonging to the dialectical world, the self must be seen as an active tension, the tension of the othering process between itself and its context. Reification of this tension would otherwise return the self to the static world of objects, and would lead to the disappearance of freedom. We can therefore say that freedom is a manifestation of self through, and against, the Other; or rather, *freedom is self in action*. This is so both in the intellectual realm and in the experiential realm.

Patrick's rebellion was an attempt to escape the state of falseness he had been imprisoned in, a false self that was molded according to the needs of the family, social pressures, and the like. But he only traded a state of false existence for one of oppositional inexistence. Even if we consider the rebellion as part of a developmental trajectory, his self remained equally fragmented and unfree, and in neither case can it be said to truly be, to exist. It was the recognition of his interexistence that marked the emergence of his existence, of his self.

Interexistence should be understood as an activity that includes aspects of both Patrick's prerebellious and his rebellious states. His prerebellious state was a surrender to his context, while his rebellion was stuck in denial of that context. The activity of self could be described as the simultaneous acceptance of and resistance to his context. His postrebellious identification with both of his parents was markedly different from his unquestioned surrender but retained elements of it. So if acceptance without resistance collapses into surrender, then resistance without acceptance remains stuck in denial. The dialectical activity of the self, this "selfing," becomes part of the context as well, and the therapeutic relationship is correctly viewed as formative of the context, that in turn forms the self, that forms the context again. This "selfing" interplay is freedom. The two are for all intents and purposes interchangeable.

Freedom as movement resonates best with Patrick's emerging agency that eludes any attempt to capture it in a static frame. The emergence of self and the emergence of agency are both manifestations of this dialectical flow. Patrick's self developed through its active "interexistence" with his determining context, and his agency simultaneously grew through the recognition and acceptance of its limitations. Privileging one pole of the dialectic to the detriment of the other leads to the petrification of the dialectical flow, and to the disappearance of agency. For instance, Patrick's initial hubris of self and the denial of his determining context can be seen as leading to the paralysis that wiped out any sense of freedom and that brought him to therapy.

As we have seen, this is also the case conceptually. In a world consisting exclusively of discrete entities, the self is the equivalent of a billiard ball bumped around the pool table; the self is viewed as just another billiard ball and has no autonomy. Without autonomy, the self also loses any genuine meaning. Postmodern critiques appropriately call into question the notion of self as a discrete entity, but they often move on to declare the "death of the subject," and agency along with it. That would be appropriate only if one were to interpret the self as a discrete entity to begin with, which, as we have seen, does not provide the necessary conceptual grounding for any relevant understanding of selfhood, and of agency. If we view the self as a movement, it must possess some degree of autonomy. I would suggest we use the term *self-as-agent*, thus supplanting both *self* and *agency*.

A final parallel between the philosophical realm and lived experience should be noted. An important point in the intellectual debate has been the impossibility of "locating" and "finding" freedom in a world of disparate objects. The same applies experientially where the search for freedom must be accompanied by a "letting go," just as the paradoxical simultaneity of acceptance and resistance marks the emergence of the self.

Patrick's initial fight for his freedom was a significant improvement over the inauthentic life of surrender he had previously been living. He fought against oppressive forces and parents who were his context. But, as we saw, fighting it only strengthened it, and trying to flee from it only sharpened its internal grip. Patrick's search for freedom seemed futile precisely because his struggle was confined to a world of hard, disparate objects.

It was only once Patrick was able to reconfigure his world from one of disparate objects to one of connections that new possibilities opened up and that his "fundamental I" emerged. This transition suggests the notion of a developmental trajectory for agency (Gentile 2001) that would be expressed through changes both in relating to the world (from resistance to acceptance) and in ways of thinking (from analytical to dialectical). The psychoanalytic journey often carries the hopes of reaching destinations such as "cure," "self-understanding," and "self-realization," but the plain discovery is that these goals are at best only partially reached, that the journey is riddled with compromises, and that, in the end, one winds up not far from where one started. But that is precisely the whole difference. Once one gives up on the endlessly complicated detours of false selves and inauthentic living, the life project to "be oneself" brings us back, one hopes, to one's self.

References

Bergson, H. 1959. Essai sur les données immédiates de la conscience. Paris: Presses Universitaires de France.

DeLong, H. 1970. *A profile of mathematical logic*. Reading, Mass.: Addison-Wesley.

Dennett, D. 1984. *Elbow room*. Cambridge, Mass.: MIT Press.

Freud, S. 1935. *A general introduction to psychoanalysis*. New York: Liveright Press.

Freud, S. 1949. *The Ego and the Id*. London: Hogarth Press.

Freud, S. 1953. *The interpretation of dreams*. London: Hogarth Press.

Frie, R. 2002. Modernism or postmodernism? Binswanger, Sullivan, and the problem of agency. *Contemporary Psychoanalysis* 38(4):635–674.

Gatch, V and Temerlin, M. 1965. Belief in psychic determinism and the behavior of the psychotherapist. *Review of Existential Psychology and Psychiatry* 5:16–25.

Gentile, J. 2001. Close but no cigar: The perversion of agency and the absence of thirdness. *Contemporary Psychoanalysis* 37(4):623–654.

Guntrip, H. 1969. *Schizoid Phenomena, Object Relations, and the Self*. N.Y.: I.U.P. Press.

Harris, E. 1987 *Formal, transcendental, and dialectical thinking*. Albany, N.Y.: SUNY Press.

Hofstadter, D. 1979. *Gödel, Escher, Bach*. New York: Vintage.

James, W. 1956. *The will to believe (and other essays)*. New York: Dover.

Knight, R. 1946. Determinism, freedom, and psychotherapy. *Psychiatry* 9:251–262.

Lefcourt, H. 1973. The functions of the illusion of control and freedom. *American Psychologist* 28:417–425.

Merleau-Ponty, M. 1966. *Phenomenology and perception*. Trans. C. Smith. London: Routledge and Kegan Paul.

Nagel, E., and Newman, J. 1958. *Godel's proof*. New York: New York University Press.

Nagel, T. 1986. *The view from nowhere*. New York: Oxford University Press.

Satinover J. 2001. *The quantum brain*. New York: Wiley.

Sauvayre, P. 1995. On the dialectics of agency. *Journal of Theoretical and Philosophical Psychology* 15(2):144–160.

Sauvayre, P., and Auerbach, C. 1990. Free will, identity, and primary creativity. *New Ideas in Psychology* 8(2):221–230.

Skinner, B. F. 1971. *Beyond freedom and dignity*. New York: Vintage.

7 Dimensions of Agency and the Process of Coparticipant Inquiry

John Fiscalini

The concept of psychological agency, with its implications of personal responsibility, unique individuality, and free will, has had a complicated and controversial history in philosophical inquiry, psychological theory, and clinical praxis. This chapter examines the problematic of agency from the perspective of the emerging clinical paradigm of coparticipant inquiry in contemporary psychoanalytic theory and practice. To account for the role of agency in lived experience, I argue that it is necessary to move beyond the one-person psychology of classical psychoanalysis and the two-person psychology of interpersonal psychoanalysis, both of which undervalue agency as a relevant clinical concept. Instead, I articulate the role of agency as a guiding clinical principle in the paradigm of coparticipant inquiry. This paradigm pays particular attention to the personal, interpersonal, and multidimensional experiences of the self and views the self and agency as inextricably linked. The therapeutic importance of psychological agency is elaborated with the use of a clinical case example, as are the curative roles of personal responsibility and interpersonal responsiveness. The chapter begins with an examination of contrasting perspectives on the question of agency within the history of psychoanalysis.

Agency in Contrasting Clinical Models

For some psychoanalytic theorists of an experiential or existential sensibility, psychological agency represents a psychic given: the inborn and inalienable human capacity to originate psychological experience and action. This agentic perspective views the individual as fundamentally proactive and self-determining, as inherently imaginative and uniquely creative. From this analytic perspective, the exercise of one's will is central to the selfic generation of new experience and to the spontaneous expression of one's singular psychology.

This proactive view of psychic agency stands in sharp contrast to the dismissive formulations of those psychological and psychoanalytic theorists who reject the concept of psychic agency and unique individuality. Consider, for example, the behaviorist theories of B. F. Skinner (1971) and the positivist interpersonal psychoanalytic concepts of Harry Stack Sullivan (1940, 1954). Both evidence a Lockean tabula rasa view of the individual as essentially reactive, determined and conditioned by his or her psychological and social surround, defined, as it were, by others. One's self is born, thus, in the psychological and moral judgments of significant others.

Historically, two clinical models, representing vastly different and incompatible therapeutic sensibilities, have dominated psychoanalytic praxis. This was marked, in the early years, by the clinical ascendancy of the classical paradigm—the impersonal, nonparticipant analyst as "objective" mirror. This is the model of analytic inquiry prescribed by Freud ([1912] 1959) and practiced most widely by classical or neoclassical analysts. The clinical hegemony of orthodox psychoanalytic theory and practice, however, was swept aside by the revolutionary "interpersonal turn" (sometimes called "relational turn") in psychoanalysis. This tectoniclike shift in psychoanalysis from a drive theory and impersonal technique to an interpersonal therapy and relational theory gave rise to the second paradigm—the interpersonal or relational analyst as intersubjective participant-observer.

These two major psychoanalytic perspectives differ in highly significant ways, yet they are similar in an important respect. Both reject or discount the concept (and therapeutic value) of psychological agency and free will. Freud believed that all experience and behavior is determined by prior causes. Psychic determinism, born in the play and push of instinctual drive, is viewed as a fundamental feature or characteristic of the psychoanalytic situation. Freud ([1924] 1962, 112) explicitly and categorically stated that the "deeply rooted belief in psychic freedom and choice . . . is quite unscientific and must give ground before the claims of a determinism which governs mental life." Thus, so much for agency and free will, which are portrayed as illusory concepts, figments of our defensive need to feel powerful and to deny our limitations and limits. For the reactionary theorist, psychological agency is a defensive mirage, an illusion.

This psychoanalytic sensibility is paralleled in the therapeutic conceptions of Sullivan. The primary architect of interpersonal psychoanalytic theory and its most influential theorist, Sullivan (1940) explicitly repudiated the notion of personal agency and the will. He was adamant in his belief that

> a great deal of time and effort is wasted in discussion of will power, choice, and decision. These three terms which refer to products of acculturation in the home, endure and are functionally very important because they are potent terms of rationalization in our culture. . . . I know of no evidence of a force or power that may be called will, in

contradistinction to the vector addition of integrating tendencies . . . not interventions of some sort of personal will-power. . . . Decision, about which many patients have much trouble—their indecisiveness—is intimately connected with the illusion of choice, in turn entangled with dogmatic assertions of "freedom of the will." (p. 188)

Sullivan also was critical of what he called the "delusion of unique individuality." Moreover, he defined personality as the "hypothetical entity which we posit to account for interpersonal relations." He goes on to say: "That there are particular human lives, each with a unique career line, I no more deny than I do the fact that I am a particular person who has a particular dog . . . [but] the immutably private in my dog and in me will always escape the methods of science" (pp. xi–xii). Not true, have replied such thinkers as the philosopher of science Anthony Moore (1984), and the influential interpersonal psychoanalyst Benjamin Wolstein (1981, 1997). Sullivan's positivist dismissal of agency and unique individuality was, according to Moore, a misreading of Percy Bridgman's (1935) operationalism.

In striking contrast to the classical and to the traditional interpersonal psychoanalytic rejection of the concept of psychological agency, European analysts identified with the existential-phenomenological analytic tradition embraced such concepts as will, agency, freedom, and responsibility and emphasized their therapeutic importance in the practice of *Daseinsanalysis*—the psychological analysis of our existential condition, or our "being-in-the-world." Concepts of agency, responsibility, freedom, and will, spurned by traditional analysts, were placed at the very center of clinical inquiry by the philosophically oriented existential analysts. These otherwise neglected concepts are primary in the clinical writings of such early existential European analysts as Binswanger (1964), Jaspers (1963), and Boss (1963), who carried forward the therapeutic implications of such existential-phenomenological philosophers as Heidegger ([1927] 1962), Sartre ([1943] 1956), Buber ([1921] 1970), and Merleau-Ponty ([1945] 1963). This clinical approach is, of course, grounded in the insights of Nietzsche ([1873] 1954), Kierkegaard ([1844] 1944), and Husserl ([1913] 1962), who might be considered the spiritual and philosophical forebears of contemporary humanistic and existential therapy and its agentic study of the human psyche.

These new and fresh existential and phenomenological ideas and approaches were brought, almost single-handedly, to the United States by the existentially oriented American interpersonal analyst Rollo May (May, Angel, and Ellenberger 1958). They gained some popularity in North America during the 1960s. Many in the psychoanalytic world adopted or adapted some existential concepts, incorporating them into their practice as best they could. The existential-phenomenological perspective had more of an impact among analysts of an interpersonal or broadly relational bent. It had less influence on classical or neoclassical analysts. Existential-phenomenological theories held much in common with those of the humanistic movement in psychology, described by some as the "third force" in psychology (the other two being behaviorism and Freudian psychoanalysis). With time, its influence and popularity waned; the force of existential-humanistic concepts began to fade, although they left their mark on many therapists. Some interpersonal analysts welcomed these new ideas on agency and the will as complementary to their own. Yet for many analysts, particularly those in the mainstream, existential and phenomenological procedures have become a forgotten language, a neglected and foreign set of ideas. Existential-phenomenological analysis seems to have had its day. The relative neglect of agency in North American psychoanalysis seems to mirror May's (1967, 1969) criticism of the widespread loss of a sense of self and agency in our modern society. Nevertheless, existential psychology continues to analytically inform those who are open to its singular ideas and practices. Perhaps this openness bespeaks a potential interest in *coparticipant* analytic concepts of agency and will, which I discuss later in this chapter.

It sometimes seems to me that the arguments against the freedom of will, become, in their strident determinism, an obsessive pursuit of some kind of universal order. I view agency and will as psychic givens, self-evident and axiomatic realities. Without these twin givens, how do we account for human creativity, spontaneity, intuition, responsibility, or any kind of personal forward thrust? Perhaps an answer, or partial answer, lies in an acceptance of our paradoxical nature—that our behavior and experience are both determined and free.

Agency and the Self

Psychological agency, or one's view of it, is linked to one's implicit or explicit psychological concept of the "I" and "me"—the working theory of the nature of the self. The various psychoanalytic conceptions of the psychological self take on specific theoretical and clinical significance. See, for example, the selfic conceptions of Fromm (1947; Fromm, Suzuki, and DeMartino 1960); Horney (1950); Sullivan (1940, 1954); Rogers (1951); Kohut (1971, 1977); Winnicott (1958); Mitchell (1988); and Fiscalini (2004).

For the psychoanalyst, as for any close observer of the human psyche, the notion of the self—the "I" or "me"—is critical to the understanding of human experience and behavior. The psychological study of the self traditionally has divided into the study of the self-as-proactive-process (*self as agent*) or the self-as-reflexive-social-experience (*self-representation or self-image*). Theorists have tended to focus their study on one or the other of these defining aspects of clinical inquiry. Those selfic processes that are seen as self-as-agent are designated proactive parts of the ego (the "I"), whereas those that form parts of the self-concept or self-image are referred to as reflexive aspects of the self or "me." The self-as-reflected-appraisal, or "me," is made up of the opinions and evaluations of others. This reflexive self-as-object comprises what I call the *interpersonal self*, the socially defined self—in William James's (1890) phrase, the "social self," or what we could call the *other-within-the-self*.

In sharp contrast, the self-as-proactive-process refers, in rough measure, to that broad set of selfic processes and potentials that I call the *personal self*. This includes the innately given psychological potentialities and self-fulfilling capacities of the individual. The personal self includes aspects of James's "spiritual self" and "pure ego."

This division of the self into self-as-subject and self-as-object reflects a central controversy in psychological and psychoanalytic theories of the self—whether the psychic self is socially constructed or a personal psychic given. Is the self uniquely individual? Simple or complex? A multidimensional dynamism, both personal and interpersonal in nature?

Foremost among the psychological self theorists of his time, James' comprehensive chapter on the self in his 1890 *Principles of Psychology* still stands as a classic treatise on the subject. A generation later, James's fellow American, the renowned psychiatrist and interpersonal theorist Harry Stack Sullivan, was influenced and informed by James's pragmatic philosophy and democratic spirit. Sullivan was also profoundly influenced by the American thinker Charles H. Cooley's (1902) looking-glass concept of the self and by the American social philosopher George Mead's (1934) view of the reflexive self as socially constructed. In the process, Sullivan developed what came to be the most extensive and detailed study of the psychoanalytic self as an interpersonal phenomenon.

Sullivan's field perspective on the self as emergent communal (interpersonal) experience is, in my estimate, the psychoanalytic theory of the self that is the most sophisticated, though one-sided, statement of an "agentless" theory of psychoanalytic inquiry. This social or interpersonal theory of the self, however, only satisfies half of what is needed for a fully rounded psychoanalytic concept of the self. A sound theory of psychoanalytic coinquiry, practiced rigorously and comprehensively, requires a complementary notion of an individual or personal self—a concept, in other words, of an irreducible human striving to fulfill one's unique psychic promise.

The Multidimensional Self

The evolution of new forms of participant or coparticipant practice, with their emphasis on a therapeutic dialectic of the personal (human singularity) and the interpersonal (human similarity), calls for a new, multidimensional concept of the self. As I have previously argued (Fiscalini 2004), the self may be conceptually divided into five significantly different domains of selfic motivation, functioning, and self-threat. These are the sensual, personal, interpersonal, personalized, and relational selves (and their specific self threats are, respectively, fear, dread, anxiety, apprehension, and loneliness). Each selfic dimension circumscribes a major aspect of the psychological self and is complexly interrelated with the other dimensions. All the dimensions are clinically important, but I focus in this chapter on the therapeutically pivotal dialectic of the personal and the interpersonal selves and their diametrically opposed relationships to psychological agency.

The multidimensionality outlined here, which is not to be confused with the question of a multiplicity of variable self states or multiple selves, reconciles, or at least accepts, the paradox that we are all simultaneously communal and individual beings. From birth, we are embedded in, and part of, a series of social fields of experience and behavior, and yet always, in some way or ways, uniquely individual. All of us, as Sullivan (1940, 1954) and later Kohut (1971, 1977) so well understood, are inescapably part of others; yet, in deeply meaningful ways, we are also, as Fromm (1947) emphasized, apart, inviolably separate. We all live in solitude as well as in contact with others, each of us seeking an optimal balance of solitude and connection—of the personal and the interpersonal.

The Interpersonal Self

Sullivan, like Cooley and Mead before him, viewed the self as a social product. The self, for Sullivan, is born in interaction with others, shaped by the inherent human need to avoid anxiety. For Sullivan, the self encompasses all living that is known to consciousness as well as the vast system of unconscious defensive processes, or security operations, which keep the phenomenal or personified self intact and unchanged. This extensive set or system of reflexive psychic processes and defensive, self-protective patterns constitutes the selfic domain of the interpersonal self.

The interpersonal self, as noted previously, cannot, by itself, provide a theoretical foundation for a full coparticipant psychoanalytic inquiry. It does not account for concepts of will, agency, intention, and other proactive selfic processes essential to a coparticipant psychoanalytic inquiry. Although the interpersonal self articulates a central dimension of coparticipant inquiry, a full appreciation of the radical possibilities of coparticipant inquiry requires a concept of those creative and proactive psychic processes and potentials that I call the *personal self.*

The Personal Self

The dynamism of the personal self comprises that set of psychic dynamics, processes, motives, actions, and goals that are marked by the human reach for self-fulfillment and self-expression (Fiscalini 1990). The personal self may be defined as the innate and immediate proactive selfic striving to live out one's unique individuality. It includes the drive to develop and express one's originality—one's own psychological powers and capacities, personal and interpersonal.

The personal self defines the *personal source of one's experience and psychological action—feeling, thinking, wishing, willing. It is the self-moving originator of psychic experience*. The personal self represents the innate and proactive striving to actualize our true nature, selfness, or uniqueness. It is the source or set of processes that form the beginnings of creativity, spontaneity, play, and those processes we call will—intending, determining, choosing, deciding, initiating. It is the *source of psychological agency*. The personal self encompasses both one's active, organizing self (the selfic set of processes that operationalize or organize mental representation and psychic and behavioral activity) and one's proactive, creative self (all those processes involved in the reach for self-fulfillment).

The group of processes that I call the personal self refers to each person's *agentic* and self-generative striving to fulfill his or her true being, or what Fromm (1947; Fromm, Suzuki, and DeMartino 1960) calls the "active center of the self," what Wolstein (1981, 1983, 1997) calls the "I" or "first-personal, uniquely individual self," and what Winnicott (1958) and others call the "true self." As previously noted, it includes such processes as creativity, activity, curiosity, play, and elements of what Farber (1966) calls "will." The personal self and the selfic processes it comprises are recognized in the humanistic thrust of Leslie Farber's (1966), Rollo May's (1967), and Erwin Singer's (1965) writings; in Erich Fromm's (1947) ideas on individuality and self-realization; and perhaps most prominently, in Benjamin Wolstein's (1981, 1983, 1997) extensive and detailed studies of "first-personal processes," or "unique individuality."

The human psyche, in its selfic aspects, is characterized by a fundamental dialectic between its communal and its uniquely individual dimensions, and between its strivings for social adaptation and for self-fulfillment and self-expression. This dialectical nature of the psyche, of human selfness and relatedness, is reflected in the clinical dialectics of those dynamisms that I call the *interpersonal self* and the *personal self*, the universal search for interpersonal security and for personal creativity.

The personal self comprises processes of will, autonomy, agency, and creativity, among other aspects of unique individuality. It thus represents the self-subject side of the psyche. Though it may be developmentally influenced by interpersonal experience, its core is inviolably personal and private, uniquely individual and nonrelational. Our inborn psychological potentials and proclivities interact with our social surround from the first moments of life. We individually exist, from the very beginning, within a social field, but we are not reducible to that field. Our personal selves, like our interpersonal selves, represent fundamental and irreducible aspects of our complex and multifaceted psyches.

In the coparticipant clinical situation, there is a continuous dynamic tension and dialectic between our forward-moving or "progressive" needs for fulfillment, satisfaction, and love and our limiting or "conservative" needs for personal orientation and interpersonal security. The tensions of loneliness, dread, and fear represent selfic needs that are inherently contradictory to those that lead to anxiety and apprehension.

Clinical Implications of the Personal Self

In the psychoanalytic situation, when the analyst or therapist is open to this psychic dimension in the patient, he or she may hear strivings for personal fulfillment, where previously only manifestations of anxiety, loneliness, or fear were felt. What, from the perspective of interpersonal security (the interpersonal self), may seem like psychopathology, defensiveness, or resistance may, from the perspective of personal fulfillment, be understood as idiosyncratic moves toward individuation, autonomy, and personal growth.

Patients' strivings for self-fulfillment may be seen in creative and original formulations or perceptions of themselves and others; in developing abilities to bear anxiety, guilt, grief, disappointment, and other distressing emotions and experiences; in increasing capacities to be alone in the presence of the analyst; and in the effort to open up to the analyst and to take in the analyst's formulations and interactive invitations.

In the analytic situation, as in life, thwarted striving for self-fulfillment is evidenced in various defensive experiences or behaviors. The need for self-fulfillment, a human imperative, often finds symptomatic expression in wistful longings for self-achievements of one sort or another; efforts to restore self-esteem; feelings of irritability and rage; depression; a vague and persistent sense of uneasiness; and various addictive or compulsive ways of trying to simulate a sense of aliveness and to compensate for, or mask, pervasive feelings of inner constriction, emptiness, or deadness.

The broadening of psychoanalytic theory to include a self-fulfilling and agentic dynamic has important therapeutic implications. First of all, it contributes to a greater and more explicit appreciation of patients' therapeutic needs for relational affirmation of their strivings to actualize their psychic potentials. Such relational interventions may be technically intended and explicit, but they often happen implicitly and unconsciously, in the inadvertent therapeutic relatedness that defines the *living-through* process, which subtends the working-through process (Fiscalini 1988). This sort of experience may account, in part, for unexpected therapeutic successes that would otherwise be improbable given the patient's seemingly unfavorable therapeutic attitude or aptitude (as, for example, a limited receptivity to or capacity for interpretive insight).

The explicit inclusion of a self-fulfilling motive in psychoanalytic theory expands the range of clinical interpretation in the coparticipant psychoanalytic situation. With an expanded interpretive ear, the coparticipant analyst may discern previously unrecognized agentic self-actualizing themes in the patient's narrative reports as well as in their interactive coparticipation in the analytic dyad.

Consider, for example, the following clinical vignette. The analyst returns from a brief holiday, and in the following session the patient, Mrs. A, expresses a strong curiosity about the analyst's holiday experiences and her relation to her husband and children during the vacation—where she and her family went; what they did, what they liked and did not like, how this differed or was similar to previous holidays, and so on. The patient, married and with children herself, has exhibited a similar passionate curiosity on a few other, seemingly unrelated, occasions. It is not new behavior, but relatively rare. The curiosity has an intrusive and insistent tone, which suggests a defensive dynamic, but at the same time, it has an alive quality to it. How are we to understand the patient's curiosity? A separation anxiety? An expression of dependency? Jealousy? Hostile envy? As a defensive sexual derivative, perhaps a strongly activated primal curiosity? Or is it a controlling wish to know secrets about the analyst? Perhaps it represents a wish to know how the analyst enjoys herself and relates to her family on such occasions so the patient can model her own behavior; the analyst knows that the patient tends to be symbiotic and overly dependent and looks to others to tell her how to live. Or is it all a defensive evasion of some other, more anxious, analytic topic? Or a way to put the analyst on the defensive? These and other defensive uses of the patient's curiosity are all possible, and on the basis of previous work, some seem probable. But if we shift from the perspective of interpersonal security, or self-protective defensiveness, we can also view the patient's behavior from the standpoint of a drive toward relational intimacy, a wish to know about the analyst and to know who the analyst is. Perhaps the intrusive and insistent quality bespeaks a defensive fear that the patient's transferential love of the analyst or interest in her will not be accepted. Is her curiosity, then, an essentially timid, if defensively aggressive, form of love? A bid for closeness? The analyst (perhaps relaxed by her vacation) is uncharacteristically more relaxed and open in answering several of the patient's questions. Has the patient, emboldened, in turn, by the analyst's openness, become more open herself, freer than usual, momentarily less inhibited in asking the questions she has yearned to ask? Is the patient thus seeking a transferential intimacy, a relational closeness, rather than acting in a distancing and defensive resistance?

The analyst is concerned that she is abetting a defensive curiosity on the part of the patient, and wonders about her possible countertransferential collusion in this. But is the analyst's countertransference of a different nature—is it, instead, her inhibition, her tightness, in answering questions on previous occasions? Has the analyst, in fact, been involved in a chronic transference-countertransference replay of a parental dampening of the patient's childhood aliveness and capacity to wonder? Has the analyst countertransferentially contributed to a characteristic and defensive incuriosity on the part of the patient? The analyst notes her own previous incuriosity about the patient's experience of curiosity, or more broadly, of the patient's relationship to her imagination. The analyst notes, with a sharpened awareness, the patient's general tendency to be incurious about herself and her life. The patient's fear of using her own psychic resources is experienced by the analyst with a vividness previously unfelt. The analyst becomes more curious about the patient's curiosity and its defensive and self-striving aspects. Why is the patient generally not curious about herself and her analytic participation? Has she simply been inhibiting her curiosity, fearful of expressing it? What are the conditions of her curiosity? What frees (or inhibits) this capacity? Or its expression? Perhaps the badgering tone of the patient's questioning hides a deeper and truer curiosity. The patient's curiosity, in other words, can now be seen as more than an instrumentality in the service of interpersonal security, relational intimacy, or sensual satisfaction. It also can be seen as the expression of a deep desire for psychic self-fulfillment.

An analytic awareness of psychic agency and the dynamism of the personal self contributes to a greater and more explicit sense of the patient as an analytic copartner, one far more psychically resourceful and therapeutically capable of collaborative and responsible coparticipatory inquiry than might be predicted by conservative neoclassical psychoanalysts who hold a regressive (and authoritarian) theory of motivation. Although the ability to do analytic work is highly individual, and conditioned by each patient's unique life experiences, the more progressive view of the individual as proactive, agentic shaper of his or her fate allows, I think, for a generally healthier, more optimistic, and more respectful view of the patient and his or her agentic capabilities. It allows for a more open, nonauthoritarian, and ultimately freer, concept of analytic inquiry.

An analytic appreciation of patients' innate needs for personal fulfillment facilitates, for example, the recognition of their desire and abilities to develop or define their own personal metapsychology. Or more radically, the coparticipatory viewpoint, with its inbuilt notion of the analytic centrality of the personal self (and psychological agency), supports the concept that patients and analysts may together form or create the methodology that works best for them, that suits their unique psychic capacities and necessities.

This view of the patient also emphasizes the patient's ultimate responsibility for his or her maladaptive and unfulfilling life. Thus, in the analytic situation, the patient is held responsible for the resistive aspects of his or her coparticipation, seen as more capable of working productively with therapeutic confrontation of any neurotic desires and defenses than is commonly thought. Consequently, the coparticipant analyst strongly encourages the patient to directly experience and explore the personal roots of his or her anxiety, even if it makes for an uncomfortable analytic experience. In other words, the notion of a personal (agentic) self supports a more direct, confrontive, and coparticipant analytic approach than is characteristic of more conservative or traditional analytic approaches to praxis.

Whereas the concept of an interpersonal self introduces the analytic themes of interpersonal influence and vulnerability, the concept of the personal, agentic, self provides the analytic themes of personal resilience and responsibility. In fact, without at least an implicit concept of personal agency, a psychoanalytic process could not be established. No matter how diminished one's awareness of agency may be, some sense of agency is required for analytic work, or for any kind of psychotherapy, for that matter. The emphasis in coparticipant inquiry is to strengthen the autonomous personal self (agency) rather than to reassure the insecure and other-directed interpersonal self. More is asked of the patient; consequently, more is found, and then given.

Premised on the concept of a personal self and a clinical dialectic between it and the dynamism of an interpersonal self, the coparticipant analytic approach maintains that patients carry within them the inner strength, psychic resources, and existential freedom to shape their own truths and future living. Our needs for self-fulfillment, like those for satisfaction and love, stand in inevitable conflict with those for interpersonal security and safety.

In their prolific and often eloquent writings on humankind's psychological dilemmas, the humanistic interpersonalists Erich Fromm and Rollo May repeatedly point to our fears of self-expression and individuation. Both point to our common existential plight—our essential aloneness, inescapable mortality, and ultimate powerlessness before nature—and to our need to create a personally meaningful relatedness to ourselves, others, and the world. This requires a dynamic concept of personal agency—of a capacity for proactive experience; in Arieti's (1972) words, a "will to be human."

On Coparticipant Inquiry

As noted earlier, clinical psychoanalysis has been dominated by two major clinical paradigms: the classical and the interpersonal models of inquiry. An evolutionary shift in clinical thought, however, has been slowly taking place, offering a new, and increasingly important, analytic perspective, which emphasizes the self-as-agent. This emerging third clinical paradigm, *coparticipant inquiry*, represents a new view of the analyst and his or her patient.

Coparticipant inquiry builds on and radically extends the clinical tenets of the previous psychoanalytic paradigms, especially those of analytic mutuality and psychic agency. This paradigm integrates the individualistic emphasis of classical theory and the social focus of participant-observation. As a unique form of clinical participation, coparticipant inquiry is defined by a radical emphasis on patients' and analysts' relational mutuality, psychic symmetry, coequal analytic authority, and the therapeutic use of immediate experience (Fiscalini 2004).

The concept of psychoanalytic mutuality, with its subthemes of interpersonal responsivity (or openness to influence) and personal responsibility (or psychic agency), first found expression in the radical practice of the Hungarian analyst Sandor Ferenczi. Though Ferenczi's experiments in "mutual analysis" ultimately proved unworkable (see Ferenczi [1931] 1988), his creative sense of a vital experiential psychoanalysis has become increasingly influential in contemporary psychoanalytic practice.

Coparticipant inquiry represents both a one-person and a two-person psychology. It avoids the reductive individualism of the classical paradigm, which traditionally has deemphasized the structuring impact of the analytic field and the therapeutic significance of field forces. Similarly, coparticipant inquiry avoids the reductive social determinism of the participant-observer paradigm, which as practiced, often has failed to take sufficient clinical account of unique individuality and human agency, and of will and personal responsibility. In fact, some theorists with an existential and experiential interpersonal sensibility (Frie 2002, 2003; Frederickson 2001, 2003; Mills 1999) have recently criticized relational and interpersonal analysts for their relative neglect of human will and agency. All psychoanalyses, however conceptualized, are coparticipatory integrations, always involving two unique individuals interrelated in a continuous and complex series of intersubjective transactions and mutual influences, each person contributing to and partly shaping the other's clinical experience (Ehrenberg 1992).

In brief summary, coparticipant inquiry is characterized by several clinical features: a view of the analytic situation as an interpersonal field; a focus on the analysis of personal agency and unique individuality; a view of analysts and patients as coanalysts continuously involved in the mutual analysis of their relationship; a radical individuation of interpretive myth and metaphor and of analytic method; a technically freer, more self-expressive, and spontaneous inquiry is supported. This includes, among myriad other therapeutic factors, an active use of the self; openness to the agentic; repudiation of mythic concepts of analytic neutrality and anonymity and acceptance of radical self-disclosure; and attention to the therapeutic promise of immediate experience, as opposed to the traditional focus on the therapeutic primacy of interpretation. These principles of coparticipant inquiry comprise a view of the analyst's expertise as residing, not in his or her "expert" knowledge of metapsychologically derived psychodynamics or institutionally determined "proper" technique, but in his or her capacity for facilitating and participating in an alive and imaginative inquiry.

The Interpersonal Field

The concept of the psychoanalytic situation as an interpersonal field is central to coparticipant theory. Patients and analysts are seen as interactively forming a therapeutic relationship marked by psychic symmetry, mutual influence, and relational reciprocity. In this shared experiential field, patients and analysts live out their loving and hating transferences and countertransferences, self-protecting resistances and counterresistances, confusing anxieties and counteranxieties, and maturing and centering relatedness. In their shared communicative and affective fields of experience, patient and analyst, in continuous agentic relation to one another, observe, analyze, and work through mutual problems and possibilities in living.

Psychological field theory, adapted from the late nineteenth-century physics of Faraday, Maxwell, and Herz, first found psychological expression in the early twentieth-century field-theoretical perceptual and psychological studies of the Gestalt school of Koffka (1935), Kohler (1947), and, later, in the personality studies of Kurt Lewin (1935). Implicit in much of contemporary thinking on psychoanalytic therapy, field theory historically found its earliest and most systematic presence in Sullivan's interpersonal psychoanalytic concepts. Thus, for contemporary interpersonal analysts, as for Sullivan, transference is seen as a field process. In fact, those contemporary analysts, interpersonal or otherwise, who practice a more radical form of coparticipant inquiry consider transference an inextricable part of a complex transference-countertransference matrix.

Thus, in coparticipant inquiry *both the analyst's and the patient's personalities are studied, by both patient and analyst.* Transference and countertransference are seen as mutually formed experiences, variable amalgams of the unconscious experience of both patient and analyst, rather than exclusively endogenous expressions of either coparticipant's closed intrapsychic world.

This view of transference and countertransference as field processes points to the general significance of "context" or "surround" in the assignment of meaning. Context is defined in manifold ways in coparticipant psychoanalytic inquiry. Any psychic act of the individual patient—a feeling state, an attitude, a pattern of behavior—may be seen in such contexts as the patient's personal and interpersonal history; the contemporary, or "here and now" interpersonal context; the pattern of previous sessions; the psychic reverberations and themes of the immediately preceding session; the anticipated next one; the pattern of intercurrrent extraanalytic events; and, of course, the situating cultural and historical values and ways of seeing and believing—the place, times, and prevailing belief systems in which this all happens. What is considered contextually relevant in any situation is, of course, itself contextually determined.

However, a psychoanalytic field emphasis on contextual analysis can lead to an excessive focus on the social or interpersonal environment and to a relative neglect of the individual and the intrapsychic. The field perspective, though clinically invaluable, runs the risk, when practiced to an interpersonal extreme, of reducing the individual to his or her relational participation. A rigid focus on contextual meaning leads to an overemphasis on the determinative effects, or "contextual impact," of social or psychological fields-of-force on their constituent coparticipants. A radical figure-ground methodology is emphasized: the part can *only* be understood by a study of the whole. From this one-sided perspective, to separate figure from ground, part from whole, is invariably to distort—events, processes, individuals can only truly be known contextually.

Without an implicit or explicit concept of agency and individuality, a field theory must, inevitably, regard patient or analyst as contextual victim—coercively "transformed" by the press of the surrounding field. With the atrophy of agency, influence becomes hypertrophied. All becomes a matter of the Other—of how "you" *make* "me" love, hate, fear, desire, and so on. Experience thus comes from without, rather than from within. Herein lies the danger of an overly interpersonalized or contextualized psychological study of another. Absent a theory of a personal self, psychoanalytic field theory becomes overcontextualized—the singularity or individuality of the patient and analyst gets lost in the field, as it were. And agency goes unaccounted for.

A rounded coparticipant inquiry requires an agentic concept of the "I," the person as an active, striving being. Of course, patient and analyst influence one another—continually so in fact. If this were not true, there would be no therapy. Analyst and patient, however, are neither determined nor defined by their mutuality—affected by, impacted on, influenced by it, but not determined by it. If this were not so, we would, in fact, confront psychological situationalism in the extreme. A full account of a comprehensive coparticipant inquiry requires a notion of active or proactive selfness. Coparticipant analysis, in its radical emphasis on patients' and analysts' expressive coparticipation in the therapeutic field, implies a concept of psychic centeredness, psychological agency, and personal singularity.

Dynamics of the Personal Self

Coparticipant inquiry, then, is characterized by a unique dialectic. On the one hand, coparticipant inquiry represents a radical interpersonal concept of *co*partnered inquiry. There is a ready appreciation of the centrality of field dynamics, and this is radically expressed in a form of mutual analysis. At the same time, coparticipant inquiry, in its more radical or comprehensive forms, is characterized by a complementary emphasis on the unique individuality of the analytic coparticipants. This personal focus, when integrated in an ongoing dialectic between the radically social and the uniquely individual, distinguishes this form of psychoanalytic inquiry.

Coparticipant psychoanalytic inquiry is premised on the dialectic of the dynamisms of the personal self and the interpersonal self. It represents *both* a one-person *and* a two-person psychology, rather than just a one-person psychology (as in Freudian orthodoxy) or a two-person psychology (as in most contemporary relational or interpersonal approaches).

The dynamism of the *interpersonal self*, as noted earlier, refers to that selfic domain or aspect of personality that arises out of a person's inherent need to socially adapt to the surrounding world of others. In Sullivan's phrase, the self—which I call the "interpersonal self"—represents the "sum of reflected appraisals" by emotionally significant others. This representational patterning of "me" (or various "me's") is, for Sullivan, the inevitable product, and the eventual producer, of social acculturation and adaptation, reflecting as it does, the universal human concern with social approval.

In sharp contrast, the dynamism of the *personal self* refers to the individual striving for self-realization or personal psychic fulfillment. It defines the uniquely individual and agentic proactive aspects of a person's selfness. Thus, the personal self brings to the coparticipant inquiry's interpersonal field philosophy an individualistic and "existential" (in the sense of experiential) focus on emergent agentic processes of will, choice, intention, self-determination, and the like.

This has obvious clinical implications for coparticipant practice and for the ways in which patients are viewed. The patient is not seen simply as the suffering, transferential injured child—the victim of unempathic circumstance—as many would have it. In coparticipant inquiry patients' interpersonal injuries and transferential fragility are noted and worked with; but, importantly, the patient is also seen as a resourceful and active being. Explicit recognition of the psychic dimension of the personal self, which Wolstein refers to as the "psychic center of the self," allows or encourages the analyst to look for and to facilitate the patient's awareness and articulation of his or her unique psychological powers and perspectives. This recognition of patients' (and analysts') personal selves, of their unique individuality and agentic capability, is vital to the clinical establishment of coparticipant inquiry. It leads, when fully and authentically practiced, to a more open, nonauthoritarian, and freer concept of inquiry.

Integral to a radical, comprehensive coparticipant inquiry is the notion that each member of the analytic dyad possesses a singular psychic selfness that actively seeks, however unconsciously, its own unique directions and development. It is the source, the psychic means or agency through which the patient (or analyst) generates clinical courage; faces fears; bears grief, guilt, anxiety, shame, and other dysphoric emotion; forms and formulates unique insights; and makes possible the working through and "living through" of transference and countertransference. This singular selfness, or individual uniqueness, is also the psychic source for one's "choice" of neurosis, and for one's neurotic "choices."

The concept of a personal self—the "I"—in dynamic relation to an interpersonal self—the "me"—also profoundly affects the contemporary analyst's concept of the intersubjective or interpersonal field. For the more conservative coparticipant analyst, unique individuality remains implicit, and the therapeutic focus is on the interactive interplay between analyst and patient and their mutual impact on one another. In other words, field forces and dyadic adaptation form the locus of therapeutic inquiry and study. In this form of coparticipant inquiry, the individual, in a sense, is reduced to the field. In a more developed, comprehensive form of coparticipant inquiry, involving the concept of a self-generative personal self, the uniquely individual strivings of the coparticipants are more complexly considered. The individual is not reduced to the dyadic field; nor, as in Freudian clinical orthodoxy, is the field reduced to the individual. In essence, it can be said that coparticipant inquiry represents the clinical marriage or merger of the interpersonal and personal selves—simultaneously aware of the individual and social dimensions of the human psyche.

In coparticipant inquiry, this sense of selfic origin, which we can know directly, immediate and unmediated, guides our analytic explorations and observations, which, in turn, result in consonant clinical actions, "chosen" spontaneously, and specifically for the singular analytic moment. The patient is seen as a therapeutic collaborator, capable of initiating or participating as a coequal in the mutual analysis of transference-countertransference phenomena. Therapeutic capability inevitably carries analytic responsibility. Patients are not only personally resourceful and interpersonally responsive (i.e., open to influence); they are also, in the final analysis, responsible for the success or failure of their therapy. In coparticipant inquiry, analysts and patients are held accountable for their experience and desires—for generating their unique anxieties and resistances. The coparticipant focus on patients' therapeutic capacities, and their attendant analytic responsibilities, ultimately derives from the coparticipant emphasis on patients' sense of agency, or personal selfness—that is, on our human capacity to make choices.

References

Arieti, S. 1972. *The will to be human*. New York: Quadrangle Books.

Binswanger, L. 1964. *Being-in-the-world*. New York: Basic Books.

Boss, M. 1963. *Psychoanalysis and Daseinsanalysis*. New York: Basic Books.

Bridgman, P. 1935. *The logic of modern physics*. New York: Macmillan.

Buber, M. 1970. *I and thou*. New York: Scribner. (Original work published 1923.)

Cooley, C. 1956. *Human nature and social order*. Glencoe, IL: Free Press. (Original work published 1902.)

Ehrenberg, D. 1992. *The intimate edge*. New York: Norton.

Ewen, R. 1993. *Theories of personality*. Hillsdale, N.J.: Erlbaum.

Farber, L. 1966. *The ways of the will*. New York: Basic Books.

Ferenczi, S. 1988. *The clinical diary of Sandor Ferenczi*. Trans. M. Balint and N. Z. Jackson. Cambridge, Mass.: Harvard University Press. (Original work published 1931.)

Fiscalini, J. 1988. Curative experience in the analytic relationship. *Contemporary Psychoanalysis* 24:125–141.

Fiscalini, J. 1990. On self-actualization and the dynamism of the personal self. *Contemporary Psychoanalysis* 26:635–653.

Fiscalini, J. 2004. *Coparticipant psychoanalysis: Toward a new theory of clinical inquiry*. New York: Columbia University Press.

Frederickson, J. 2001. There's something "youey" about you. *Contemporary Psychoanalysis* 36:587–617.

Frederickson, J. 2003. Eclipse of the person in psychoanalysis. In R. Frie, ed., *Understanding experience: Psychotherapy and postmodernism*. New York: Routledge.

Freud, S. 1959. Recommendations to physicians on the psycho-analytic method of treatment. In *Collected papers*, vol. 2, 323–333. New York: Basic Books. (Original work published 1912.)

Freud, S. 1962. A *general introduction to psychoanalysis*. New York: Washington Square Press. (Original work published 1924.)

Frie, R. 2002. Modernism or postmodernism? Binswanger, Sullivan, and the problem of agency in contemporary psychoanalysis. *Contemporary Psychoanalysis* 37:635–674.

Frie, R. 2003. *Understanding experience: Psychotherapy and postmodernism*. New York: Routledge.

Fromm, E. 1947. *Man for himself*. New York: Harper and Row.

Fromm, E., Suzuki, D. T, and DeMartino, R. 1960. *Zen Buddhism and psychoanalysis*. New York: Harper and Row.

Hall, C., and G. Lindzey. 1957. *Theories of personality*. New York: Wiley.

Heidegger, M. 1962. *Being and time*. London: SCM Press. (Original work published 1927.)

Horney, K. 1950. *Neurosis and human growth*. New York: Norton.

Husserl, E. 1962. *Ideas concerning a pure phenomenology and phenomenological philosophy*. New York: Collier. (Original work published 1913.)

James, W. 1890. *Principles of psychology*. New York: Holt, Rinehart and Winston.

Jaspers, K. 1963. *On the nature of psychotherapy*. Chicago: University of Chicago Press.

Kierkegaard, S. 1944. *The concept of dread*. Princeton, N.J.: Princeton University Press. (Original work published 1844.)

Koffka, K. 1935. *Principles of gestalt psychology*. New York: Harcourt.

Kohler, W. 1947. *Gestalt psychology*. New York: Liveright.

Kohut, H. 1971. *The analysis of the self*. Madison, Conn.: International Universities Press.

Kohut, H. 1977. *The restoration of the self*. Madison, Conn.: International Universities Press.

Lewin, K. 1935. *A dynamic theory of personality*. New York: McGraw-Hill.

Macmurray, J. 1992. *The self as agent*. New York: Humanity Books. (Original work published 1957.)

May, R. 1967. *Psychology and the human dilemma*. New York: Norton.

May, R. 1969. *Love and will*. New York: Norton.

May, R., Angel, E., and Ellenberger, H. 1958. *Existence: A new dimension in psychiatry and psychology*. New York: Basic Books.

Mead, G. H. 1934. *Mind, self, and society*. Chicago: University of Chicago Press.

Merleau-Ponty, M. 1963. *Phenomenology of perception*. New York: Humanities Press. (Original work published 1945.)

Mills, J. 1999. Unconscious subjectivity. *Contemporary Psychoanalysis* 35:342–347.

Mitchell, S. 1988. *Relational concepts in psychoanalysis*. Cambridge, Mass.: Harvard University Press.

Moore, A. 1984. Unique individuality redeemed. *Contemporary Psychoanalysis* 20:1–32.

Nietzsche, F. 1954. *The portable Nietzsche*. Ed. W. Kaufmann. New York: Viking Press. (Original work published 1873.)

Rogers, C. 1951. *Client-centered therapy*. Boston: Houghton.

Rychlak, J. 1979. *Discovering free will and personal responsibility*. New York: Oxford University Press.

Sartre, J.-P. 1956. *Being and nothingness*. New York: Philosophical Library. (Original work published 1943.)

Singer, E. 1965. *Key concepts in psychotherapy*. New York: Random House.

Skinner, B. F. 1971. *Beyond freedom and dignity*. New York: Knopf.

Sullivan, H. S. 1940. *Conceptions of modern psychiatry*. New York: Norton.

Sullivan, H. S. 1954. *The psychiatric interview*. New York: Norton.

Taylor, R. 1964. *Determinism*. In P. Edwards, ed., *The encyclopedia of philosophy,* vol. 2. New York: Macmillan.

Winnicott, D. W. 1958. *Through pediatrics to psycho-analysis*. New York: Basic Books.

Wolstein, B. 1981. The psychic realism of psychoanalytic inquiry. *Contemporary Psychoanalysis* 17:399–412.

Wolstein, B. 1983. The pluralism of perspectives on countertransference. *Contemporary Psychoanalysis* 19:506–521.

Wolstein, B. 1997. The first direct analysis of transference and countertransference. *Psychoanalytic Inquiry* 17:505–521.

III Social and Cultural Contexts

8 Psychological Agency: A Necessarily Human Concept

Adelbert H. Jenkins

At the dawn of the twenty-first century, notions of psychological agency are under siege in the social sciences. One source of that critique is familiar. It comes from those, encouraged by recent advances in neuroscience, who believe that psychological and experiential phenomena can be accounted for by "more basic" physiological and biochemical events. On this biological view there is little room for an independent sense of choice and freedom such as is important to the concept of agency. Such a position, which is an example of one kind of "reductionism" (Bergner 2004; Slife and Williams 1995), is fully consistent with the broad mechanistic perspectives that have underlain the reigning conceptual paradigms in American psychology.

Another assault on agency comes from a somewhat unexpected direction. It comes from a group of scholars, critical of the broadly objectivist traditions in psychology, who have been identified with a "postmodern" and "social constructionist" perspective. While the constructionists' perspective is compatible in some ways with recent critiques of Western psychology (examples of such critiques are those by Martin and Sugarman 1999 and Richardson, Fowers, and Guignon 1999), the constructionists go further by arguing for an almost exclusive emphasis on the formative effect of social experience on the person. On this view, a central theme is the subordination of the individual person, who is seen as embedded in social, linguistic, and historical contexts and who as a person, or subject, is not only shaped, but also subverted by the contexts in which she or he exists (Frie 2003). The social constructionists, then, can also be seen to have laid siege to the notion of psychological agency, though they have done so from a quite different theoretical direction than have the neuroscientists.

In this chapter I argue that a developed conception of psychological agency is an essential component of a theoretical effort to understand human individuality and experience. A conception of agency attempts to describe the psychological processes that enable individuals to affect in their own right the flow of events in which they are engaged. Some years ago the Harvard psychologist Robert White (1959, 297), in his critique of the predominating drive-reduction models of the day, had noted that "something important is left out when we make drives the operating forces in . . . human behavior." To bring back what was "left out" he developed his view that organisms, particularly the higher mammals, possess an independent capacity for "effective" and "competent" interaction with their environments. Later the humanistic psychologist Isidore Chein (1972, 6) developed his view of the human being as "an active, responsible agent . . . who insists on injecting [himself or herself] into the causal process of the [surrounding] world." The major premise of this chapter is that while biological and sociocultural frameworks make essential contributions to our understanding of human experience, if independent psychological processes are not also considered necessary in accounting for human functioning, something important is still being left out.

In speaking to that "missing" component for understanding human experience, I will ground my approach to agency in Rychlak's (1988) *logical learning theory* perspective, which he developed as a "rigorous" take on humanistic psychology. His framework is a part of the movement that grew in psychology in the latter third of the twentieth century to challenge the extant philosophical traditions in the field. While many humanistic theories of agency can be considered general psychological perspectives on human behavior, such notions are particularly illuminating when they consider how people address challenges in living. I will use the logical learning theory perspective first to briefly highlight agency themes that can be seen in selected recent discussions of psychotherapy. I will then indicate how the notion of agency that I am advancing here contributes to an understanding of the psychological adaptation of people of color in the United States. My aim is not to argue that individual psychological processes are the fundamental aspects of human experience. No one becomes human except through participation in the processes of a particular culture. My point is that accounting for the complexity of human life, both in its strengths and its liabilities, requires multiple conceptual vantage points. No one level of analysis alone is sufficient; however, the understanding provided by the dimension of psychological agency is necessary.

Agency: The Missing Link

To hold biological or, as will be our particular concern in this chapter, sociocultural critiques of agency up to review is not to deny the significance for behavior of these two domains of explanation. Just as the importance of human biological functioning cannot be denied, there can be little argument with the idea that social and cultural processes are necessary to the existence of the human being. As Philip Cushman (1995, 17–18) argues, for example,

> Culture infuses individuals through the social practices of the everyday world, shaping and forming in the most fundamental ways how humans conceive of the world and their place within it. . . . Culture is not indigenous "clothing" that covers the universal human; rather it is an integral part of each individual's psychological flesh and bones. . . . Culture . . . is "sedimented" in the body. This is what is meant by the social "construction" of the individual.

On this view, the person can appropriately be seen to be not just *in* the culture but *of* the culture.

However, I believe that the more forceful statements of the social constructionist position take this perspective to a problematic point. For example, Kenneth Gergen (1985, 271) notes that the aim of social constructionist theorists is to shift the "explanatory locus of human action . . . from the interior region of the mind to the processes and structure of human interaction." More pointedly, he argues that "for social constructionism . . . the chief locus of understanding is not in 'the psyche' but in social relationships. All that psychology traces to mental origins, [social] constructionists might wish to explain through microsocial process" (Gergen 1997, 735, 724). Such a way of formulating things appears to dismiss the need for the consideration of distinct *psychological* processes in contributing to the construction of meaning. This position fails to take account of different independent causal contributions to human meaning and experience (Rychlak 1993).

To be fair, some postmodern theorists have seemed to recognize the potentially problematic aspects of the constructionist stance. For example, even as he puts particular emphasis on the social construction of the self, Philip Cushman, who is a psychotherapist, attempts to engage some of these issues in his insightful volume *Constructing the Self, Constructing America* (1995). However, he does not fully resolve them, in my opinion. At one point in his book he acknowledges that there must be some way of accounting for how we "think critically, oppose the status quo, and have independent thoughts" (p. 292). His "philosophical hermeneutic" position is that we are not just influenced by one monolithic culture but that we live at the intersection of sometimes conflicting cultural traditions, which give "alternative perspectives, traditions, or alternative aspects of a tradition [for us] to draw upon" (p. 293). This seems quite apt. However, the question then becomes, what accounts for the choices we make from the alternatives available at these junctures? In response Cushman seems to suggest, "Our *ability to find* [italics added] other traditions or aspects of our indigenous tradition" helps us oppose what we come to disapprove of (p. 293). But just what is this "ability to find" other points of view? One suspects that to the extent that this is a stable aspect of human functioning, one that helps the individual transcend a given set of circumstances, at least in understanding a situation, it is an aspect of individuality that is not constructed by, and hence *not* reducible to, cultural processes. Attempting to understand human experience without a theoretical way of accounting for individual agency, especially for those working in a clinical context, does not seem plausible. As Frie (2003, 3) notes, "Without a psychological agent who develops, changes, and learns, the therapeutic process appears to lose its meaning." The approach to agency that I outline here is one way of indicating how people create the meaning that they use to govern their lives.

A Humanistic Approach to Agency

On the logical learning theory (LLT) view a psychological agent is a being who can in principle conform to, add to, oppose, or disregard sociocultural and/or biological stimulation. In brief overview, this position argues that (1) subjectively held intentions are as important causally as are drives and environmental forces in governing the way people behave; (2) "dialectical" thinking, the imaginative capacity to bring alternative conceptions of meaning to life situations, is frequently used by people to guide their behavior; and (3) as human mental capacity comes at experience, it actively structures, it does not just passively register, stimulus input. These are interrelated propositions at the core of the LLT framework, which cannot be explored in depth here (see Rychlak 1994). In this chapter we are particularly interested in the first two notions pertaining to causation and meaning.

The first point in the LLT framework emphasizes that human behavior and experience can only be fully understood in terms of all four of the notions regarding causation that Aristotle (1952, 271) codified two millennia ago: "material," "efficient," "formal," and "final" causes. On the one hand, the individual is necessarily influenced by the material- and efficient-cause factors of life. These terms refer to the physical substances within and around us and the forces of the natural world that affect our behavior. However, in addition we cannot understand what a person does without understanding the intentions and reasons (the formal- and final-cause components) that make up his or her experience and also contribute to behavior. That is, we are interested not only in the forces that impel people but also the *purposes* for the sake of which they act. Thus, through the pursuit of individually generated ends, people are important causal factors in their own lives; they are not just the passive pawns of surrounding objects and forces.

Psychoanalytic and humanistic therapists seek to help their clients become more attuned to the intentions for the sake of which they act. In so doing the therapist necessarily takes, in LLT terminology, an "introspective" (i.e., subjective) point of view on the client's life—that is, she or he takes the *actor's* perspective. By contrast, the mechanistic theorist in attempting to account for human events primarily in terms of material- and efficient-cause conceptions relies on "extraspective" or third-person descriptions. This is a view outside of, and without central causal regard to, the actor's experience. The effort to account for human experience and behavior solely in terms of one or two of these causal concepts alone is one way of defining a *reductionistic* approach. (As I have noted, the current explanatory emphasis on human biological features is an example of such a perspective.) Thus, one of the philosophical problems of a strong social constructionist position that tries to account for psychological experience in terms of sociocultural inputs is that it rules out the final-cause principles—the intentionality and purposiveness—that cannot be solely accounted for in social/environmental terms. Again, the key term here is *solely*—that is, in this conception of multiple causation in human affairs we recognize that the social context is *one* of the crucial contributing factors to the form and possibilities for execution of individual intentions. However, an independent "mental" capacity to set intentions and goals is a necessary aspect of psychological agency for the individual. I will have more to say about this shortly with respect to the clinical situation. At this point we might ask, Are there features of human mentality that allow for an independent capacity to set independent intentions, enabling the person to shape the environment? An affirmative response to such a question is proposed by the LLT approach to meaning.

The LLT perspective proposes that meaning relations can be usefully categorized as "demonstrative" or "dialectical." Demonstrative meaning refers to designations of a situation in a relatively singular and precise way, making for unequivocal connections between a symbol and its referent (Rychlak 1988). In such a thought mode we think by using specific concepts that exclude confusing options about a situation. (Thus, a tree is a plant, not a kind of animal.) However, we are also inherently able to appreciate the alternative—in fact, the opposite—ways of construing what seems to be a firmly structured social or physical circumstance. On this view a given term suggests alternate possibilities, and sometimes can only really be understood when the opposite meaning is implicitly taken into account. (Our location of the position of something that is "up there," for example, is in relation to a conception of "down here.") A crucial feature of this "dialectical" thinking style is people's capacity to acknowledge and imagine alternatives. There is always more than one way to conceive a situation, which "demands that the human being affirm some . . . meaning at the outset for the sake of which behavior might then take place" (Rychlak 1988, 295). This implies that individuals contribute to their lives by how they (intentionally) *choose* to frame events within the contexts in which they find themselves. The psychoanalyst Marshall Edelson (1971, 25), writing in another context, has expanded on this capacity further: "[The human being] symbolizes the invisible. . . . [She or he] alone is able in the presence of 'yes' to imagine 'no,' in the absence of 'anything' to imagine 'something,' in the presence of 'that which is' to imagine and act in terms of 'that which is not,' and in any situation to imagine alternatives and their possible consequences."

Such a perspective is fully consistent with some of the postmodern "constructionist" points of view in the broad sense. There is no assumption that reality is waiting to be discovered (Howard 1991). As Edelson (1971, 27–28) notes, "While 'real' external reality may be presumed to exist independently of its apprehension, it cannot be known except symbolically—as part . . . of psychic reality. . . . [Even] science does not involve direct knowledge of 'real' reality but an interpretation of reality in a particular framework of meaning." The assumption is that the *person* brings a psychological capacity to organize experience and thus contributes to the meaning of the transaction with the social context. This necessary contribution of the individual is an important point that some postmodern perspectives miss. However, it should be emphasized again that in this encounter, the actors do not stand outside of the world of events. They carry out dialectical cognitive activities in the situations they are engaged in. On this view, then, agents approach the world from birth with active mental processing by which they conceptually structure experience, thereby helping to determine how things are known. Granted that a culture establishes powerful guidelines for "seeing" and "knowing," it is ultimately up to individuals to decide that in order to "get along" with their group, they will "go along" with what is expected. In principle the person, *able to appreciate the opposite,* could do otherwise—though, granted, at possibly great cost to the self. The emphasis in a humanistic view of agency is on the person's active contribution to the outcome of events.

Earlier I noted Philip Cushman's (1995, 293) reference to the human "ability to find other traditions" to resolve or bring useful change to a social circumstance. I propose that this ability rests at least partly in the human being's native capacity to imaginatively construct situations in dialectical ways. It is the ability, having a sense of one's own intentions, to imagine a path that may be quite at variance with the conventional wisdom of one's culture. Again, this is not the activity of the solitary, isolated subject operating outside of the arena of his or her situatedness. This feature of human adaptive ability can only operate within the determinative physical and social framework of which the person is a part. (See Jenkins's (2001) discussion of the work of the Confucian scholar Tu Wei-ming (1985) in this regard.) However, this human dialectical imaginative capacity is not reducible to the social framework in the sense of being accounted for or caused solely by that framework. I contend that this idea of agency is compatible with recent developments in conceptions of psychotherapy and is particularly valuable in considering issues pertaining to multicultural psychology. Let us turn first to some illustrations of how the agency notion fits in psychotherapy.

Psychotherapy as Enhancement of Agency

Most approaches to psychotherapy are promoted as efforts to increase the client's freedom to live life more fully. On the view presented here this involves enhancing the client's psychological agency (Jenkins 1997). The notions of freedom and agency do not necessarily imply isolated individualism; the goal of enhancing freedom refers to helping individuals become more able to participate in culture in ways that both they and the culture consider meaningful. Even so, it is not possible to do away with a consideration of certain *processes* of individual function that operate both within and outside the therapy context. For example, notwithstanding the social constructionist themes in his writing, Cushman (1995) clearly has a conception of the individual as an identifiably active and responsible contributor to the events in which she or he is engaged. In one case example, he notes that contrary to the client's view of herself, it is the therapist's job not to view her as a passive victim of neglect and abuse. Instead she should be viewed "as an *active* agent, constrained by her complicity with particular social practices in her world, but also potentially *empowered* by her embrace of alternative social arrangements" that the therapeutic process offers her and that she can find or forge in certain segments of society (p. 296; emphasis in the original). Clearly such terms as *active agent*, *complicity*, and *embrace* reflect an implicit goal for her to become aware of herself as a choosing, responsible person through her individual actions and decisions within her encompassing relational structure.

Psychotherapies with a psychodynamic or humanistic orientation have continued to evolve over the decades (Todd and Bohart 1999). Some of these therapies are presenting a clearer conception of the client as a proactive participant in the psychotherapy process. Such notions are commensurate with the idea of active agency being discussed here. Examples of this trend are Roy Schafer's "action language" approach to psychoanalysis and the recent scholarship on the "active client" by the humanistic psychotherapist Arthur Bohart.

"Action Language" as Humanistic Agency

Various writers commenting on traditional psychoanalysis have called attention to two diverging philosophical perspectives in Freud's thinking that can be abstracted from his voluminous writings (Cameron and Rychlak 1985; Holt 1972; Ricoeur 1970; Rychlak 1981). For example, Holt (1972) identified both "mechanistic" and "humanistic" images of the human being in Freud's work. Put very briefly, in the mechanistic view the person is primarily an *object* of forces acting from within and around him or her. In the humanistic image the person is seen as an *actor* independently capable of choice and responsibility even in the context of a field of impacting stimuli.

In his "action language" approach to psychoanalysis, Schafer (e.g., 1976, 1983) has made a rather extensive attempt to spell out what could be called the humanistic side of Freudian theory. In my view his perspective is implicitly grounded in many of the same philosophical principles that inform the LLT framework. (See a more thorough discussion of this point in Jenkins 1992.) Schafer (1976, 361) has noted that "the person as agent has always stood at the center of psychoanalytic understanding." Thus, "Action is human behavior that has a point; it is meaningful human activity; it is intentional or goal-directed performances by people; it is doing things for reasons" (p. 139). From the LLT view action is not just physical behavior; it includes wishing, believing, and expressing emotions. This is consistent, too, with Edelson's (1988, xxiii) characterization of psychoanalytic theory as an "intentional psychology." Action, which in this framework encompasses unconscious as well as conscious mental activity, "cannot be fully described by an independent observer acting alone, for it is not . . . mainly a social psychological concept. For instance, unconsciously the same insult may be an excremental action for one person, a castrating action for another, and perhaps both for a third" (Schafer 1983, 101). That is, for the telic theorist, who insists on the inclusion of the final cause explanatory principle, behavior is not either primarily a neurological or a sociocultural concept alone. Actions must be understood as subjectively derived meanings being lived out within efficient- and formal-cause contexts. Thus, in life situations, which are admittedly saturated with culturally prescribed mandates and implications, one can still not understand what people do or what they experience without taking into account the meanings that actors impose on the contexts they are in.

Maladaptive behavior represents a set of actions, too. Seen psychoanalytically, psychic conflict reflects intentions held unconsciously that operate antagonistically to other conscious or unconscious intentions. That is, the client has been acting in order to bring about certain ends or actively wishing that certain end states could come about, while experiencing these activities as not having been performed by him or her. A neurosis is not something simply suffered passively; it "is created and arranged and protected" (Schafer 1983, 111). Psychoanalytic therapy, briefly put, involves clarifying with the client what she or he is doing, and making sense of it—that is, gaining understanding of the reasons for the actions, so that in this reevaluated perspective the client's "sense of danger is diminished and he or she can open as well as reopen the possibilities of action" (p. 112).

This last sentence brings me back to the client's existential situation of inevitably confronting the plurality of experience in psychotherapy. As I have noted, the person is required to affirm or make a decision about what is the (personally) meaningful way of making sense of a situation: "This affirmative necessity is another one of those active roles assigned to mind by humanists, because which pole of a bipolarity [or a set of alternatives] is affirmed . . . is up to the individual and *not* to the environment" (Rychlak 1988, 295). One takes one's stand within the (dialectical) alternatives conceivable in a given experience. Once affirmed, a given alternative can become the standard way to look at a situation within conventional "reality." At this point the person may quite likely move to a "demonstrative" perspective and take the affirmation about the given situation as the *only* correct way to view it.

On this view of psychopathology, clients' narrative constructions of themselves and their circumstances lock them into repetitively self-defeating and socially limited ways of being. Through participating in a sensitive therapeutic process clients come to recognize that the way they have been construing the world has made a crucial contribution to their plight. They come to recognize that they can participate in the process of constructing meaning in their lives in a different way and thereby reclaim a greater degree of freedom. In one sense they move back to a new "preaffirmative" point, a point where they can begin to see alternatives in experience and can consider new options for conceptualizing their circumstances. This "humanistic" view of the psychoanalytic process is obviously quite consistent with conceptions of therapeutic action in other therapies as well. (For example, the Control-Mastery perspective on psychoanalytic therapy puts the client's active efforts to master unconscious conflicts at the center of theoretical understanding (Silberschatz 2005).)

Put another way, psychotherapy can be seen to help an individual become more "aware" in one sense of that word. In the LLT framework *awareness* is defined as "appreciation of the arbitrariness in experience"— that is, "knowing that something else might be taking place in a life circumstance" (Rychlak 1988, 354). On a dialectical view it suggests that there are inevitably other ways of conceiving an event. In that regard psychotherapy is a process, as Edelson (1971, 117) put it, that "increases the capacity of its participants . . . to attain voluntarily a state of becoming more fully awake." This perspective does not hold that the client should be in search of *the* single basic causative meaning. That would be contrary to the dialectical orientation in principle. The assumption in this more hermeneutic view is that achieving useful constructions about aspects of one's life opens new—and probably also unsettling—possibilities for self-exploration and self-understanding. Useful formulations that are constructed are not endpoint descriptions of the self but rather way stations in the continuing development of one's self-understanding in the shifting contexts of life: "The fact that one has discerned *further* meaning, *weightier* meaning, *more disturbing meaning* . . . or *more carefully disguised* meaning than that which first met the eye or the ear does not justify the claim that one has discovered the ultimate truth that lies behind the world of appearances—the 'real' world" (Schafer 1983, 8; italics in the original).

Consider, for example, a depressed young woman who comes to the understanding in therapy that she had unconsciously developed the belief during her childhood years that her lively, pleasurable interest in life as a child was generally worrisome and depressing to her mother. As a result, she gradually developed and maintained an ascetic and socially inhibited lifestyle, which has extended into adulthood, partly to appease and maintain her relationship with her mother. As she becomes clearer on this construction of her history, she becomes open to new ways of thinking about herself and open to new possibilities for action. But her new conceptions of her potential may also unearth disturbing competitive feelings toward her mother, perhaps reflected in wishes to prove herself a more capable person than her mother. Hopefully her sorting out and working through the variety of new conceptions about herself that emerge in therapy are by no means the end of her growth process. Presumably what she gains from therapy is not just a new set of contents or understandings about herself but perhaps, even more important, the extension of her dialectical capacity and the use of this ability to be open to the alternatives in her experience in a way that helps her live more productively.

The Client as Active Self-Healer

In the discussion so far we have characterized all persons as agents who try to organize the meaning of situations for themselves so that they can be causally effective as they engage the world. When people are coping with adaptive problems, this involves the crucially important capacity first, to imagine the world in ways different from how it is presented. Then they work to bring that conception into being, as much as the determining context will allow. It can be said that people coming to psychotherapy are experiencing a constraint on their sense of agency. On the one hand this predicament could be described as an experience of "demoralization" (Frank and Frank 1991). On the other hand in turning to psychotherapy people are actively struggling to marshal available resources as best they can. The theme of the client as active agent in the therapy process is brought to the next logical level by Bohart and Tallman (1999). A brief outline of this perspective will indicate the relevance of their ideas to this discussion.

While it is generally agreed that change can occur only when the client is sufficiently "motivated," the typical view of the psychotherapy process tends to center change on the agency of the therapist, as embodied in his or her capacity to make appropriate technical interventions. However, in contrast to this tradition Bohart and Tallman (1999, 14) argue that "the primary healing agent in psychotherapy is the client." The therapist is seen basically as a helpful and necessary facilitator of this process. These authors note that people are continually engaged in actively solving problems in their daily lives and in overcoming significant problems on their own. Clients bring the same attitude into psychotherapy, although it is presumably being carried out in an ineffective way. In broad overview, the therapist's job is to use his or her professional skills to guide and support the client's natural self-healing activities.

In their description of the client's role in the therapy, Bohart and Tallman provide what amounts to a close analysis of clients' agentic activity. In the therapy process clients are performing a number of actions, in Schafer's definition of that term. For example, as they talk they are *thinking* about themselves in relation to what they are saying, and what the therapist is saying and doing; they are *experiencing* the therapist, experiencing themselves with respect to the therapist, and reexperiencing prior events; and they are *matching* their current experience with the therapist to prior interactions with significant figures from the past and present. "In sum they are as active and generative in psychotherapy as therapists are. . . . The client is the intelligence that ultimately makes the therapy process run" (Bohart and Tallman 1999, 15). While the therapist is seen as having general professional expertise, the client is the only expert on himself or herself. As a process expert tailoring his skills to the client's needs, the therapist helps clients to "clarify their problems . . . develop and define potential solution pathways . . . and [then] find ways of attaining that solution" (p. 16).

Bohart and Tallman argue that a "client-as-self-healer" model accounts for research results on psychotherapy at least as well as, if not better than, the more typical "medical model" in which the therapist as wise expert, acting *on* the patient, is the central conception. They cite in particular that large body of recent research that seems to show no broad superiority of one kind of therapy over any other, the so-called Dodo bird verdict (Wampold 2001). For Bohart and Tallman this implies that different clients in their search for help actively make use of therapists in the ways that are unique to their needs. This means that positive outcomes are frequently a function of how the client makes use of therapist techniques, not necessarily whether the intervention has the specific effect the therapist intended. Further, if one therapist does not seem to be helping, clients often move on to another therapist. While the therapist-intervention model here seems to favor something of an "integrative" approach, Bohart and Tallman oppose practice that is technique-centered: "The key variables appear to be the ability of therapists to establish a relationship with clients, reach them, and get them to open up and invest their energies in the therapy process" (p. 288).

To review the discussion so far, in taking a different position from the strict social constructionist view regarding human individuality, I have maintained that in all contexts of adaptation the human is a proactive being who constructs meaningful postulates about his or her experience and works continuously in order to bring about the circumstances for evaluating and executing them. While I affirm that people are in crucial ways constituted by culture, human experience and behavior also derive from the functioning of people's psychological agency, defined as the ability to conform to, add to, oppose, or disregard sociocultural and/or biological stimulation. I have particularly emphasized the human propensity to think *dialectically,* the capacity to imagine opposite or alternative possibilities in the presence of a given situation. Thus, an important part of the work of psychotherapy is with clients' imaginal processes, encouraging them to become more "aware"—that is, take a more open perspective toward alternate possibilities for conceiving their circumstances. This of course involves struggling with powerful emotions and habitual defensive reactions. However, psychotherapy is most effective when the client comes at least implicitly to recognize and claim his or her agency in the therapeutic situation and in life. In this discussion of agency and psychotherapy I have focused on that aspect of LLT having to do with meaning. Now I wish to turn this discourse to a brief consideration of psychological issues of people of color in America. My emphasis on the human potential for imaginative resourcefulness in dealing with problems in living provides a vantage point for seeing the pertinence of the LLT perspective to issues of cultural diversity.

Agency and Multiculturalism

To fully appreciate the contribution of an agency concept to the psychological situation of people of color in America, we must step back and take a short, selective look at American history and culture. Over a hundred years ago the noted African American intellectual, W. E. B. DuBois ([1903] 1994, 9), stated: "The problem of the twentieth century is the problem of the color-line—the relation of the darker to the lighter races of men in Asia and Africa, in America and the islands of the sea." This has turned out to be a profoundly prophetic statement.

It would be consistent with a social constructionist approach to argue that a group's adaptation to its historical circumstances involves shared ways of conceiving its situation in the world in the interests of survival. On this view, as we have seen, knowledge and experience, indeed "mentality" itself, are primarily the product of social interactions and role performances as these are structured within particular social and historical contexts. It is no secret that racial bias has been endemic to the culture and institutions of the United States throughout its history. A social constructionist perspective would appropriately emphasize racist institutions in America as a particular construction by dominant cultural groups within the particular American social-historical situation (Kovel 1984).

In the latter half of the twentieth century as the nation was forced to address racism more seriously, the tendency in the accumulating social science literature reflected the common practice of looking within minority communities and people of color themselves for the sources of the social disadvantage that affected their personal and collective destinies. As a result, the victims of individual and institutional racism in the white society were made responsible for their own plight. For example, Ramirez (1998) commented on the repetitiveness in social science descriptions of such phrases as "sense of inferiority" and "identity crisis" to refer to psychological characteristics of Mexican Americans. The sociologists Robert Crain and Carol Weisman (1972, 26) in their extensive study of African-American adults expressed their view that racial segregation had seemed to rob black persons of "some vital aspect" of their personalities, preventing them from functioning sufficiently well to realize their ambitions. In their book *The Mark of Oppression* (1962, 297), the psychiatrists Abraham Kardiner and Lionel Ovesey even went so far as to say that as a result of centuries of oppression "the Negro has no possible basis for a healthy self-esteem." Little attention was given to the role of white society in creating problems for ethnic minorities.

Equally as important as this tendency to blame the victims for their predicament, social scientists seemed to show an almost complete lack of understanding of the resilience and resourcefulness that people of color frequently showed in their efforts to survive and transcend oppressive conditions. Relying as they did on their traditional "extraspective" stance as observers, but in fact also constrained by their own culturally engendered views, many social scientists showed an almost complete lack of interest in studying the effective and constructive aspects of the psychological functioning of minorities.

In the past few decades ethnic minority social scientists have presented forceful critiques of Western psychology and have articulated new psychological frameworks for understanding cultural diversity (e.g., Guthrie 1998; Jones 2004; Mio, Barker-Hackett, and Tumambing 2006; Ramirez 1998). With respect to the concerns of this chapter, in my writing I have argued that it is precisely at the point of trying to fully characterize the ways minority people have taken on societal injustices that a complementary view is needed (Jenkins 1989, 1995). A concept of psychological agency is necessary to supplement the explanatory perspective that comes from relying on the determinative force of the social context alone. Something is missing here, too, if one does not include this crucial component in one's framework.

Interestingly enough, more adequate characterizations of the lives of people of color have been available throughout the twentieth century. Many literary scholars of color—poets, essayists, and novelists—have been quite adept at depicting the psychological situation of people in minority communities. As members of the marginalized communities themselves they perhaps have had a special vantage point, described earlier as an "introspective" view, for considering things missed by "objective" observers who are not members of these groups. Many examples could be cited. For instance, the conception of African Americans as people who have *actively* grappled with their fate rather than simply permitting themselves to be shaped by circumstances is reflected in the self-proclaimed mission of the celebrated African-American writer Ralph Ellison. In one essay he noted that he set himself the goal "to commemorate in fiction . . . that which I believe to be enduring and abiding in our situation, especially those human qualities which the American Negro has developed despite and in rejection of the obstacles and meannesses imposed upon us" (1964, 39). One can see here the depiction of people able to (dialectically) imagine their humanity and further its development in opposition to the societal pressures that they faced.

Pursuing this idea, we can see that the theme of "overcoming" was central to the productions of the writers of the Harlem Renaissance of the 1920s. In one of his most famous poems, Langston Hughes (1926) captured the spirit that was part and parcel of the common black person's everyday life. There he portrayed an old woman reminding her son that

Life for me ain't been no crystal stair.
It's had tacks in it . . .
And places with no carpet on the floor—
Bare. . . .
But all the time
I'se been a-climbin'on . . .
And sometimes gon' in the dark
Where there ain't been no light.
So, boy, don't you turn back. (p. 187)

In his celebrated novel *Invisible Man* (1952), Ralph Ellison enunciates the theme of resilience and resistance. In the opening passages of the novel, an old black man is lying on his deathbed. He calls his son (the father of the protagonist of the novel) close to him and says,

"Son . . . I never told you, but our life is a war and I have been a traitor all my born days, a spy in the enemy's country ever since I give up my gun back in the Reconstruction. Live with your head in the lion's mouth. I want you to overcome 'em with yeses, undermine 'em with grins, agree 'em to death and destruction, let 'em swoller you till they . . . bust wide open. . . . Learn it to the younguns," he whispered fiercely; then he died. (pp. 19–20)

The writer notes that "they thought the old man had gone out of his mind. *He had been the meekest of men*" (p. 20; italics added). One sees here the dialectical stance he had taken—meekness to mask enduring hostility, in the service of his underlying intention (goal, purpose) to defy the white power structure.

More recently, the award-winning African-American writer, John Edgar Wideman (1994, 102–103), observed in one of his essays that

> the historical mind of African people captive in the American South learned how to "get over." From daily encounters with this land, its peoples, weather, its tasks, this "mind" fashioned visions, dreams . . . with the density, the hard and fast integrity of rungs on an iron ladder. . . . The unwillingness of southern whites to . . . acknowledge black humanity . . . were palpable barriers. . . . The minds of my forebears found means to negotiate paths over, under, around, and through this resistance . . . even when the punishment for conceiving the barriers, let alone . . . resisting them, was death.

In these eloquent characterizations of the historical struggle of African Americans we can see important aspects of what LLT proposes as psychological agency. In spite of society's obstacles, which were aimed at keeping black people in a subhuman state, these people even in their everyday contexts "fashioned visions, dreams"—they constructed plans and goals—which were the *opposite* of and *alternative* to that which seemed objectively possible in their social circumstances. They worked consistently to carry out their intentions of not letting themselves be dehumanized, and thus they survived individually and as a people.

The power of the dialectical imagination can be seen among other people of color as well. The way that some Japanese Americans handled World War II internment is an example. Following the attack on Pearl Harbor and the outbreak of war between Japan and the United States, over 100,000 Japanese Americans were put into "internment" camps away from their homes on the West Coast with few of their material or financial assets. Based on interviews with former internees, the sociologist Ronald Haak (1970) found that many of these people had shown far more agency in the face of their debilitating hardships than is generally recognized. In one Arizona camp that he takes as an example, he notes that after consulting with neighboring Indian tribes the internees learned to grow plants and vegetables that could be adapted to that environment. They amply supplemented their food allotment, and from profits earned they were able to help camps in less fortunate circumstances. The Arizona camp became a showcase during the war years to visiting state officials.

The apparent cooperativeness of the internees did not come from a sense of capitulation or inferiority as a people, but seemed rather to emanate from a prideful ethnic heritage of humility, sacrifice, and hard work under duress. In the face of certain harsh facts of external reality the internees in the Arizona camp took a clear dialectical perspective on their circumstances. They were able to conceive of and explore alternatives to the problems presented to them and they turned these problems into possibilities for alternate action. In the face of "barren" they conceived of "fertile" and brought it to pass; in the face of official hostility they conceived of the possibility of tolerance and cooperativeness from white society and acted so as to make that more likely. The internees did not simply retreat passively but imagined proactively what might sustain a sense of worth consistent with their conception of themselves. Clearly they were intent on developing and maintaining their "human qualities . . . despite and in rejection of the obstacles and meannesses imposed" on them, in Ellison's terms. It is not hard to translate these vignettes into examples of people exercising the *psychological* processes of agency as I have presented that concept here. Granted the necessary and desirable contribution of culture to being human, the history of people of color in America would have been extremely limited if their capacity to construct reality were *only* a function of the imposed role relationships and the dominant group's interpretation of the sociocultural traditions as to what should constitute their humanity. Their humanness has also been fashioned from their active strivings to bring to bear alternative conceptualizations of who they were onto the American experience.

Psychotherapy in the Ethnic Minority Context

The above discussion pertains to the adaptations of ethnic minority people in their daily lives. Managing the problems of living poses challenges for everyone. Racism has obviously made this process particularly difficult for people of color. When a sense of "demoralization" becomes too great, ethnic minority persons, like other people, contemplate their options. People of color have been less likely than Euro-Americans to rely on traditional mental health services first, and have been more likely to look within their communities or families for solace (Sue and Sue 2003). When they do come they are likely to be cautious and to shield themselves in various ways. They may come with suspicions about how fairly they will be dealt with by the mental health establishment and whether mental health workers will be able to reach across cultural barriers and respond sensitively to their needs. Even when the therapist is an ethnic minority person, she or he may still be identified as part of the "Establishment" (Sue and Zane 1987). As we know, psychotherapy allows clients to conceptualize and reflect on their experience in the world. African Americans and people of varying socioeconomic circumstances are quite able and willing to do that if given the opportunity (Helms and Cook 1999; Sue et al. 1991).

Some years ago Barbara Lerner (1972) described an investigation of short-term, psychodynamically oriented therapy in an inner-city community mental health center. The therapy was helpful to many of these people. Her client group was a diverse sample. It included "a Black Muslim incapacitated by an illness that had no physical basis, a suicidal prostitute, a welfare mother who abused her children . . . a child molester fearful of the police . . . a factory worker who felt that people on television were ridiculing him and broadcasting his deficiencies, and so on" (p. 33). Not all of the group were poor or black. But

> the one thing all of these people had in common was a sense that something inside themselves prevented them from struggling effectively to realize their full psychosocial potential. None of them discounted real and often terrible external obstacles to such a realization, but all of them were dissatisfied with their ability to mobilize their own resources in the struggle against external obstacles. (p. 33)

These were people who had a clear sense that their agency, their "capacity to generate circumstances . . . compatible with the execution of their intentions" (Chein 1972, 6), was hampered as a function of their own personal adaptive histories and they turned to psychotherapy in the hope that it could help them confront their social circumstances more effectively.

The literature has suggested that the early sessions of the psychotherapy contact are particularly important with clients of color and one must bring a particular kind of attentiveness to work in these sessions before other aspects of therapy can begin (Block 1981; Griffith and Jones 1979; Sue and Sue 2003; Sue and Zane 1987). Gibbs (1985) has proposed a set of "micro-stages" that therapists often must go through in the earliest sessions with African-American clients as the latter assess whether the therapist is truly socially egalitarian in their personal attitudes. These clients are likely to leave quickly if their subtle evaluations of the therapist do not prove reassuring. While there are cautions regarding the way working- and lower-class minority clients, especially, may approach psychotherapy, perspectives that recognize clients as active agents in the process should be particularly useful. Consistent with the insights of essayists and novelists, psychologists have noted the active style that African Americans tend to bring to coping challenges. Carolyn Block (1981, 179) suggests that "the Black culture stresses early in life the ability to 'do it.' Emphasis is placed on the active—managing difficult situations without showing stress." Gibbs's conception (1985) of the client actively "testing" the therapist in the relationship is fully consistent with Bohart and Tallman's (1999) idea of the client's active efforts at self-healing and with the idea of African Americans as approaching life problems in a "can-do" mode.

For some scholars, dysfunctional behavior not due to biological aberration comes primarily as a natural response to the considerable injustices that society selectively imposes on people as a function of race and class. It is true that minorities and the poor need to have the oppressive conditions that have been fostered by social institutions lifted from them. Real and profound social change is called for—the kind that actually allows for equality of opportunity.

Many in disadvantaged communities are engaged in the enduring struggle of working for a more liberated social milieu. But when people are also saddled with their own personally generated problems, they are not in the best position to work for their own self-determination. Thus, as Lerner (1974, 53) notes,

> What [socially dispossessed] people reduced to a state of psychological impotence usually need is a restoration of their sense of personal power, which will ultimately allow them to join with their fellows in an organized group struggle for social change—one in which they will be less vulnerable and more effective. Generic psychotherapy is fully compatible with social change because it is an attempt to restore personal power—self-understanding, self-control, self-direction, and self-esteem—through the development of an honest, empathic, egalitarian relationship with another human being, the therapist.

In this sense, as we noted earlier, psychotherapy is designed to help everyone achieve a greater sense of freedom—the freedom to conceive and thereby achieve a wider set of positive possibilities.

Conclusion

I have argued here that a notion of individual psychological agency is necessary in order to account for human experience and behavior. I have taken particular issue with the postmodern viewpoint that posits the human being as primarily constructed by sociocultural factors. We are to an important degree constituted by culture and, of course, biology; however, we are also more. From the point of view presented here, saying that the larger gestalt of culture shapes individual functioning is the equivalent of saying that the social context serves as the grounds or the basis for psychological processes of establishing meaning. The person is an active and responsible agent who chooses from among the possibilities for conceiving a situation. The importance of an agency concept is highlighted when we are concerned with describing how people handle challenges to coping. In this chapter I chose as illustrative certain recent developments in psychotherapy and the way people of color have struggled with social oppression in the United States. I suggested that the psychotherapy process works by opening a client's imaginative and experiential capacities to more fruitful alternatives for engaging their circumstances. With regard to people of color, I have maintained that their psychological survival in America has depended historically on the use of their agency to reconceptualize the negative images and situations presented to them, thereby finding their own sense of worth and personhood. At a broad philosophical level, portraying persons as agents represents them as a part of the causal process that determines the flow of events in which they are engaged. It avoids the potentially reductive notion that a single causal vantage point is a sufficient basis for understanding the complexity of human functioning.

Finally, another implication of this discussion is worth mentioning. Agency is relevant to what the clinical psychologist Sheldon Korchin (1976) has called "the clinical attitude," which focuses the clinician on the uniqueness of the particular person. As Korchin notes, "A psychological approach is *clinical* to the extent that it attempts to understand people in their natural complexity and in their continuous adaptive transformations" (Korchin 1976, 23; italics in the original). When Bohart and Tallman (1999) give full respect to clients' readiness to make use of the therapist in their particular and unique ways of organizing their experience, they are implicitly advocating Korchin's conception of the clinical attitude. When Ellison's old man acknowledges that he has been a "traitor," contending with his white oppressors by trying to "overcome 'em with yeses" and "undermine 'em with grins," we recognize that only a conception of personhood that acknowledges someone's inevitable insistence on acting for the sake of his or her (perhaps hidden) goals can possibly account for the natural complexity that is the human experience. As people mobilize their agency they master their difficulties, bring about "adaptive transformations," and even have an impact on the sociocultural context that ultimately sustains them.

References

Aristotle. 1952. *Physics*. In R. M. Hutchins, ed., *Great books of the Western world*, vol. 8, 257–355. Chicago: Encyclopaedia Britannica.

Bergner, R. M. 2004. Is it all really biological? *Journal of Theoretical and Philosophical Psychology* 24:30–49.

Block, C. B. 1981. Black Americans and the cross-cultural counseling and psychotherapy experience. In A. J. Marsella and P. B. Pedersen, eds., *Cross-cultural counseling and psychotherapy*, 177–194. Elmsford, N.Y.: Pergamon Press.

Bohart, A. C., and Tallman, K. 1999. *How clients make therapy work*. Washington, D.C.: APA Books.

Cameron, N., and Rychlak, J. F. 1985. *Personality development and psychopathology: A dynamic approach*. Boston: Houghton Mifflin.

Chein, I. 1972. *The science of behavior and the image of man*. New York: Basic Books.

Crain, R. L., and Weisman, C. S. 1972. *Discrimination, personality and achievement: A survey of northern Blacks*. New York: Seminar Press.

Cushman, P. 1995. *Constructing the self, constructing America: A cultural history of psychotherapy*. Reading, Mass.: Addison-Wesley.

DuBois, W. E. B. [1903] 1994. *The souls of Black folks*. New York: Dover.

Edelson, M. 1971. *The idea of a mental illness*. New Haven, Conn.: Yale University Press.

Edelson, M. 1988. *Psychoanalysis: A theory in crisis*. Chicago: University of Chicago Press.

Ellison, R. 1952. *Invisible man*. New York: Signet Books.

Ellison, R. 1964. That same pain, that same pleasure: An interview. In R. Ellison, ed., *Shadow and act*. New York: Signet Books.

Frank, J. D., and Frank, J. B. 1991. *Persuasion and healing*. 3rd ed. Baltimore: Johns Hopkins University Press.

Frie, R., ed. 2003. *Understanding experience: Psychotherapy and postmodernism*. New York: Routledge.

Gergen, K. J. 1985. The social constructionist movement in modern psychology. *American Psychologist* 40:266–275.

Gergen, K. J. 1997. The place of the psyche in a constructed world. *Theory and Psychology* 7:723–746.

Gibbs, J. T. 1985. Establishing a treatment relationship with Black clients: Interpersonal vs. instrumental strategies. In C. Germain, ed., *Advances in clinical social work practice*, 184–195. Silver Spring, Md.: National Association of Social Work.

Griffith, M. S., and Jones, E. E. 1979. Race and psychotherapy: Changing perspectives. In J. H. Masserman, ed., *Current psychiatric therapies*, vol. 18, 225–235. New York: Grune and Stratton.

Guthrie, R. V. 1998. *Even the rat was white: A historical view of psychology*. 2nd ed. Boston: Allyn and Bacon.

Haak, R. O. 1970. Co-opting the oppressors: The case of the Japanese-Americans. *transaction: Social Science and Modern Society* 7:23–31.

Helms, J. E., and Cook, D. A. 1999. *Using race and culture in counseling and psychotherapy*. Boston: Allyn and Bacon.

Holt, R. R. 1972. Mechanistic and humanistic themes in Freud's thought. *Psychoanalysis and Contemporary Science* 1:3–24.

Howard, G. S. 1991. Culture tales: A narrative approach to thinking, cross-cultural psychology, and psychotherapy. *American Psychologist* 46:187–197.

Hughes, L. 1926. Mother to son. In *Selected poems of Langston Hughes*. New York: Knopf.

Jenkins, A. H. 1989. Psychological agency: A crucial concept for minorities. *Theoretical and Philosophical Psychology Bulletin* 9:4–11.

Jenkins, A. H. 1992. Hermeneutics versus science in psychoanalysis: A rigorous humanistic view. *Psychoanalytic Psychology* 9:509–527.

Jenkins, A. H. 1995. *Psychology and African Americans: A humanistic approach*. 2nd ed. Boston: Allyn and Bacon.

Jenkins, A. H. 1997. Free will and psychotherapy: The enhancement of agency. *Journal of Theoretical and Philosophical Psychology* 17:1–13.

Jenkins, A. H. 2001. Individuality in cultural context: The case for psychological agency. *Theory and Psychology* 11:347–362.

Jones, R. L., ed. 2004. *Black psychology*. 4th ed. Hampton, Va.: Cobb and Henry.

Kardiner, A., and Ovesey, L. 1962. *The mark of oppression*. Cleveland: Meridian Books.

Korchin, S. J. 1976. *Modern clinical psychology*. New York: Basic Books.

Kovel, J. 1984. *White racism: A psychohistory*. 2nd ed. New York: Columbia University Press.

Lerner, B. 1972. *Therapy in the ghetto: Political impotence and personal disintegration*. Baltimore: Johns Hopkins University Press.

Lerner, B. 1974. Is psychotherapy relevant to the needs of the urban poor? In D. A. Evans and W. L. Claiborn, eds., *Mental health issues and the urban poor*, 49–54. Elmsford, N.Y.: Pergamon Press.

Martin, J., and Sugarman, J. 1999. *The psychology of human possibility and constraint*. Albany: State University of New York Press.

Mio, J. S., Barker-Hackett, L., and Tumambing, J. 2006. *Multicultural psychology: Understanding our diverse communities*. New York: McGraw-Hill.

Ramirez, M. 1998. *Multicultural/multiracial psychology: Mestizo perspectives in personality and mental health*. 2nd ed. Northvale, N.J.: Aronson.

Richardson, F. C., Fowers, B. J., and Guignon, C. B. 1999. *Re-envisioning psychology: Moral dimensions of theory and practice*. San Francisco: Jossey-Bass.

Ricoeur, P. 1970. *Freud and philosophy: An essay on interpretation*. New Haven, Conn.: Yale University Press.

Rychlak, J. F. 1981. *Introduction to personality and psychotherapy: A theory-construction approach*. 2nd ed. Boston: Houghton Mifflin.

Rychlak, J. F. 1988. *The psychology of rigorous humanism*. 2nd ed. New York: New York University Press.

Rychlak, J. F. 1993. A suggested principle of complementarity for psychology: In theory, not method. *American Psychologist* 48:933–942.

Rychlak, J. F. 1994. *Logical learning theory: A human teleology and its empirical support.* Lincoln: University of Nebraska Press.

Schafer, R. 1976. *A new language for psychoanalysis*. New Haven, Conn.: Yale University Press.

Schafer, R. 1983. *The analytic attitude*. New York: Basic Books.

Silberschatz, G., ed. 2005. *Transformative relationships: The Control-Mastery theory of psychotherapy*. New York: Routledge.

Slife, B. D., and Williams, R. N. 1995. *What's behind the research: Discovering hidden assumptions in the behavioral sciences*. Thousand Oaks, Calif.: Sage.

Sue, D. W., and Sue, D. 2003. *Counseling the culturally diverse: Theory and practice*. 4th ed. New York: Wiley.

Sue, S., Fujino, D. C., Li-tze, H., Takeuchi, D. T., and Zane, N. W. S. 1991. Community mental health services for ethnic minority groups: A test of the cultural responsiveness hypothesis. *Journal of Consulting and Clinical Psychology* 59:533–540.

Sue, S., and Zane, N. 1987. The role of culture and bicultural techniques in psychotherapy: A critique and reformulation. *American Psychologist* 42:37–45.

Todd, J., and Bohart, A. C. 1999. *Foundations of clinical and counseling psychology*. 3rd ed. New York: Longman.

Tu Wei-ming. 1985. Selfhood and otherness in Confucian thought. In A. J. Marsella, G. DeVos, and F. L. K. Hsu, eds., *Culture and self: Asian and western perspectives*, 231–251. New York: Tavistock.

Wampold, B. E. 2001. *The great psychotherapy debate: Models, methods, and findings*. Mahwah, N.J.: Erlbaum.

White, R. W. 1959. Motivation reconsidered: The concept of competence. *Psychological Review* 66:297–333.

Wideman, J. E. 1994. *Fatheralong: A meditation on fathers and sons, race and society*. New York: Vintage.

9 Sexual Agency in Women: Beyond Romance

Linda Pollock

Young women in our culture face a range of difficulties as they mature and come into their own as sexual beings. Some of their difficulties are culturally based, shared to some extent with other women and arising from, among other factors, the fear that female sexuality arouses in our culture. Other difficulties are psychological, relating to their ability as individuals to recognize their embodied feelings, to engage fully in mutually reciprocal relationships, and to take responsibility for their own decisions.

This chapter introduces the idea of sexual agency—drawing from psychological theories about the development of a capacity for interpersonal mutuality—as the ability to take responsibility for, and direct, one's own sexuality. Sexual agency allows a woman to recognize her sexual feelings and to make decisions about whether, when, and with whom to act on those feelings. It is her power to navigate the internal conflict that pits her sexual arousal against her values and beliefs.

I suggest in this chapter that sexual agency is an important, if often unarticulated, aspect of women's healthy sexuality. If we believe that sexuality exists only as a socially embedded concept that does not exist outside cultural parameters, or that agency is merely a marker of individual atomism, then the concept of sexual agency can be neither helpful nor relevant in a discussion of healthy functioning. If, on the other hand, we understand sexuality to be, at its most essential level, embodied, and to some extent independent of its meaning in the culture, and if we believe that agency, like other characteristics of healthy adult functioning, develops within a social context and coexists with values of trust, loyalty, and interdependence, then the concept of sexual agency is valuable.

This question—whether agency is a marker of individual atomism or whether it develops and functions within a social context—has been extensively explored by feminist scholars. In their recent book, Catriona Mackenzie and Natalie Stoljar (2000) introduce the idea of "relational autonomy," a construction of the term *autonomy* that gives primacy to values of human connection. They frame autonomy as one of the building blocks of agency, which has traditionally privileged the values of independence, isolation, and self-sufficiency over values of dependency and interconnection (see Gardiner 1995; Mackenzie and Stoljar 2000; Nelson-Kuna and Riger 1995). In contrast to other feminist readings (Gilligan 1993), Mackenzie and Stoljar argue that autonomy, and by extension, agency, do not necessarily connote atomism and separation. Because agents' identities are formed within a context of social relationships and shaped by social factors such as race, class, gender, and ethnicity, identity, and thus agency, are multidetermined and derived from an intricate web of influences and relationships. The goal of human development is framed as having less to do with individuation and more to do with creating and sustaining relationships of empathy and mutual intersubjectivity (Held 1993; Mackenzie and Stoljar 2000).

Rather than standing as a singular body of thought, feminist theory incorporates many and varied viewpoints. Postmodernism, sharing the stage with symbolic theory, metaphysical theory, care theory, and diversity theory, itself reflects a diversity of perspectives. In their analysis of the positioning of the constructs of agency and autonomy within different schools of feminist thought, Mackenzie and Stoljar posit that postmodern theories understand the notion of autonomy to be a conceit of the Enlightenment in its emphasis on positivism.

Postmodernism charges that defenders of Enlightenment ideals make the notion of autonomy complicit with the structures of subordination to keep entire groups of people marginalized and powerless (Code 1995; Mackenzie and Stoljar 2000). When postmodernism focuses primarily on difference and "Otherness," for example, autonomy is understood to be a historically, culturally, and socially specific ideal masquerading as a universal norm. As it suppresses individual differentiation, the fictionally unanimous concept of autonomy sets the scene for oppression (Mackenzie and Stoljar 2000, 11). Foucault's theories of power, which comprise another perspective in postmodern thought, deny the very possibility of political agency, asserting that no free will can escape the forces of power. Because individuals are constructed by the culture, they have no capacity for true choice, for making decisions unaffected by the powers that be (Bartky 1995).

Psychoanalytic postmodernism presents another challenge to agency. Psychoanalytic theorists focus on the assumption that agency always involves a person's capacity for self-awareness, psychic unity, and self-mastery. Psychoanalytic thought—which from its inception in Freud's writings has taken issue with the idea of self-mastery, holding that people are by nature conflict-ridden, self-deluded, and driven by unconscious desire—has provided fertile ground for postmodern assertions. We cannot know each other directly; we can know only about each other's subjectivity, the ever-shifting result of transient thoughts and feelings determined more by our institutions than by our individual experiences. Although classical psychoanalytic theory has supported the paradigm of domination by legitimizing male-dominated power structures, postmodernism has, in part, compensated for this implicit political stance by deconstructing the idea of the authoritarian analyst.[1]

The difficulty with these various postmodern perspectives is that they seem to leave little room for sexual agency. If a woman's sexual arousal is understood as a "cultural fallacy" and more generally as a "social construction," she cannot embody her sexuality; it is as if she cannot trust the messages coming from her own body. If gender and sexuality are essentially discursive and culturally mediated, if autonomy is impossible, it is hard to conceptualize sexual agency.

Mackenzie and Stoljar, however, make a good case for a redefinition of agency incorporating values of connection and interdependency. A similar case can be made for sexual agency, incorporating aspects of mutuality and positioning sexuality as, at its most essential level, embodied. Although we are fundamentally social and cultural beings, we are never wholly determined by our relational contexts, and although our psychic worlds are basically contextual, embodied sexuality emerges with the first adolescent hormones, and to that extent, is independent of its meaning in the culture. The experience and expression of the body always occur within the sociocultural contexts in which we are embedded. Yet our fundamental embodiment can never be entirely reduced to these contexts. It is in this spirit that I offer thoughts about sexual agency and its importance in the lives of young, heterosexual women.[2] I am suggesting that it is difficult for young women in our culture to develop a healthy sense of sexual agency, and that we can look at that difficulty from two directions: from the meaning of heterosexual female sexual desire in this culture and from the level of psychological maturation that sexual agency requires. The chapter illustrates theoretical arguments with brief clinical vignettes.

Social Constructs

One of the primary ideological frameworks in our culture, domination—exemplified by the structure of male hegemony (Eisler 1995)—has a profound effect on our understanding and experience of gender (Benjamin

1988; Bordo 1993; Chodorow 1978; Held 1993; Irigaray 1985; Lorde 1984; Rich 1983). We relate to each other in hierarchical terms, and we construct sexuality in these same terms. Our culture finds domination erotic—power itself is sexy—and we tend to think about sex as a dangerous and destructive force (Debold, Wilson, and Malave1993; Eisler 1995). From a feminist viewpoint, the equation of sex with violence creates fear and a need for control, channeling men's sexual desire into domination and women's sexual desire either into the terror of victimization or the comfort of romance (Fine 1988; Debold, Wilson, and Malave1993).

Emerging from psychoanalytic postmodernism in the 1970s and 1980s, poststructuralist scholars explore how gender is created and destabilized within the structure of language itself. Focusing on masculinity and femininity as *subject positions* within language, for example, Sandra Bartky (1995) explores the way binary constructions (male/female, language/silence, rational/irrational, moral/immoral, light/dark) support male hegemony: the first term is valued over the second term. Valued terms comprise the structures of Western thought. Devalued terms represent the feared things that our culture works to control, suppress, or exclude. Femininity in this paradigm is constructed as Otherness, and female sexuality is to be feared.

Carrying poststructuralist ideas back into psychoanalytic theory, the French feminist school overlays the classical idea of the Oedipal struggle with Lacanian thought. For women to take a subject position, in Lacan's work, means having only one kind of sexuality: passive, vaginal, reproductive, and heterosexual. Extending Freud's thought to the logical extreme, female sexuality does not exist as an entity in itself in our phallocentric culture: female anatomy is defined as the absence of a penis; female pleasure lies in being filled (Irigaray 2003).

Many North American feminist theorists, focusing less on the literary and the abstract and more on the impact of social constructs on the lives of individuals, emphasize the role that our culture's rigid definitions of sexuality and gender play in the oppression and control of women (Rich 1983; Bartky 1990). They point out that things are seldom what they seem. Simple things—like a compliment about how nice you look today, the opening of a door, a joke, a piece of advice from a psychologist—can reveal themselves as more malevolent—a threat, an insult, a degrading comparison, a reminder that women are inferior.

Imagine a patient talking in psychotherapy about wanting to make herself attractive, by having her hair cut, wearing makeup, and donning stilettos. Is she expressing a false need constructed by a culture fixated on locking women into a value system that measures them only by their attractiveness to men? Or is she expressing the manifestation of a more primitive need to express the love of her body by adorning it? Uncertainty about how to understand such questions, confusion between the personal politics of oppression and the behavior of someone not only gendered but also sexual, lies at the heart of many women's conflicts around their own sexual desire.

Conflict between a felt urge and a sexuality defined by repudiation emerged in therapy with a patient I will call Susan, who entered psychotherapy for the first time in her senior year of college. She had just had an abortion, having gotten pregnant the first time she had sex, with her boyfriend. Although she had been raised Catholic and was conflicted about her moral stance on abortion, she had not been able to face the possibility of carrying the baby to term, given the pregnancy's potential impact on her family, her college career, and her entrée into the business world after graduation. Susan's struggle when entering therapy was with guilt: she thought that what she did was wrong and that her motivation for the abortion had been weakness.

In the aftermath of the abortion—indeed, the next eighteen months seemed more like an aftermath of her abortion than they seemed to mark her college graduation or her first job—she became more and more distanced from her sexual desire. She had wanted to make love with her boyfriend when she had gotten pregnant, but she was not to feel that desire again during the course of the therapy. Her countenance changed. She cut off her long, sexy hair into a short, unisex cut and instead of wearing the tight jeans and sweater of a college student she acquired a wardrobe of conservative, somewhat unflattering business suits typical of professional work attire at that time. She continued to date the same boyfriend but their sex life grew rigidly polarized. His desire for her continued, while she struggled unsuccessfully to find any remnant of her own libido and desire. Susan's guilt about the abortion and her image of herself as weak overwhelmed her fragile identification as a sexual being.

Once at college and away from familial pressure to conform, she had been able to play with her image as a woman who incites desire. She had enjoyed flirting and making the first advances toward the decision to have sex. But the cruel irony of her immediate pregnancy ended her foray into sexualized adulthood. She took refuge in an androgynous presence and acted out her conflict with her sexual desire in her relationship with her boyfriend. She could not enjoy her role as either a sexual subject or a sexual object.

The images of female sexuality that abound in our culture exemplify the sex of a consumer culture, sex that breed insecurity and gender inadequacy, sex in which women are sexual only as objects. The women in these images are not subjects, not the initiators of sexual desire, not people to hold responsible for decisions about their sexuality. They are objects, passive recipients, silent bodies, whose power lies in their incitement of male desire. The choice these images present to the viewer is binary. A woman can take on the role of sexual object or she can avoid sex altogether. The choice is that of whore or virgin, slut or victim, neither of which is a sexual subject in her own right. The women who exist outside these parameters, not limiting themselves to the binary choice, tend to be seen in our culture as predators. They are sexual, like whores, but they reject their own debasement. Active in their lust, they are considered truly dangerous.

For her groundbreaking book on teenage sexuality, Deborah Tolman (2002) interviewed adolescent girls who described the forced dichotomy of whore and virgin. Girls who express sexual desire are seen as "bad" girls, who deserve any consequences they suffer. And girls themselves enforce the duality: they are just as likely to dole out the punishment as they are to be the target (Tolman 2002; White 2002).

The prohibition in our culture against women's active desire is familiar to almost any psychoanalyst. We hear women articulate their fear of desiring, being needy, of being seen as dependent, hungry, wanting, desperate. The defense is against need itself, as much as it is about sexual desire. The conflict emerges between a woman's embodied desire and her values and beliefs. The difficulty is not simply that women do not let themselves experience desire. It is that women are in deep conflict about their image of themselves as people-who-desire.

Tolman repeatedly cites the passivity with which girls in her study related to their sexuality. Although a greater number of the girls were already sexually active than would have been true several years before,[3] they talked about their experiences and their social world almost exclusively without mention of a personal decision about it.

Providing girls with a way to acknowledge their sexual behavior without facing the taunts and the damaged reputations that the label of "loose girl" or "slut" carry, the passive voice obscures girls' active choice, giving them a socially condoned way to make sense of and describe their sexual experiences (Tolman 2002; Cassell 1992; Debold, Wilson, and Malave1993; Wolf 1997). But passivity undermines girls' pleasure and their confidence in their bodies by obfuscating the power of their deepest cravings. It robs girls of their vitality and their capacity for joy in the experience of bodily sensations as they make the transition from girlhood to adolescence (Debold 1991; Pipher 1994; Tolman 1994).

As the inevitable disconnection becomes routine, the passive stance tears a rift between girls' desire for pleasure and their desire for emotional connection, weakening both. We expand the gap between girls' narratives about connection and the sexual feelings hidden in their bodies by encouraging them in their dreams of romance and relationships, and in their quest for perfect beauty, while remaining silent about their sexual longings. We put girls under systematic pressure not to feel, know, act on, or speak about their sexual desire (Tolman 2002; Fine 1988).

In the end, girls disconnect from their sexual desire because it is too dangerous, destroying the vital connection between their power and its primitive physical source. Without that connection, girls lose their appetites for living and their inner sense of direction and meaning. (Debold, Wilson, and Malave1993) When a girl is ignorant of her own sensations, she is especially vulnerable, not only to the pressure from other individuals, but to the pressure of the social constructs themselves. This is an uncomfortable state, denying physiological processes and containing the subsequent anxiety that, in turn, fuels the denial and repudiation of her own sexual desire (Tolman 2002). Girls disconnected from the source of their own desire can grab onto the plethora of consumer goods marketed directly to their insecurity (Lorde 1984). As they lose their agency as autonomous people, they create new images for themselves and gain an air of certainty by resorting to male-invested cultural scripts for desire and success (Debold, Wilson, and Malave1993).

Other times girls' desire is subverted into a passion for the intense control and resistance manifested in eating disorders (Bordo 1993; Debold, Wilson, and Malave1993). Anorexia offers them an opportunity for some of the experiences generally reserved for men—self-mastery, self-transcendence, expertise, and power over others through the effort of their own will—permitting girls to enter the male world while maintaining the innocence of childhood. Debold (1991, 179) writes that "they reconstruct their desire as they disfigure themselves." In effect, they skip from an innocent childhood experience to an androgynous experience in the male world, bypassing almost completely the experience of sexual agency, and thus desire and mature gender identification too.

The corresponding axiom is that boys are innately sexual but girls are not (Bartky 1990; Debold 1991; Debold, Wilson, and Malave 1993; Tolman 2002; Fine 1988). Our well-defended belief holds sexual desire as an embodied drive, difficult to control, necessary to satisfy, aggressive to the point of violence, and very much male (Tolman 2002). In our patriarchal world, male desire is so pervasive and so integral to the culture that girls use that construct to interpret their own experience of desire. Thus conceived, sexual desire stands in opposition to traditional constructs of femininity, precluding it from the array of feelings and behaviors that we expect from girls or that they expect from themselves (Tolman 2002; Valvadre 1987).

A twenty-four-year-old woman I will call Marie entered psychotherapy with pervasive guilt about her sexual behavior. She wanted to learn how to say no. A successful graduate student, she described the way she went about relationships with men as "stupid." She would get sexually involved with a man quickly, often the same night she met him, and after one or two dates the man would drop her. Her first reflections on her behavior made her aware that she would sleep with a man because she was afraid that if she did not, the man would not like her. Essentially, she framed her desire as a reflection of his desire. Her concern was not that she might be putting herself in danger from violence or disease, but that she was too "easy." It was about being different. It was not normal, she thought, for a woman to be so promiscuous. Was her self-esteem so low that she thought she did not deserve more than a one-night stand? Was her need for affection so desperate that she took love wherever she could find it?

The treatment was facilitated less by teaching her to say no than by helping her understand why she was saying yes. We talked about the role she played in the sexual negotiations, and began to surmise that she was in fact the initiator in many of the situations. It was not just the man but she as well who wanted the sex. We talked about how much she enjoyed herself, and it became clear that while she very much enjoyed the sex act itself, it was the closeness, the promise of instant intimacy, that so compelled her. Her worst disappointment emerged in the man's withdrawal after one or two nights. The sexual intimacy that satisfied at least temporarily her need for connection also seemed to preclude the development of a deeper relationship with the man. Her promiscuity was a defense against intimacy.

Once she was able to accept her own sexual desire, she was able to set limits on its expression. The sense of rejection and unworthiness in which she was embedded gave way to a sense of choice, and an awareness that she could make decisions in her own best interest.

The idea that sexual desire is the province of men, not women, has evolved in recent years, but in a direction that makes it even more difficult to sort out emotionally. Sexual expression is freer and more commonplace now among young women. They wear outfits that would have branded them as loose in previous generations. There is also permission for women to act more sexually aggressive than before. Millions of women now expect sexual pleasure in their lives, and there is a general expectation that sex is supposed to be pleasurable for both women and men (Berman 2005; Clayton 2007; Leiblum and Rosen 2000; Schnarch 1997; Sheehy 2007). Evidence of sexual empowerment is embedded in therapy sessions and in casual conversations with young women as well as appearing on the covers of women's magazines and in the expanding market for male impotence drugs, which have moved beyond the market of men struggling with impotence to include younger and healthier men, who use the drugs for self-confidence in an era of sexually aggressive women.

So the illusion in this generation's culture is that women have a lot more sexual freedom. The irony, of course, is that they have no more sexual freedom than did their mothers' generation. The virgin/whore dichotomy remains a powerful narrative (Perel 2006; Tishkoff 2006; Tolman 2002). Girls still grow up with a fear of being labeled a slut by their classmates. Men are still seen as the primary initiators of sexual behavior and the authors of desire. Women are still in charge of limiting sexual behavior, and they still feel the danger of making the wrong choice (Valvadre 1987). This is the new paradox of desire: women need to protect themselves *from* men while making themselves attractive *to* men (Tolman 2002).

Basic to the task of successfully negotiating this new paradox of desire—to decode the cultural messages and make decisions about whether and how to express her sexuality—is a young woman's ability to feel her embodied feelings, thoughts, and emotions, and her ability to function at a relatively complex level psychologically.

Psychological Constructs: Making Meaning

In his book *In over Our Heads: The Mental Demands of Modern Life* (1994), Robert Kegan describes human development in terms of stages: successively more complex ways of responding to the world around us. He describes our ways of organizing experience as not simply replaced as we grow but subsumed into more complex systems of mind. This is a radical concept, and one that adds a useful perspective to the way we understand young women's sexual desire.

The first of Kegan's stages, including children from age two to about age six, is governed by the *principle of independent elements*. Their attachment to their immediate environment makes their thinking fantastic and illogical, their feelings impulsive, and their relationships egocentric.

In the shift from the first stage to the second stage, children undergo a qualitative change in the way they organize their thinking, their feeling, and their relationships. They leave fantasy behind, moving into a concrete world that conforms to the laws of nature; they become fascinated by the limits and possibilities within that world. Governed by the *durable category*, the second stage takes children from age six into their teen years. During this stage, they begin to understand that things have consistent properties.

Terriers belong to the dog family. Wolves are also part of that family, but they are not dogs. A person can feel angry and resist the temptation to yell. When someone drops a ball, it falls at a certain speed. Because they have developed the ability to organize things in terms of predictable properties or characteristics, their thinking can become concrete and logical, their feelings can transcend the immediate moment, and they can understand that other people have their own point of view. This is the age at which children protest that things aren't fair. They are savvy to rules and they pride themselves on knowing what the rules are. They can understand disagreement.

The deep structure of each of these developmental stages is the subject-object relationship. Each stage differs in terms of what is subject and what is object, but every stage is constituted by a subject-object relationship.[4] The *subject* in each stage is the set of elements with which the child is identified or in which she is embedded.[5] In the first stage of life, the infant is embedded in impulses, so impulses are the subject in stage 1. The term *object* refers to the set of elements with which the child interacts. They are constructs that the child can manipulate in some way, by thinking about them, being responsible for them, relating them to each other, controlling them, internalizing them, or performing some other action on them. We *are* subject. We *have* object. The child cannot be responsible for, in control of, or reflect on that which is subject. But the most interesting part is this: what the child takes as subject and what she takes as object are not fixed. They are transformed during these developmental shifts, each time into a more complex structure. What was subject becomes object, and something new and more complex becomes subject. As she shifts between stages, the child is freed from the previous subject, suddenly able to *have* it rather than *being had* by it.

Once a child evolves the second stage from the first, for example, she is ruled by her ongoing needs rather than by her impulses. She becomes proud of her ability to distinguish concrete reality from the mere appearance of things. The momentary impulse of the immediate perception moves from being the subject of her experience to being the object.

The third of Kegan's stages, the one whose birth we witness as adolescents come into their own in their teen years, is governed by the *principle of cross-categorical knowing*. The newfound ability to focus on the interaction *between* durable categories rather than simply focusing *on* them releases the person from concrete thinking and simplistic emotional logic. She begins to think abstractly, and she develops the capacity to reflect on her own emotional states. Socially, she develops the capacity for loyalty and can identify with a community of people or ideas larger than herself. Emotionally, she can begin to take responsibility for her actions; she can possess agency.

Kegan gives an example of the concrete thinking characteristic of the second order of mind: A judge asked the young man brought before him on theft charges how he could steal from people who had trusted him. The young man answered, quite sincerely, that it is very hard to steal from people if they do not trust you (p. 39).

This adolescent had not yet made the transition to the third order of mind. In Kegan's terms, he had no self organized in such a way that reflection would lead to a report of internal conversation. There is no agency, no sense of real intention or responsibility. For a stage 2 adolescent, a request for self reflection leads to a narration of logically sequential behavior.

One of the developments that we expect to see around this time in patients' lives is a significant change in the nature of their friendships. Moving from a latency state in which a friend is someone with whom the patient identifies strongly, someone who is very much like herself, someone who fits the model of what Sullivan (1953) described as a chum, the patient making the transition to a third-order state develops a capacity to co-construct interpersonalism. When the inevitable differences and conflicts arise between two friends, a second-order adolescent will tend to experience the conflict as a betrayal; she will tend to see the friend as suddenly representing a competing point of view and thus not acting as a true friend. Once the adolescent begins to make the shift into third-order consciousness, she will begin to try to restore her sense of an identification between the two views rather than dismissing the friendship. She will begin to dislodge her identification with her own categorical point of view to facilitate the reparation of the interpersonal split. In the process of dislodging her fixed identity and adding to it one or more characteristics that would facilitate the repair of the rift in the friendship, she develops a more fluid sense of identity and paves the way for the emergence of true cross-categorical knowing.

Sexual Agency

To apply Kegan's terms to adolescent sexuality, once a young woman has made a shift from stage 2 durable-category thinking to the ability to frame cross-categorical interactions characteristic of stage 3, she can develop sexual agency. She becomes able not only to *be* sexual but also to *have* sexuality. She can make decisions about it, play with it, act aggressively with it, act passively with it. She can reflect on it and direct it. She can act as a sexual subject as well as a sexual object.

For many young women, it turns out to be easier and safer to do what is expected: to have sex in a prescribed context, to restrict themselves to heterosexual choices, to limit their sexuality to the role of silent recipient, to identify with passive sexuality, to avoid the power of the erotic (Lorde 1984). That essential power lies in the dialectic, the back-and-forth movement, between the assertion of control and the longing to be engulfed, between aggression and submission, between the roles of subject and object (Valvadre 1987 Lorde 1984; Debold, Wilson, and Malave1993; Benjamin 1995). In our rigidly gendered culture, there is little movement between those gender-specified poles. And when there is no dialectical movement, no trading of roles between the subject and the object, the doer and the done-to, the lover and the beloved, eroticism itself tends to stagnate (Valvadre 1987) and sexual agency disappears.

Doing "what's expected" involves eradicating any trace of the predator, the aggressive, of what Rollo May (1969) called the daimonic, the urge to affect others, to make certain that we are valued, and what Jessica Benjamin (1995) has described as the inextricable counterpoint to recognition. Healthy sexuality requires a give and take of love and hate, nurturing and aggression (May 1969; Lorde 1984; Valvadre 1987). With too much aggression one person is overpowered. With too little aggression there is no real connection. When we let our image of sexuality dissolve into an effete, overcultivated image of tenderness, when we let ourselves stay immersed in the romanticism and sentimentality that characterizes the kind of watered-down sexual desire permitted women in our society, we lose much of what is vital in sexuality (Benjamin 1995; May 1969; Valvadre 1987). May (1969, 21) wrote, "There is required [in sexuality] a self-assertion, a capacity to stand on one's own feet, an affirmation of one's self in order to have the power to put one's self into the relationship."[6]

The capacity to put one's self into a relationship begins in early childhood, as we train our children in gender identity. Nancy Chodorow's (1978) reconceptualization of the Oedipal crisis from a feminist viewpoint laid the framework for a new understanding of gender. Because boys, in their differentiation from their mothers in early development, relinquish the mother as the primary love object to identify with a gender that is not hers, they resolve their gender identity relatively early and tend to see the objects of their desire as Other. The process is straightforward rather than dialectical (Valvadre 1987). Women, as a result of their identification with a gender that is also their mothers', tend to remain longer within the mother's orbit. The relinquishment of girls' primary love object is not as absolute as is the boys'; girls' Oedipal period is characterized by the continuation of pre-Oedipal attachments and sexual oscillation in the Oedipal triangle (Chodorow 1978). Girls go through a process of relinquishment and differentiation, but they do so without establishing the mother as radically Other. So as girls mature they tend to identify with the desire and pleasure of the Other as readily as they do with their own. When combined with a strong sense of self, that tendency becomes part of a woman's agency—the power to connect with the Other while remaining in touch with her self. But when that tendency is coupled with a weaker sense of self, a woman will identify only with the Other's desire and will lose track of her own needs and longings (Valvadre 1987).

In her book *Like Subjects, Love Objects: Essays on Recognition and Sexual Difference* (1995), Jessica Benjamin sets out an intersubjective understanding of connection and separation in early development not as points at opposite ends of a continuum, but as states that exist together. In the early months of life, a baby experiences herself as one with her mother: indistinguishable and omnipotent. At the point of realizing that she is indeed a separate and distinct person, the baby needs her mother to respond to her: "At the very moment of realizing our own independent will, we are dependent upon another person to recognize it" (pp. 36–37). Interpersonal dependency begins with the first moment of autonomy. As the child develops the capacity for categorical thinking, the tension between connection and separation takes the form of a tension between assertion of the self and recognition of the Other.

Extending Benjamin's metaphor into adult life, there is a similar paradoxical relationship between the roles of sexual subject and sexual object. At the very moment of recognizing her own power as a sexual subject, a woman becomes dependent on another person to respond. As she recognizes her own subjectivity, she recognizes the other person as separate and distinct. As she learns to initiate sexual contact, she begins to learn that she can also respond to another's entreaties. As she moves through and beyond the limitations of our social constructs to take on the role of sexual subject, she enables herself to participate also as a sexual object. It is the capacity to move back and forth between the roles of sexual subject and sexual object that defines the basic function of sexual agency. The woman who is locked *into* the role of sexual object and the woman who is locked *out of* the role of sexual object are equally stymied: neither can be a full agent of her own sexual experience.

A patient I will call Amy sought psychotherapy at the age of nineteen, wanting help with sexual problems she was having with her boyfriend. They had had sex for the first time two years earlier, which she described as quite unpleasant and even painful. When she entered therapy she and the boyfriend were living together; they occasionally attempted intercourse, but always unsuccessfully. Her pain and anxiety made any kind of sexual contact intolerable for her.

Amy was unable to imagine herself as sexual or even gendered. She identified herself as strong and smart, yet equated femininity with weakness and ineptitude, all the while longing to experience the sexual in herself and others.

She loved to talk about sex. She described crushes on male Hollywood action heroes and would make quick, provocative comments about her own sexual interest in them, with a certain quality reminiscent of a male adolescent commenting on a woman, like, "Ooh, he makes me hot!" and "Yeah, wowwa wowwa!" Yet she was intensely reticent to explore the issues more deeply. The fun was on the surface; when we made forays into deeper exploration, the playfulness and the sexuality would disappear.

Amy was also reticent to explore the transference, but seemed enchanted with me. She began to remake her physical image, drawing on her impressions of women around her. She got a French manicure, a new stylish haircut, new edgy glasses, and prided herself on her ability to find funky clothing.

Gradually the area of playfulness, the range of topics that she could tolerate exploring, expanded to include fantasies about sexual forays and vicarious reiterations of the sexual exploits of her work colleagues. Her sexual fantasies always involved a mythical Hollywood hero; she was always the aggressor, usually inflicting some kind of pain on the man. The fantasies contrasted sharply with her relationship with her boyfriend, not just in terms of their overt sexuality, but in terms of her access to her own aggression. She talked about her boyfriend in a sentimentalized way, her voice rising noticeably in pitch as she crooned about him sweetly. The place where she began to come alive—to make some sort of a connection between her powerful erotic fantasies and stories and her deadened, sentimentalized emotional life—was in her deep frustration at the distance between those two states.

It was a striking characteristic of Amy's sexual fantasies that they represented sex as a one-way phenomenon. There was no reciprocity in her sadistic fantasies with action heroes: she was able to act out the role of sexual subject in a way she could not do in real life, but the role of sexual object remained abhorrent to her. She was blocked—as a result of early childhood abuse at the hands of her brother, and her dreaded identification with a passive, unprotective, and colorless mother—from the experience of objectification. She was unable to trust sufficiently in the emotional context around her to ever surrender control.

Benjamin (1995) labels the state at which mother and child can exchange roles *complementary structure*. This structure "organizes the relationship of giver and taker, doer and done to, powerful and powerless. It allows us to reverse roles, but not to alter them. In the reversible relationship, each person can play one role at a time: one person is recognized, the other negated; one is subject, the other object" (p. 43).

This is the predominant mode of relating for late adolescents. When a young woman is involved in a relationship characterized by complementary structure, there is, at any given point in time, an imbalance of power. Only one person is active at a time. Only one person is seen. The power can shift from one person to the other, but the landmark of complementary structure is that the choice is binary: the person can choose either role but cannot combine them. The person who is the subject holds the power to acknowledge or not, to see what is hidden, to reach the core of the object's self (Benjamin 1995).

Eventually, if the relationship does not develop beyond the structure of complementarity, the erotic play stagnates. Without the dialectic, sex is no longer playful (Valvadre 1987). Sexual tension gradually abates, as the master overpowers the other's subjectivity. The complementary structure becomes rigid, and sensuality is replaced by control. Omnipotence emerges, the object is completely assimilated, and the conquest becomes meaningless, leading to a narrative exhaustion, in the inevitable moribund outcome of objectification (Benjamin 1995; Valvadre 1987).

The alternative, in a healthy relationship characterized by sexual agency, is for complementarity to give way to mutuality. The shift begins with a recognition that the other person has her own reality (Benjamin 1995). Benjamin pulls from Winnicott's concept of cross-identification, emphasizing the person's emerging capacity to put herself in the place of the other, based on mutual understanding. The shared understanding brings with it a sense of pleasure, and heralds the development of mature sexual agency.

Indeed, the stage of mutuality, or co-constructed interpersonalism, to use Kegan's term, brings with it the ability for a young woman to surrender herself in an intense sexual experience, without losing her subject position. The separation between self and Other is suspended: the experience is that of merging with another person. But it is not an experience of being controlled. The young woman loses herself while retaining wholeness; she is seen in the deepest and most personal way, even while recognizing the Other. On a physical level, the state of mutuality is about having reciprocity in a sexual encounter: the ability to give and receive pleasure simultaneously. On an emotional level it is the ability to desire another person who has the capacity to transform you. On a deeper, psychic level it is the ability to engage in a choreography of cocreation and mutual recognition: the ability to lose yourself in another person while maintaining a sense of personal wholeness. It is the ultimate point of erotic union (Benjamin 1995, 184). It is the fulfillment of sexual agency.

Implications

A young woman's capacity for healthy sexual agency requires her to recognize and challenge our culture's limiting constructs about female sexuality, to remember how to inhabit and respond to her own body, and to reach a certain level of cognitive and psychological maturity. As agents in the culture, adults can expose girls to experiences that will encourage them to stay connected to their bodies in a spirit of play.

One of the most important things in an adolescent girl's life, predicated on her attainment of Kegan's second level of development, is her status in a group of girls, all of whom live in the cultural context of the mixed message of female objectification and the deeply embedded understanding that good girls "don't want it." As they begin the transition to adolescence, girls who may have enjoyed their own bodies—girls who have been active, playful, and happy with themselves—enter a time when the continued enjoyment of their bodies would involve playing with their sexuality. At that point everything changes. Playfulness, and the capacity to take pleasure in their own physical prowess, are relegated to the world of childhood, while sexuality, in all the seriousness with which we construct it in this culture, becomes their focus (Kagan 1972; Pipher 1994). Girls force themselves into an image of femininity, reconstructing themselves to fit their ideal of feminine perfection. This transformation into an unfeeling, disconnected, disembodied state makes sexual agency unreachable.

One of the reasons (and there are many reasons) that adolescents ignore warnings and information about safe sex is that the statistics and dire predictions of the sex education discourse seem to have little to do with the excitement and arousal that girls feel in flirting, kissing, and petting. Girls' early sexual experiences do not feel like the experiences about which adults have warned them. The warnings feel irrelevant.

Subjectivity and thought itself emerge from a grounding in bodily experience (Frie 2003a; Gendlin 2003). If concerned adults do not make the topics of the body speakable, they will remain enshrouded in silence, obscurity, and denigration. Girls will hear only the discourses offered in the public sphere. Even though the current sex education curricula mark progress in their effort to encourage the verbalization of sexual anatomy and functions, they tend to reinforce the predominant social construct that sex presents a serious danger to young women (Tolman 2002; Fine 1988).

We can encourage mothers to help their daughters become aware of their own desire. Direct communication about desire and embodied sexuality is especially important in the context of the deafening silence with which our culture deals with female desire. Mothers who pay attention to sensual pleasures in their own lives, and discuss some of those pleasures with their daughters, affirm desire in the broadest sense, teaching girls that physical pleasures are important and that desire and eroticism are about more than sex. Mothers who talk with their daughters about the work they do, and their passion for it, encourage daughters to pursue passions outside the realm of relationships. Mothers who listen for reflections of desire in their daughters' conversations open a discourse about sexuality. Mothers who do not cloak their stories in what Debold (1991, 177) calls conventions of feminine goodness open the way for their daughters to shape lives beyond the text of the romance story. In talking with daughters about their dreams and desires, in being open about the painful compromises they have had to make between work and love, and in being honest about the impact that cultural constructs have had on their lives, mothers give their daughters some of the support they need to shape a life outside our consuming culture of beauty. So many women live with deep silences about parts of their own sexual histories. Remaining silent not only misses the opportunity to educate adolescent girls about the realities of sex and passion, but it leaves the girls vulnerable to a repetition of their mothers' own mistakes and leaves us complicit in ensuring the continuity of the values of male dominance and female victimization for another generation.

Equipped with an awareness of the rigid gender roles that infuse the experience of young women in this culture, we are better able to understand and articulate the struggles young women face. Our ability to recognize and speak about the forces that restrict and demonize a young woman's physical sensations helps to give her a conscious choice about how to respond to those forces. Acknowledgment that the culture in many ways loathes and fears women, acting to control and oppress them, helps young women confront the misogyny around them. Making misogyny speakable gives girls a chance to see beyond the cultural stereotypes of virgins and whores, and to express their own sexuality in ways not constrained by those stereotypes. Our striving to keep girls connected with their changing bodies lets us help those girls, and the women they become, hold onto the power of embodied desire. We can help them recognize the ways the popular media collude with the prevailing norms of male-dominated sexual experience that encourage girls to participate in the narratives of romance and sentimentality.

We can help adolescent women make the developmental shift necessary for sexual agency to emerge. A young woman functioning in what Kegan calls a second-order perspective can articulate the differences between the physical and the contextual components of her experience. In conceptualizing the inherent paradoxes—of wanting to take and wanting to be taken, of wanting to make herself attractive to men while protecting herself from them, of wanting to be active and wanting to surrender—she will come to understand that she is in a bind, that she has to choose and either way she will lose a part of her experience. And we, as adults in the culture, should know that the frustration a young woman feels being locked in that bind, limited to dyadic roles, can itself provide some of the impetus necessary for her to make the transition to the more mature stage and in turn to a full and healthy capacity for sexual agency. The frustration becomes the motivation for change. This is important not just because it frees women to experience the full range of their own sexuality, but because it sets the scene for the emergence of a broader understanding, and a transcendence, of the rituals of power and identification.

Notes

1. The postmodern call for a loosening of rigid classical techniques has had its hand in the evolution of psychoanalytic theories prevalent today.

2. In this chapter I focus on the experience of heterosexual women living in a culture permeated by assumptions about female sexuality that almost entirely exclude the experience of lesbian sexuality. Male desire and our cultural concepts of eroticized male dominance provide the underpinnings for female objectification and define the heterosexual viewpoint from which the virgin/whore construct emerges, becoming the central dichotomy for heterosexual women. For lesbian women, who construct their sexuality in a cultural context equally bounded but perhaps not as permeated by male dominance as the mainstream heterosexual context, the central dichotomy is more likely to focus on monogamy versus multiple partners.

3. According to Tolman's (2002, 8) estimates, 65 percent of girls have had sex by the age of eighteen, whereas only 49 percent of girls in 1995 had had sex before the age of nineteen.

4. Kegan's use of the terms *subject* and *object* differs from the way feminists, intersubjectivists, or self psychologists use the terms. Kegan uses the word *subject* to refer to the elements with which a child identifies. With the word *object* he refers to those things with which the child interacts.

5. Since this chapter focuses on the experiences of late-adolescent women, I use the feminine pronoun throughout. Kegan was not gender-specific.

6. May (1953, 160) presaged the emergence of the concept of agency from the earliest of his writings on existentialism, defining human freedom as the capacity to take

a hand in our own development and to define who we are. The postmodern call for a loosening of rigid classical techniques has had its hand in the evolution of psychoanalytic theories prevalent today.

References

Bartky, S. L. 1990. *Femininity and domination: Studies in the phenomenology of oppression*. New York: Routledge.

Bartky, S. L. 1995. Agency: What's the problem? In J. K. Gardiner, ed., *Provoking agents: Gender and agency in theory and practice*. Chicago: University of Illinois Press.

Benjamin, J. 1995. *Like subjects, love objects: Essays on recognition and sexual difference*. New Haven, Conn.: Yale University Press.

Benjamin, J. 1998. *The bonds of love: Psychoanalysis, feminism, and the problem of domination*. New York: Pantheon.

Berman, L. 2005. *The passion prescription*. New York: Hyperion.

Bordo, S. 1993. *Unbearable weight: Feminism, Western culture, and the body*. Berkeley: University of California Press.

Butler, C. 2002. *Postmodernism*. New York: Oxford University Press.

Cassell, C. 1992. Still good girls after all these years. In D. Steinberg, ed., *The Erotic Impulse*. New York: Putnam.

Chodorow, N. 1978. *The reproduction of mothering*. Berkeley: University of California Press.

Clayton, A. 2007. *Satisfaction: Women, sex, and the quest for intimacy*. New York: Ballantine Books.

Code, L. 1995. *Rhetorical spaces: Essays on (gendered) locations*. New York: Routledge.

Code, L. 2000. The perversion of autonomy and the subjection of women: Discourses of social advocacy at century's end. In C. Mackenzie and N. Stoljar, eds., *Relational autonomy: Feminist perspectives on autonomy, agency, and the social self*. New York: Oxford University Press.

Debold, E. 1991. The body at play. In C. Gilligan, A. Rogers, and D. Tolman, eds., *Women, girls, and psychotherapy: Reframing resistance*. New York: Haworth Press.

Debold, E., Wilson, M., and Malave, I. 1993. The power of desire. In *Mother daughter revolution: From betrayal to power*. New York: Addison-Wesley.

Eisler, R. 1995. *Sacred pleasure: Sex, myth, and the politics of the body*. New York: HarperCollins.

Fine, M. 1988. Sexuality, schooling, and adolescent females: The missing discourse of desire. In M. Gergen and S. Davis, eds., *Toward a new psychology of gender*. New York: Routledge.

Freud, S. 1957a. A special type of object choice made by men. In *The standard edition of the complete psychological works of Sigmund Freud*, vol. 1, 163–175. London: Hogarth Press. (Original work published 1910.)

Freud, S. 1957b. On the universal tendency to debasement in the sphere of love. In *The standard edition of the complete psychological works of Sigmund Freud*, vol. 1, 179–190. London: Hogarth Press. (Original work published 1912.)

Frie, R. 2003a. Introduction: Between modernism and postmodernism: Rethinking psychological agency. In R. Frie, ed., *Understanding experience: Psychotherapy and postmodernism*. New York: Routledge.

Frie, R. 2003b. Language and subjectivity: From Binswanger through Lacan. In R. Frie, ed., *Understanding experience: Psychotherapy and postmodernism*. New York: Routledge.

Gardiner, J. K., ed. 1995. *Provoking agents: Gender and agency in theory and practice*. Chicago: University of Illinois Press.

Gendlin, E. 2003. Beyond postmodernism: From concepts through experiencing. In R. Frie, ed., *Understanding experience: Psychotherapy and postmodernism*. New York: Routledge.

Gilligan, C. 1993. *In a different voice: Psychological theory and women's development*. Cambridge, Mass.: Harvard University Press.

Haffner, D. 2001. *Beyond the big talk*. New York: Newmarket Press.

Held, V. 1993. *Feminist morality: Transforming culture, society, and politics*. Chicago: University of Chicago Press.

Irigaray, L., Porter, C., and Burke, C. 1985. *This sex which is not one*. Ithaca, NY: Cornell University Press.

Irigaray, L. 2003. The sex which is not one. In L. Cahoone, ed., *From modernism to postmodernism: An anthology*. Malden, Mass.: Blackwell.

Kagan, J. 1972. A conception of early adolescence. In J. Kagan and R. Coles, eds., *Twelve to sixteen: Early adolescence*. New York: Norton.

Kegan, R. 1994. *In over our heads: The mental demands of modern life*. Cambridge, Mass.: Harvard University Press.

Leiblum, S., and Rosen, R., eds. 2000. *Principles and practice of sex therapy*. New York: Guilford Press.

Lorde, A. 1984. Uses of the erotic: The erotic as power. In *Sister outsider*. Freedom, Calif.: Crossing Press.

Mackenzie, C., and Stoljar, N., eds. 2000. *Relational autonomy: Feminist perspectives on autonomy, agency, and the social self.* New York: Oxford University Press.

May, R. 1953. *Man's search for himself.* New York: Norton.

May, R. 1967. *Psychology and the human dilemma.* New York: Norton.

May, R. 1969. *Love and will.* New York: Norton.

Meyers, D. T. 2000. Intersectional identity and the authentic self? Opposites attract! In C. Mackenzie and N. Stoljar, eds., *Relational autonomy: Feminist perspectives on autonomy, agency, and the social self.* New York: Oxford University Press.

Nelson-Kuna, J., and Riger, S. 1995. Women's agency in psychological contexts. In J. K. Gardiner, ed., *Provoking agents: Gender and agency in theory and practice.* Chicago: University of Illinois Press.

Perel, E. 2006. *Mating in captivity: Reconciling the erotic and the domestic.* New York: HarperCollins.

Pipher, M. 1994. *Reviving Ophelia: Saving the selves of adolescent girls.* New York: Random House.

Pollock, L., and Slavin, J. 1998. The struggle for recognition: Disruption and reintegration in the experience of agency. *Psychoanalytic Dialogues* 8:857–873.

Rich, A. 1983. Compulsory heterosexuality and lesbian experience. In A. Snitow, C. Stansell, and S. Thompson, eds., *Powers of desire: The politics of sexuality.* New York: Monthly Review Press.

Schnarch, D. 1997. *Passionate marriage: Keeping love and intimacy alive in committed relationships.* New York: Henry Holt and Co.

Sheehy, G. 2007. *Sex and the seasoned woman.* New York: Ballantine Books.

Slavin, J., and Pollock, L. 1997. The poisoning of desire: The destruction of agency and the recovery of psychic integrity in sexual abuse. *Contemporary Psychoanalysis* 33:7.

Sullivan, H. S. 1953. *The interpersonal theory of psychiatry.* New York: William Alanson White Psychiatry Foundation.

Tishkoff, D. 2006. *Madonna/Whore: The myth of the two Marys.* Bloomington, Ind: AuthorHouse.

Tolman, D. 1991. Adolescent girls, women and sexuality: Discerning dilemmas of desire. In C. Gilligan, A. Rogers, and D. Tolman, eds., *Women, girls, and psychotherapy.* New York: Hawthorne.

Tolman, D. 1994. Doing desire: Adolescent girls' struggle for/with sexuality. *Gender and Society* 8(3):324–342.

Tolman, D. 2002. *Dilemmas of desire: Teenage girls talk about sexuality*. Cambridge, Mass.: Harvard University Press.

Valvadre, M. 1987. Body and erotic power. In *Sex, power and pleasure*. Ontario: The Women's Press.

White, E. 2002. *Fast girls: Teenage tribes and the myth of the slut*. New York: Scribner.

Wolf, N. 1997. *Promiscuities: The secret struggle for womanhood*. New York: Random House.

10 Navigating Cultural Contexts: Agency and Biculturalism

Roger Frie

In contemporary psychology the terms *agency* and *culture* are often seen to be at odds with one another. After all, agency is traditionally defined as referring to a person's self-expression, based on freedom and individual choice. Discussion of agency tends to emphasize the person's autonomy, a focus that risks turning the person into a solitary actor, separate from the world of events. As a result, agency can seem like an abstraction with little or no relation to the contexts in which a person exists. A cultural or multicultural perspective in psychology, on the other hand, seeks to understand the person through the lens of culture and society. Individual behavior is not defined in isolation, but in terms of the cultural positions that a person occupies.

The aim of this chapter is to suggest that far from being separate or opposed, agency and culture are in fact deeply intertwined and interdependent. People are inescapably shaped by the culture in which they live. Culture is inherent in the social practices of the everyday world, be they language, rituals, tradition, religion, economy, or politics. As Clifford Geertz (1973, 49) has remarked, "There is no such thing as a human nature independent of culture." At the same time, culture is constantly being transformed as individuals negotiate common meanings through social interactions. The question of how people make and remake their culture, and specifically the manner in which individual psychology is organized and experienced within culture, points to the role of agency. In this sense, agency and culture are mutually reinforcing, in such a way that the analysis of one must always include the other.

The interaction of agency and culture is particularly evident in bicultural experience. Broadly stated, biculturalism refers to an individual's experience of two different cultural traditions. In the North American context, biculturalism is perhaps best understood as the interaction between a dominant and nondominant culture. While the function of culture in biculturalism has been widely studied, the importance of agency for understanding bicultural experience has only recently become a topic of consideration (Jenkins 2001;

Markus and Kitayama 2003b; Miller 2003). The study of biculturalism provides a framework for understanding how agency is both culturally shaped and individually articulated.

In this chapter, I contend that psychological agency plays a key role in enabling bicultural individuals to navigate different sets of cultural norms and is important to the achievement of bicultural competence. Agency is a situated and emergent process of reflection, informed by personal history, and fundamentally embedded in our biological and sociocultural contexts. Agency is never simply an isolated act of choice, but is shaped by the contexts in which it is expressed. As such, agency can never exist outside of its cultural contexts, but neither can the potential for action and the creation of meaning be reduced to purely cultural terms.

To study the role of agency in biculturalism, I begin by providing a brief overview of the conceptual frameworks commonly used to explain cultural experience, particularly the process of acculturation and biculturalism. I then focus on South Asian immigrant experience. Drawing on a brief clinical example, I examine how agency contributes to the psychological development and functioning of the bicultural person. I conclude by proposing a culturally situated concept of agency.

Conceptual Frameworks and Their Limitations

To study the psychological dynamics at work in bicultural experience, psychologists often rely on conceptual frameworks. I begin by addressing how these frameworks are conceptualized and applied in practice and suggest that they need to be refined and accorded a more delimited role. In much theory and research during the past two decades, for example, the concepts of individualism and constructivism, and independence and interdependence, have been used to capture the different worldviews of Western and non-Western cultures. Whereas individualism is often defined as assigning central importance to the person and giving less significance to sociocultural influence, collectivism sees group cohesiveness as paramount. In collectivism, personal goals and uniqueness are less significant aspects of the larger social and cultural group.

Individualism and collectivism have traditionally been seen as separate and opposed. According to this view, the individualistic self is prevalent in Western European and North American cultures, whereas many Asian cultures hold the view that the self is strongly connected to the family, group, and community. Within this framework, independence is seen as the central attribute of individualism, and interdependence is viewed as the central attribute of collectivism. A landmark study by cultural psychologists Richard Shweder and Edmund Bourne in 1984 summarized a large amount of cross-cultural literature. Their study identified two ideal types of self: a Western concept that is autonomous, abstract, and independent, and a non-Western notion that is context-dependent, socially defined, and interdependent.

At about the same time, this perspective was supported by anthropologists (Dumont 1980; Marriott 1976), who read South Asian religious and philosophical writings as indicators of a culture deeply at odds with Western culture. These anthropologists suggested that South Asian cultures, especially dominant Hindu forms, grant value principally to the collective. They concluded, perhaps in a one-sided manner, that South Asian cultures derogate individuals to the point that the Western concept of the individual is not very helpful in the study of Indian societies. The difficulty, as Holland et al. (1998, 29) point out, is that accounts of the self derived from analysis of the talk and texts of specialists are often partial and may not coincide with the self construed by popular genres of speaking and acting.

Depictions of Western representations of the self can be similarly one-sided. While conceptions of the self in psychology often bespeak a person who is autonomous and bounded, developmental and feminist psychologists challenge this view and argue that it is precisely the ability to relate and care about others that defines the nature of much human experience. For many feminists, the emphasis on the singular self reflects a Western, male-dominated emphasis on rationality and individualism, leading Carol Gilligan (1986, 249) to remark that "when others are described as objects for self-reflection or as the means to self-discovery and self-recognition, the language of relationships is drained of attachment, intimacy, and engagement. The self, although placed in the context of relationships, is defined in terms of separation."

Gilligan's (1993) analysis of the masculine assumptions of traditional moral psychology highlights the exclusion of an "ethic of care" in psychology. Gilligan questions the reasoning behind Lawrence Kohlberg's view of autonomy as the goal of moral and psychological development. For Gilligan, the morality of a caring orientation arises through the individual's ability to develop a connected sense of self. In contrast to Kohlberg, she sees interpersonal responsiveness and caring as fully developed and moral.

Since Gilligan first introduced her ideas, theories of gender and development have become more complex, mirroring the way identities are experienced as multiple and fluid. Yet the ability to separate from one's family and develop one's independence and autonomy is frequently seen as a sign of psychological maturity in popular Western culture, and is entrenched in traditional theories of psychological development (see Mahler, Pine, and

Bergman 1975). In contrast, recent developmental research focuses on the emergence of a social self. Studies on topics ranging from attachment research (Fonagy et al. 2005) to early infant development (Stern 1985), and mother-infant interaction (Beebe and Lachmann 2002) all demonstrate the ongoing social foundations of human experience. The goal of human development, on this view, has less to do with individuation than with creating and sustaining relationships of mutuality.

As these studies suggest, there is considerable diversity in definitions of self-experience within and across cultures. Meta-analyses by Oyserman, Coon, and Kemmelmeier (2002) support this view. They conclude that "multicultural models, which categorize variations in world view based on racial, ethnic, or national group membership, might be unwarranted" (p. 373). One noteworthy finding, for example, was that among forty-six studies of national groups, European American subjects were found to be higher in collectivism than were Korean and Japanese subjects. At the same time, mixed findings were noted among thirty-five studies of European Americans and subjects from other groups in the United States. Overall, findings from Oyserman, Coon, and Kemmelmeier seem to indicate that while the constructs of collectivism and individualism reflect some general differences among societies, they may be more relevant to understanding how persons perceive collective and individual values within their own development.

Recently, Markus and Kitayama (2003a, 2003b), whose work is most often associated with independent and interdependent models in cultural psychology (Markus and Kitayama 1991), have cautioned against concluding that all Westerners are independent in a particular way, or that non-Western cultures promote only a particular form of interdependence. Not all those who are part of an independent cultural context will characterize themselves as independent, nor will all those who engage in interdependent cultural contexts claim to be interdependent. Markus and Kitiyama suggest that while independence and interdependence are important aspects of human development and behavior across cultures, it is necessary to appreciate how they influence and affect people differently.

It thus is important to see the concepts of individualism, collectivism, independence, and interdependence not as rigid signposts, but as fluid markers. The fluidity of cultural concepts as they relate to self-understanding is highlighted by Sudhir Kakar (1995). He discusses the role of these concepts in his cross-cultural clinical practice:

> In spite of the cultural highlighting of the inter- and transpersonal, I found my traditional Indian patients more individual in their unconscious than they initially real-

> ized. Similarly, in spite of a Western cultural emphasis on autonomous individuality, my European and American patients are more relational than *they* realize. Individual and communal, self and other, are complementary ways of looking at the organization of mental life. They exist in a dialectical relationship to each other, although a culture may . . . stress the importance of one or the other in its ideology of the fulfilled human life and thus shape a person's *conscious* experience of the self in predominantly individual or communal modes. (p. 274)

Some general distinctions can undoubtedly be drawn between different cultural perspectives. Yet as Kakar's clinical observations suggest, self experience is more complex than our conceptual frameworks typically allow for.

When considering cultural influence, dichotomous views of independence and interdependence overlook the intricacies of development and experience. At the same time, they neglect differing views within diverse cultures about what these constructs actually mean. Indeed, some critics (Miller 2002; Raeff 1997) argue that labeling cultures in general terms entails an unfair stereotyping of cultures. They suggest that individualism and independence, as well as collectivism and interdependence, are characteristic of all cultures and hence, all human beings.

The emphasis on broad cultural categories and concepts also tends to underestimate the idiosyncratic meanings, needs, and desires of personal experience. This is an important point since the process of meaning creation is both cultural *and* personal in nature. Culture provides the person with a system of common symbolic patterns through which to create meanings and organize experience (Archer 1988; Raeff 1997). On this view, culture is not an entity equivalent with group membership labels, but "a shifting continuum of shared commonality among individuals" (Harwood et al. 2002, 25). And as a result, culture is being continually transformed as individuals negotiate common meanings through social interactions (Holland et al. 1998).

While we certainly cannot stand outside of culture, we can potentially affect our place in it by exercising our situated agency. As psychological agents, we invest activities and practices with practical and personal significance in ways that can modify the sociocultural conventions within which we exist and act. Thus, as Martin, Sugarman, and Thompson (2003, 43) suggest, "Once emergent within societies and cultures, psychological beings not only continue to be affected by sociocultural practices, but also are affected by their own interpretations and conceptions of, and reactions to, such practices." This process of making and remaking culture, and of navigating our place in it, is particularly evident in bicultural experience, as individuals react to the challenges of living in two or more cultures simultaneously.

Navigating Cultural Contexts

Cultural contexts present distinct sets of "possibilities and constraints" (Martin and Sugarman 1999) that inevitably determine behavior. The question of how to navigate among multiple cultural contexts is at the heart of clinical work with immigrants and the children of immigrants (whom I refer to as "second-generation"). Although the acculturation process is commonly associated with immigrants who come from non-Western countries, it also occurs when people migrate within a society that consists of multiple cultures. Bicultural experience is frequently characterized by a combination of, and a vacillation between, feelings of belonging to the dominant sociocultural context and of being different from others in that context. Immigrants may seek therapy because of the psychological challenges they face in their newly adopted environment, and because their feelings of difference are frequently experienced negatively. The term *acculturation stress is* often used to describe this phenomena.

Traditionally, acculturation has been associated with assimilation, a view that rests on the assumption that immigrants invariably surrender or decrease their ties with their culture of origin on resettlement in the dominant culture. According to this so-called unidimensional model, acculturation takes place along a single dimension, with groups or individuals only moving over time from one pole (their traditional culture) toward another (the dominant Western culture). When acculturation is measured in such a linear manner, however, it precludes the possibility that individuals may retain various elements of their culture of origin while simultaneously learning about and living in the dominant culture. Moreover, when acculturation is viewed solely in terms of broad social categories, the specific realities of particular ethnocultural groups and the variations across groups can be overlooked. In addition, important distinctions can be made between different generations and the varied experiences of individuals in groups. In contrast to the implications of the unidimensional model, current acculturation research suggests that adaptation to the dominant culture does not preclude retention of one's ethnic culture (see Berry 1980, 1997, 2002). In his definition of acculturation, for example, Berry lists four choices of adaptation: assimilation, integration, separation, and marginalization. Of the four, integration is the closest to the notion of bicultural competence.

Whereas Berry adopts "a universalist perspective on acculturation" (Berry and Sam 1997, p. 296), Bhatia suggests that acculturation is better understood as an asymmetrical process of negotiation and mediation (Bhatia 2002).[1] In my view, the experience of acculturation in general, and of biculturalism in particular, is neither straightforward nor fixed in nature. Indeed, this process is especially problematic for second-generation children of immigrants. Whereas the parent may emigrate due to economic, social, or political circumstance and often struggle with questions of identity and the pressures to assimilate, the children of immigrants are faced with another set of challenges.

In contrast to the sequential process of socialization, children of immigrants are situated in a multicultural context beginning from birth that compromises both their family culture and the dominant Western culture. As a result, they have to deal with the demands of two different, and often opposing sets of cultural values and traditions. These children are directly confronted with the problem of how to live in the dominant North American culture and still find support from their family's cultural background (LaFromboise, T., Coleman, H. L. K., and Gerton, J. 1993). Not surprisingly, they frequently experience conflicting sets of emotional loyalties. The inability to resolve differences in the acculturation process often results in misunderstandings, miscommunication, and conflict.

The achievement of bicultural competence involves overcoming many of these challenges in order to maintain effective interpersonal relationships in two or more cultures. The process of acculturation needs to capture this ongoing bidirectional exchange *between* cultures. In my view, therapeutic work with the children of immigrants can focus on helping them to recognize, understand, and appreciate the ways they are situated both within and across cultures. Psychological agency is central to this process. The sense of oneself as agent emerges with, and allows for, the ability to navigate among different cultural norms and identities. However, it is also important to note that cultural contexts always present distinct sets of possibilities and constraints that inevitably affect and determine the course of personal experience. The process of integration and bicultural competence is not just a matter of "individual strategy" (Bhatia 2002), where one has a free choice to integrate the values of the dominant culture and own's own immigrant culture (Radhakrishnan 1996).

In the same sense, agency can never exist free of constraints. While traditional theories of agency emphasize free will and choice, the fact is that we are always participating in sociocultural contexts that shape our belief systems. We are not free to adopt whatever new understandings or perspectives appeal to us. Talk of agency and choice in the context of biculturalism is not a return to a fantasy in which the individual can be or do anything. And it is certainly not to forget the histories and material conditions that shape the context of a person's choices. This is particularly the case for immigrants whose decisions are determined by socioeconomic conditions. Indeed, the understanding of psychological agency always needs to be grounded in an awareness of the circumstances that shape our capacity to respond to situations.

South Asian Immigrant Experience

I will consider the importance of agency for the process of psychological change in a brief clinical case example, focusing on South Asian immigrant experience. Among South Asian Americans, the second generation's participation in contemporary North American culture is evidenced in diverse ways. Yet a number of dimensions of their experience stand out, including identity formation, gender, sexuality, and marriage. Indo-American and Indo-Canadian women, in particular, often experience the stresses of acculturation in ways different from men. According to the anthropologist Karen Leonard (1997, 2005), these gendered and generational tensions tend to cut across traditional South Asian cultural and religious divides.

South Asian immigrant parents may feel at a loss in terms of how to respond to their children, especially their daughters. Some parents respond by becoming more rigid. Das Gupta cites an example in which an Indo-American daughter describes her parents as engaged in a "museumization of practices." On a trip to India, she discovers that there is a wide difference between the parents' version of "Indian" and how Indians in India actually live. Her parents' version, as one might imagine, is more restrictive (Das Gupta 1997). In a "Focus on Youth" article in *India West* magazine (cited in Leonard 2005), Smriti Aggarwal quotes a Hindu father who states that girls are much more strictly controlled than boys because they can get pregnant and consequently damage a family's reputation. Aggarwal writes that the question of sex in her Indo-American generation is not being openly acknowledged. In the article she quotes a Hindu female doctor who states that 40 percent of her Indo-American patients are sexually active.

Just as sexuality and gender are powerful themes, so too is the issue of nondisclosure—not telling one's parents about the significant choices one is making in life. In a survey undertaken by Priya Agarwal (1991), for example, more than half of the young people questioned preferred to date without telling their parents. The gender and generational differences become magnified with respect to marriage. Indeed, marriage can become a situation of extreme stress for many traditional South Asian immigrant families (Das Gupta 1998). Depending on how traditional the family is, children are put in a difficult position. They must either accept parental opposition to dating and "love marriages" and trust their parents to arrange their marriages, or they must choose to marry someone themselves and risk disappointing their parents.

The complexity of psychological stressors involved in the bicultural experience of some second-generation South Asians cannot be underestimated. In my clinical work with young South Asian Americans, for example, a central issue is often how to manage the desire for self-expression with competing and conflicting cultural norms. In the case of one client, whom I will refer to as "Padma," her bicultural experience brought with it a set of challenges that seemed insurmountable and triggered the onset of symptoms of depression and anxiety. I will use this clinical case example to highlight the role of agency for navigating different cultural contexts in the achievement of bicultural competence. All identifying characteristics of the client have been changed to ensure confidentiality; that said, the themes of this case example are reflected in the experiences of many second-generation South Asian American women from traditional backgrounds.

Padma was born in North America shortly after her parents emigrated from South Asia. After leaving home to attend university, Padma had met and entered into a relationship with a man of European decent. At the time our work began, her relationship was becoming more serious as each talked about their commitment to the other. The dilemma for Padma was that her parents expected her to marry someone who was South Asian and who would possess an understanding of and commitment to the family's cultural values and traditions. In having to maintain her relationship in secrecy, she not only faced the threat of losing her parent's emotional support, but felt as though she was betraying her family and community.

Padma was fully bilingual, having lived simultaneously in two different cultural contexts. She grew up in a multicultural environment and attended a school with children from diverse ethnic and cultural backgrounds. Yet it was made clear to her early on that she was expected to marry within her own culture and remain loyal to the family's cultural traditions. The difficulties Padma experienced were both intergenerational and cultural.

Padma's sense of identity was unalterably tied to her roles and positions in each culture, yet perhaps not fully defined by any of them. The different sociocultural worlds she inhabited presented diverse sets of assumptions about how to act and what to do. She envied what she perceived as the "autonomy" of her Western peers, particularly women, who seemed oblivious of her struggle with the pressures associated with growing up simultaneously in different cultures. Her anger with her parents and the expectations they held was combined with the feeling of being treated like an object. She drew parallels between her prescribed role as a woman in her family and community and a sense of objectification. In turn, she tended to have an idealized view of the place of women in Western society and the supposed freedoms they had in choosing which roles they wished to take on.

Padma's anger with her parents often resulted in a one-sided perception of her family's culture. Once her identity as "an Other" had been more fully acknowledged, she began to consider similarities between the multiple cultural positions she occupied and eventually between herself and her family. However, empathizing with her parents was very difficult for her. It required her to experience and express the deep sense of sadness she felt about the lack of understanding on the part of her family. This process was followed by an increased curiosity about and appreciation of her family's culture. In particular, Padma's exploration of her prescribed roles as a daughter and future wife led to a more nuanced understanding of the obligations these roles entailed.

Padma's capacity for self-reflection, which was articulated in the therapeutic encounter, allowed her to consider past and present experiences in new and more tangible ways and thus demonstrated the possibility of future alternative modes of action. As we come to glimpse ourselves as agents in our worlds, it becomes possible for us to imagine new and different ways of being. Change requires both a desire and a will to open up new possibilities of being, yet our agency is always limited by the contexts in which we find ourselves. In the clinical situation, agency is rarely a matter of simple choice, just as therapeutic action is never a linear process. We may desire change but may be unable to bring it about on our own. It would be wrong to assume, therefore, that the sense of oneself as an agent is simply derived from an act of individual will and determined by such notions as autonomy and separateness. Rather, therapeutic interaction suggests that agency is an emergent process that is inherently relational. As Jessica Benjamin (1988, 12) notes, the response of the Other enables a person to feel that she is author of her actions: "Recognition is that response form the other which makes meaningful the feelings, intentions, and actions of the self. It allows the self to realize its agency and authorship in a tangible way."

The mutuality of the therapeutic setting helped Padma develop the ability to navigate the possibilities and constraints of her cultural contexts. She quickly came to understand the different sociocultural demands she faced and their implications. But mastering the affective experience of coming to terms with diverse cultural contexts presented a formidable challenge. The initial stages of this challenge took place within the therapeutic relationship.

From the outset, sociocultural differences between my client and myself were determining our understanding and experience of one another. Her struggle to exist amidst two conflicting sets of sociocultural norms was reflected and repeated in our work together. For example, her experience of therapy varied. During the early stages of our work, Padma's sense of me would fluctuate as she reflected on the male-dominated culture of her family and community, and her perceptions of the potentially liberating, but also frightening Western culture she experienced outside the home. When I challenged her she would often recoil and treat me much as she did the men in her family, with a cool and detached demeanor that masked her considerable anger. When I was supportive and empathic, she would be more likely to take a chance and reveal her feelings and wishes.

By engaging her capacity to imagine alternative modes of being and feeling, Padma began to navigate between different cultural contexts and the emotional demands they placed on her, rather than remaining entrenched in a single context. She also learned to relate in ways that were more reciprocal and respectful of her own needs and desires. This was not by any means an easy or obvious process. The therapy with Padma was dependent on a number of factors: a supportive and safe environment in which she could explore her sense of herself as an agent and learn to relate in different ways; the development of her imaginative and emotional capacity to consider alternative perspectives despite her fundamental contextualism; and a willingness to act on her understanding by using new and meaningful forms of self-expression.[2]

Our work together lasted several years and focused on helping her recognize and understand the way she was situated across cultures. Throughout this process, Padma developed an increasingly personal voice—a voice through which she began to express her own desires, not out of anger, but grounded in an appreciation for her different cultural identities. She was eventually able to find ways to speak more openly with her parents, to express her needs and thus reach a compromise that enabled her to continue her relationship as well as her connection to her immediate family—though ultimately this meant giving up the recognition that came with taking up her traditionally prescribed place within the family and community. Padma described this change in terms of a loss of a "secure" cultural identity provided by her membership in the community. But at the same time, she also said that she learned to embrace a bicultural identity, which she described as feeling "more personal" and "less imposed from outside."

It was precisely by reflecting on the gap between her individual experience and her prescribed cultural and social roles that Padma was able to consider the possibility of change. Her sense of herself as an agent meant negotiating between personal desires and diverse cultural demands. But to begin this process, she had to be able to recognize, and even appreciate, the multiplicity of her cultural contexts.

My work with Padma ended when she moved away, but was followed by a brief, though important, postscript. Several years after the completion of our work together, she contacted me again. She said that she wanted to update me and let me know how she was doing. Her situation had changed quite dramatically. Padma had broken off her relationship with her boyfriend, and was now engaged to a South Asian man. She was no longer depressed or anxious. Nor did she seem confused by the direction her life had taken—"surprised" might be a better descriptor. Padma stated that she felt secure in her decisions and described feeling fully alive in her current life. According to Padma, the decision to embrace the South Asian community, her family, and her prescribed roles resulted neither in a sense of objectification nor in a perceived loss of self. On the contrary, she said she was able to feel a sense of pride and identification through the acceptance of her various social and cultural positions. This suggests that the process of identity formation does not simply end with the achievement of bicultural competency. Rather, as Jean Phinney (1989) suggests, the meaning and importance of cultural identity continues to be revisited and explored throughout the life span.

Agency across Contexts

Padma's biculturalism raises some important questions regarding the concepts we use to examine and explain the relationship of agency and culture. For instance, can a stereotypical Western model of agency, with its emphasis on autonomy, separation, and individual will, account for Padma's decisions? Or are her actions captured by other, culturally variable forms of agency, which focus more on social and relational styles of being in the world? Clearly we need a theory of agency that is attuned to the complexity of cultural and personal experience.

Padma's experience requires us to examine the issue of culture-bound agency in more detail. In this final section I would like to suggest that the potential for agency is common across cultures, but that the experience and expression of agency is directly related to the cultural contexts in which we find ourselves. In other words, the actions people choose and how they experience their decisions will vary depending on the prevalent structure, ideas, and practices of their cultural contexts. This requires that we move beyond the belief that the individual self is merely "influenced" by sociocultural factors and contexts. It is not enough to view the self and culture as interacting variables. Rather, the experience of self, like agency, is forged within communal contexts (Martin 2007) and fundamentally embedded in culture.

For many observers, however, talk of agency in a cross-cultural milieu inevitably implies the elevation or even imposition of Western notions of separateness and individuality over non-Western societal norms. Within the clinical setting, for instance, the clinician's own values and their impact on the therapy must always be attended to. This is an important point because our understanding of agency tends to rest on normative assumptions about the value of autonomy, self-expression, freedom, and individual choice. The Western conception of agency, implicit in the so-called American Dream, is captured in the iconic image of the "Marlboro Man," which has become a global symbol of an independent lifestyle based on choice. This form of agency is inherently individualistic, guided by instrumental ends.

As we have seen, Padma's sense of herself as an agent meant navigating different cultural norms and demands, and these contexts affected the choices she made. Her desire for and experience of separation and individuation, for example, can be understood in terms of a personally oriented expression of agency aimed at self-determination. Yet when agency is only understood in terms of movement toward self-sufficiency, it adheres to a specific set of sociocultural and gender norms. As I have suggested, traditional models of self-development are value laden, broadly representing a Western, male-oriented cultural perspective. By contrast, Padma's fulfillment of family and social obligations can be understood as a relationally oriented expression of agency in which actions taken to meet interpersonal duties were experienced as personally satisfying.

This perspective on agency requires us to consider in more detail how social obligations and expectations tend to be experienced in different cultural contexts. According to research undertaken by the social psychologist Joan Miller (2003), among Hindu Indian populations individuals experience a sense of agency as their actions are oriented toward meeting interpersonal requirements, even if these actions are arduous and demanding. Miller (2003) states that fulfilling social expectations creates a sense of satisfaction: "Duty in these cases appears to derive from the individual's sense of themselves as inherently a member of a larger community, in which the social tends to be experienced as an expression of self, rather than as an external force in tension with the self" (p. 81). The fulfillment of social expectations and duties is not simply a habitualized action, nor is it any less developed than prevalent forms of agency in Western societies. On the contrary, duty tends to be closely linked to personal values and individual satisfaction. Clearly, as Miller suggests, agency can be experienced and understood in diverse ways.

Agency, on this view, always takes place by virtue of its cultural contexts, and is never simply an individual achievement. To move beyond standard Western versions of agency and self-determination, Markus and Kitayama (2003b) similarly distinguish between different types of self-experience.

They delineate two major models of agency, which they refer to as "disjoint" and "cojoint." Markus and Kitayama characterize the dominant model of the "educated" North American context as disjoint agency. In their view, disjoint agency is the expression of an individual's desires, goals, intentions—actions that affirm and realize a relatively independent self. Markus and Kitayama describe the dominant model in non-Western cultures as cojoint agency. This type of agency is associated with being responsive to others, coordinating with others, and affirming one's place in a particular social order—actions that contribute to and reflect a relatively interdependent self. Whereas disjoint agency is constructed as individual, cojoint agency is constructed as social and relational. These models of agency are prevalent across cultures and subgroups within cultures. They are interrelated and should not be understood as separate or opposed.

It is important to note the similarities between the cojoint model of agency and the work of feminist scholars (Gardiner 1995; Mackenzie and Stoljar 2000) who have coined the term "relational autonomy." In Mackenzie and Stoljar's reading, autonomy, and by extension, agency, do not connote atomism and separation. They argue that agents' identities are formed within a context of social relationships and shaped by sociocultural factors such as gender, class, and race. Relational autonomy, therefore, is a construal of the term autonomy that gives primacy to values of human connection. Similarly, the notion of agency is always derived from an intricate web of sociocultural contexts and practices, as well as from personal and relational contributions to meaning.

Cultural models of agency help individuals experience, interpret, and create meaning in their social worlds. As people participate in these worlds patterned by the structure of meanings and practices, they themselves become co-constructors of their socially shared realities. It is precisely the individual construction of experience within shared sociocultural contexts that points to the role of agency. Agency allows for the capacity to reflect, to think critically, and to oppose the status quo. In turn, personal contributions to the creation of meaning facilitate the ongoing process of cultural transmission and change.

The present considerations point to the need to move beyond the stereotypical views of agency and culture as dichotomous, and to develop more variable conceptualizations that can be used to study and explain the complexity of human experience. Individuals should not be viewed as passive entities who simply react to their situational contexts, but culturally forged agents who can potentially shape the environments they encounter. Human experience, on this view, can be understood as an ongoing process in which the person is "contextually constructed" yet to some degree also has the potential to be an "agent of construction." This culturally contextualized process is particularly relevant to bicultural experience.

The experience of bicultural individuals suggests that agency can take different forms and that the expression of agency is at once both cultural and personal. Using a clinical case example, I have suggested that the expression of "situated" agency depends on the fluid requirements of a person's contexts and that many bicultural individuals seek to actively maintain and develop their connection to multiple cultural contexts.

On this view, biculturalism is never simply an equal, bidirectional movement between cultures. For Padma, as I have suggested, the experience of biculturalism was frequently asymmetrical. To be bicultural is to be constantly moving in one cultural direction or another, depending upon one's sociocultural contexts and constraints, as well as one's personal needs and desires. The concept of integration cannot assume a seamless interaction of cultures. As Rajagopalan Radhakrishnan (1996) points out, cultural positions are frequently incompatible, if not unequal and opposed:

> When someone speaks as an Asian-American, who is exactly speaking? If we dwell in the hyphen, who represents the hyphen: the Asian or the American, or can the hyphen speak for itself without creating an imbalance between the Asian and American component?. . . . True, both components have status, but which has the power and potential to read and interpret the other on its terms? If the Asian is to be Americanized, will the American submit to Asianization? (p. 211)

Nor, I suggest, does the tension between different cultural positions and identities necessarily decrease with time. Rather, to my mind, it is the individual's ability to cope with these tensions and to find new, often innovative ways to navigate different cultural demands that characterizes bicultural competency.

The movement between cultures thus requires the bicultural individual to continually adapt and adjust to varied intergenerational, social, and cultural challenges. The ability to move between dimensions of cultural and personal experience is an important function in becoming biculturally competent, and is dependent on the process of psychological agency. Indeed, in an environment that requires the navigation and understanding of multiple choices, obligations, and cultural differences, I believe the development of agency is inherently related to a person's sense of psychological well-being.

Notes

1. Berry and Sam (1997, 296) write that, "In this chapter we take the position that despite these substantial variations in life circumstances of these acculturating groups, and despite the large variation in cultural groups that experience acculturation, the

psychological processes that operate during acculturation are essentially the same for all groups; that is, we adopt a universalist perspective on acculturation."

2. While this complex process of psychological change is difficult to capture, it can be illustrated using a hermeneutic perspective. My client's cultural outlook and shifts in experience are akin to Hans-Georg Gadamer's notion of a "horizon of understanding." Gadamer (1995) suggests that experience always takes place within the specific horizon, or frame of reference, that is a person's known and meaningful world. The horizon refers to the totality of all that can be realized or thought about by a person at a given time in history and in a particular culture. It is from the perspective of my horizon of understanding that I identify things, pose questions, and interpret and know what kind of answers make sense to me. In this sense, our embeddedness in cultural contexts gives us a familiarity with and allegiance to a particular culture. Only by moving to the edge of our boundaries, to engage with what is Other to ourselves, can there be the opening up of a space for new possibilities and cross-cultural understanding. Through the change in her horizon of understanding, my client began to see difference not as an implicitly negative trait, but as an unalterable and potentially positive aspect of her cultural identity.

References

Agarwal, P. 1991. *Passage from India: Post 1965 Indian immigrants and their children.* Palos Verdes, Calif.: Yuviti Publications.

Archer, M. 1988. *Culture and agency: The place of culture in social theory.* Cambridge: Cambridge University Press.

Beebe, B., and Lachmann, F. M. 2002. *Infant research and adult treatment.* Hillsdale, N.J.: Analytic Press.

Benjamin, J. 1988. *The bonds of love: Psychoanalysis, feminism and the problem of domination.* London: Virago.

Berry, J. W. 1980. Acculturation as varieties of adaptation. In A. Padilla, ed., *Acculturation: Theory, models, and findings,* 9–25. Boulder, Colo.: Westview.

Berry, J. W. 1997. Immigration, acculturation and adaptation. *Applied Psychology: An International Review* 46:5–8.

Berry, J. W. 2002. Conceptual approaches to acculturation. In K. M. Chun, P. M. Organista, and G. Marin, eds., *Acculturation: Advances in theory, measurement, and applied research,*17–38. Washington, D.C.: American Psychological Association.

Berry, J. W., and Sam, D. 1997. Acculturation and adaptation. In J. W. Berry, M. H. Seagull, and C. Kagitcibasi, eds. *Handbook of cross-cultural psychology: Social behavior and applications,* Vol. 3, 291–326. Needham Heights, MA: Allyn & Bacon.

Bhatia, S. 2002. Acculturation, dialogical voices and the construction of the diasphoric self. *Theory & Psychology* 12:55–77.

Das Gupta, M. 1997. "What is Indian about you?": A gendered, transnational approach to ethnicity. *Gender and Society* 11:572–596.

Das Gupta, S. 1998. *A patchwork shawl: Chronicles of South Asian women in America.* New Brunswick, N.J.: Rutgers University Press.

Dumont, L. 1980. *Homo hierarchicus: The cast system and its implications.* Chicago: University of Chicago Press.

Fonagy, P., Gergely, G., Jurist, E. L., and Target, M. 2002. *Affect regulation, mentalization, and the development of the self.* New York: Other Press.

Gadamer, H.-G. 1995. *Truth and method.* Trans. J. Weinsheimer and D. G. Marshall. 2nd ed. New York: Continuum. (Original work published 1960.)

Gardiner, J. K., ed. 1995. *Provoking agents: Gender and agency in theory and practice.* Champaign: University of Illinois Press.

Geertz, C. 1973. *The interpretation of cultures.* New York: Basic Books.

Gilligan, C. 1986. Remapping the moral domain: New images of the self in relationship. In T. Heller, M. Sosna, and D. Wellbury, eds., *Reconstructing individualism: Autonomy, individuality and the self in western thought,* 221–253. Stanford, Calif.: Stanford University Press.

Gilligan, C. 1993. *In a different voice: Psychological theory and women's development.* 2nd ed. Cambridge, Mass.: Harvard University Press.

Harwood, R. L., Leyendecker, B., Carlson, V., Asencio, M., and Miller, A. 2002. Parenting among Latino families in the U.S. In M. H. Bornstein, ed. *Handbook of parenting: vol. 4. Social conditions and applied parenting 2nd ed.* 21–46. Mahwah, NJ: Lawrence Erlbaum Associates.

Holland, D., Lachicotte, W., Skinner, D., and Cain, C. 1998. *Identity and agency in cultural worlds.* Cambridge, Mass.: Harvard University Press.

Jenkins, A. H. 2001. Individuality in cultural context: The case for psychological agency. *Theory and Psychology* 11:347–362.

Kakar, S. 1995. Clinical work and cultural imagination. *Psychoanalytic Quarterly* 64:265–281.

LaFromboise, T., Coleman, H. L. K., and Gerton, J. 1993. Psychological impact of biculturalism: Evidence and theory. *Psychological Bulletin,* 114:395–412.

Leonard, K. I. 1997. *The South Asian Americans.* Westport, Conn.: Greenwood Press.

Leonard, K. I. 2005. Asian Indian Americans. In J. Buenker and L. A. Ratner, eds., *Multiculturalism in the United States: A Comparative Guide to Acculturation and Ethnicities,* 2nd ed., 65–78. Westport, Conn.: Greenwood Press.

Mackenzie, C., and Stoljar, N., eds. 2000. *Relational autonomy: Feminist perspectives on autonomy, agency, and the social self.* Oxford: Oxford University Press.

Mahler, M., Pine, F., and Bergman, A. 1975. *The psychological birth of the human infant: Symbiosis and individuation.* New York: Basic Books.

Markus, H., and Kitayama, S. 1991. Culture and self: Implications for cognition, emotion, and motivation. *Psychological Review* 98:224–253.

Markus, H., and Kitayama, S. 2003a. Culture, self and the reality of the social. *Psychological Inquiry* 14:277–283.

Markus, H., and Kitayama, S. 2003b. Models of agency: Sociocultural diversity in the construction of action. In V. Murphy-Berman and J. J. Berman, eds., *Cross-cultural differences in perspectives on the self,* 1–57. Lincoln: University of Nebraska Press.

Marriott, McK. 1976. Interpreting Indian society: A monistic alternative to Dumont's dualism. *Journal of Asian Studies* 36:189–195.

Martin, J. 2007 The selves of educational psychology: Conceptions, contexts, and critical considerations. *Educational Psychologist* 42:79–89.

Martin, J. and Sugarman, J. 1999. *The psychology of human possibility and constraint.* Albany: State University of New York Press.

Martin, J., Sugarman, J., and Thompson, J. 2003. *Psychology and the question of agency.* Albany: State University of New York Press.

Miller, J. G. 2002. Bringing culture to basic psychological theory: Beyond individualism and collectivism. *Psychological Bulletin* 128:97–109.

Miller, J. G. 2003. Culture and agency: Implications for psychological theories of motivation and social development. In V. Murphy-Berman and J. J. Berman, eds., *Cross-cultural differences in perspectives on the self,* 59–99. Lincoln: University of Nebraska Press.

Oyserman, D., Coon, H. M., and Kemmelmeier, M. 2002. Rethinking individualism and collectivism: Evaluation of theoretical assumptions and meta-analyses. *Psychological Bulletin* 128:3–72.

Phinney, J. 1989. Stages of ethnic identity development in minority group adolescents. *Journal of Early Adolescence* 9:34–49.

Radhakrishnan, R. 1996. *Diasphoric meditations; Between home and location.* Minneapolis: University of Minnesota Press.

Raeff, C. 1997. Maintaining cultural coherence in the midst of cultural diversity. *Developmental Review* 17:250–261.

Shweder, R. A., and Bourne, E. J. 1984. Does the concept of person vary cross-culturally? In R. A. Shweder and R. A. LeVine, eds., *Culture theory: Essays on mind, self, and emotion,* 158–199. Cambridge: Cambridge University Press.

Stern, D. 1985. *The interpersonal world of the infant.* New York: Basic Books.

Contributors

John Fiscalini, Ph.D. is Associate Clinical Professor at the New York University postdoctoral program for psychoanalysis; training and supervising analyst and faculty member at the William Alanson White Institute of Psychiatry, Psychoanalysis, and Psychology. He maintains a private practice in New York. His most recent book is *Coparticipant Psychoanalysis: Toward a New Theory of Clinical Inquiry* (Columbia University Press, 2004).

Roger Frie, Ph.D., Psy.D. is Associate Professor of Psychology, Long Island University, Brooklyn Campus; Assistant Clinical Professor of Medical Psychology at Columbia University College of Physicians and Surgeons; and faculty member at the William Alanson White Institute. He also maintains a private practice. His most recent books include *Psychotherapy as a Human Science* (Duquesne University Press, 2006, with Daniel Burston) and *Understanding Experience: Psychotherapy and Postmodernism* (Routledge, 2003).

Jill Gentile, Ph.D. is a supervisor at the Institute for the Psychoanalytic Study of Subjectivity and has taught at the Manhattan Institute for Psychoanalysis, the National Institutes for the Psychotherapies, and the Psychoanalytic Institute of Northern California. Her publications explore psychoanalytic developmental phenomenology. She maintains a private practice in clinical psychology and psychoanalysis in Manhattan and in Highland Park, NJ.

Adelbert H. Jenkins, Ph.D. is emeritus Associate Professor of Psychology, New York University. He is a past President of the Society for Theoretical and Philosophical Psychology. His publications include *Psychology and African Americans: A humanistic approach,* 2nd ed. (Allyn & Bacon, 1995); "Individuality in cultural context: The case for psychological agency" in *Theory and Psychology*; and "Free will and psychotherapy" in *Journal of Theoretical and Philosophical Psychology*.

Elliot L. Jurist, Ph.D., Ph.D. is Director of the Doctoral Program in Clinical Psychology, City University of New York and Professor of Psychology, CCNY. He is editor of *Psychoanalytic Psychology*; author of *Beyond Hegel and Nietzsche: Philosophy, Culture and Agency* (MIT Press, 2000); and coauthor of *Affect Regulation, Mentalization and the Development of the Self* (Other Press, 2002, with Peter Fonagy, George Gergely and Mary Target).

Linda Pollock, Psy.D. is a past President of the Massachusetts Association for Psychoanalytic Psychology, consulting psychologist for Tufts University, and faculty member at the Boston Institute for Psychotherapy. She has lectured widely, and her work has been published in *Psychoanalytic Dialogues*, *Contemporary Psychology*, *Psychoanalytic Quarterly*, and *Contemporary Psychoanalysis*. She maintains a private practice in Boston, MA.

Jack Martin, Ed.D. is Burnaby Mountain Endowed Professor of Psychology at Simon Fraser University. His research interests are in philosophy and history of psychology, especially in the psychology of personhood. His most recent books include *Psychology and the Question of Agency* (SUNY Press, 2003, with Jeff Sugarman and Janice Thompson) and *The Psychology of Human Possibility and Constraint* (SUNY Press, 1999, with Jeff Sugarman).

Arnold Modell, M.D. is Clinical Professor of Psychiatry, Harvard Medical School, and training and supervising analyst at the Boston Psychoanalytic Institute. His most recent books include *Imagination and the Meaningful Brain* (MIT Press, 2003), *The Private Self* (Harvard University Press, 1993), and *Other Times, Other Realities* (Harvard University Press, 1990).

Jeff Sugarman, Ed.D. is Associate Professor of Education at Simon Fraser University. He is coauthor of *The Psychology of Human Possibility and Constraint* (SUNY Press, 1999) and *Psychology and the Question of Agency* (SUNY Press, 2003). He is a Fellow of the American Psychological Association, past President of The Society for Theoretical and Philosophical Psychology, and corecipient of the George Miller Award for an Outstanding Recent Article in General Psychology.

Pascal Sauvayre, Ph.D. is a supervising analyst and faculty member at the William Alanson White Institute, and the codirector of the Child and Adolescent Program at the National Institute for the Psychotherapies. His other publications on agency include "On the dialectics of agency" in *Journal of Theoretical and Philosophical Psychology* and "Free will, identity, and primary creativity" in *New Ideas in Psychology*. He maintains a private practice in New York.

Index

Psychological Agency